Invested Interests

Invested Interests

Capital, Culture,
and the World Bank

Bret Benjamin

University of Minnesota Press   Minneapolis / London

Published by the University of Minnesota Press
111 Third Avenue South, Suite 290
Minneapolis, MN 55401-2520
http://www.upress.umn.edu

Library of Congress Cataloging-in-Publication Data

Benjamin, Bret.
    Invested interests : capital, culture, and the World Bank / Bret Benjamin.
      p. cm.
    Includes bibliographical references and index.
    ISBN-13 978-0-8166-4872-6 (hc : alk. paper)
    ISBN-10 0-8166-4872-7 (hc : alk. paper)
    ISBN-13 978-0-8166-4873-3 (pb : alk. paper)
    ISBN-10 0-8166-4873-5 (pb : alk. paper)
    1. World Bank—History. 2. World Bank—Influence. 3. World Bank—Social aspects. 4. Economic assistance. 5. Globalization. I. Title.
    HG3881.5.W57B456 2007
    332.1'532—dc22

                          2006103039

Printed in the United States of America on acid-free paper

The University of Minnesota is an equal-opportunity educator and employer.

12 11 10 09 08 07   10 9 8 7 6 5 4 3 2 1

Contents

Acknowledgments

To be frank, I have many debts to settle. I plead for relief, as these brief acknowledgments cannot begin to account for, never mind repay, the generosity, support, and sustenance that so many people provided me during the process of writing this book.

The University at Albany, State University of New York (SUNY), and United University Professions provided research funds for my travels to the World Bank Archives in Washington, D.C., to the World Social Forums in Porto Alegre and Mumbai, and to numerous scholarly conferences where I have presented versions of this work. Even more important, my department secured time for writing leaves, which allowed me to complete the project. I was also fortunate to participate as a faculty lecturer in a Fulbright program in the Russian Federation, where I began to work out several of the ideas contained in the following pages; my thanks to Fulbright, and especially to Tatiana Venediktova at Moscow State University and John Ryder at the Office of International Programs–SUNY, for providing me this opportunity.

It has been a genuine pleasure to work with the staff at the University of Minnesota Press. My gratitude to Adam Brunner, Laura Westlund, Emily Hamilton, Nancy Sauro, Paula Friedman, and particularly Richard Morrison, a long-time champion of this project, who has successfully helped shepherd it through many phases.

I genuinely appreciate the professionalism and enthusiasm demonstrated by the staff at the World Bank Archives who assisted me during my research time at that facility: Lucia McGowan, Maurizio Gallerini, Sarvenaz Alikhani, Eva Kaminski, Vlada Alekankina, Elisa Liberatori-Prati (Chief Archivist), Ian Ross McAndrew, Deirdre Bryden, Chandra Kumar, Teti Goodarzi, Trudy Huskamp Peterson, and especially Bertha F. Wilson and Steve Barrett. Likewise the staff at Columbia University Oral History Research Office Collection, including David Loerke and Courtney Smith, were immensely helpful.

I learned a tremendous amount from the challenging and buoying feedback provided by all of the scholars who reviewed this manuscript in its various stages. Kate Bedford deserves special plaudits here. A political scientist who could have easily dismissed this book as the ravings of an English professor, Kate, through her serious engagement, generous commentary, and detailed critique of the manuscript pressed me to write far stronger, more nuanced arguments. This book has benefited enormously from her involvement. My heartfelt gratitude, as well, to Miranda Joseph, whose guidance and encouragement were nothing short of indispensable during my work. In addition to the countless revisions that resulted from her lucid feedback on earlier drafts, the very fact that this book exists in bound and printed form owes no small amount to Miranda's committed support for this project.

I can scarcely type the word "committed" without thinking of my friend and mentor Barbara Harlow, who has played such a formative role in my intellectual, professional, and political development. This work is a reflection of, and a tribute to, her expansive conception of the possibilities for scholarship within English studies, her precise attention to the textual details of the colonial archive, and her utterly principled political commitments.

A thanks to *all* my colleagues at the University at Albany, SUNY, who have been universally supportive, and who have fostered an atmosphere of intellectual rigor and creativity that has been enormously productive for me during my time at this institution. It is a great pleasure working with Liz Lauenstein, Regina Klym, Connie Barrett, and Kelly Williams. Steve North, Jeff Berman, Tom Cohen, Lana Cable, Doug Payne, David Wills, Helen Elam, Teresa Ebert, Rosemary Hennessy, Randal Craig, Pierre Joris, Glyne Griffith, Richard Barney, Charles Shepherdson, and Don Byrd, each in her or his own way, made valuable contributions to this book. Special mention is due to Gareth Griffiths, Marjorie

Pryse, and Helene Scheck, who read my manuscript with care and acuity.

I also would like to name the extraordinary cohort of junior faculty with whom I have had the pleasure of working during my time in the Albany English department: Mike Hill, Dina Al-Kassim, Paul Kottman, Mark Anthony Neal, Branka Arsić, Ed Schwarzschild, Lisa Thompson, McKenzie Wark, Helene Scheck, Eric Keenaghan, Hoang Phan, Jennifer Greiman, Laura Wilder, and Ineke Murakami. Even now, as I look over this list of amazing colleagues, I smile at my great fortune.

My thanks as well to the many undergraduate and graduate students, too numerous to list, with whom I have worked out so many of the ideas contained in this manuscript; most directly, this book draws heavily on what I learned from students who took my "Bandung at 50" seminars. Special thanks to the members of our Marxist reading group, from whom I continue to learn a great deal each week. I am grateful to Tara Needham in particular for her provocative responses to a draft of chapter 6, her suggestions for relevant research materials about Arundhati Roy, and her perpetually challenging engagement with the questions of transnational culture study, all of which have contributed substantively to this book.

Early versions of this project benefited from the support and critical attention of, among many others, Amitava Kumar, Lester Faigley, Chuck Rossman, Phil Doty, Toyin Falola, John Slatin, Bill Holt, Ailise Lamoreux, Gina Siesing, Sandy Soto, Paige Schilt, Lois Kim, Nick Evans, Jennifer Bean, Daniel Anderson, Vimala Pasupathi, Aimé Ellis, Rebecca Dyer, Katie Kane, Salah Hassan, David Alvarez, Joseph Slaughter, Jennifer Wenzel, and Mary Havan.

Fond thanks to the fellow *forumistas* with whom I traveled to the World Social Forums in Brazil and India: Mike Hill, Tanya Agathocleous, and Mike Rubenstein. A special *abraço* in this regard to Johnny Lorenz, with whom I twice traveled to Porto Alegre and with whom I have talked and thought about the complexities of this research project for many years. Johnny deserves much credit for sparking my interest in the WSF.

A warm note of thanks to those friends inside and outside the university who made my life in Albany so rich while I completed this project. The book owes much to the many meals, drinks, and laughs shared with Laura Mendelson, Lisa Thompson, Eric Keenaghan, Jennifer Greiman, Barry Trachtenberg, Helene Scheck, Pierre Joris, Nicole Peyrafitte, Don and Margie Byrd, Gareth Griffiths, Richard Barney, Steve Rein, Niki Haynes, and Nina Baldwin. Ed Schwarzschild, the man responsible for Sunday-Night-Movie-Night and an annual bowling debacle, deserves singling out. As do Gene and Bobby Garber, oenephiles, bon vivants, and in the case of the former, genuine trout bum. I could not have dreamed up two more wonderful, supportive friends than Lee Franklin, confectioner and ethicist at large, and Marci Nelligan, human magnet for the substitute Grovers of the world. Finally, there is good reason why Mike Hill's name peppers these acknowledgments; we have been fast friends since my job interview at Albany, and his personal and professional generosity and unwavering commitment to the greater good have been the enduring constants of my time at Albany.

Perhaps my largest debt of gratitude is owed to my family members. Their endless abundance of support, patience, and love sustained this project in innumerable ways. Effusive thanks, then, to my father, Bob, from whom I inherited the gift of calm pragmatism that has served me so well during the long process of writing this text; to my mother, Nancy, whose joyous and determined enthusiasm animates all of my work; to Jeremy and Hillit for their unqualified hospitality, their intellectual inquisitiveness, and their roles as coconspirators and contrarians; and to Woodrow, who has been a dogged supporter from the very inception of this project.

Finally, I offer loving thanks to my partner, Laura Wilder, who has lived with this book every bit as much as I have. Your compassion, radiant warmth, and honest generosity sustain me at every turn. I thank you not only for your tireless work reading and rereading drafts, not only for the million kindnesses, small and large, that you graciously performed to help me carve out time for writing, not only for the countless things that you have taught me over the years, but also for the deep, thick, everyday pleasures of our lives together.

Introduction

Accounting for Culture

"The World Bank's influence is global and total," states Muhammad Yunus, recent Nobel Prize winner and founder of the Grameen Bank in Bangladesh.[1] Bruce Rich, author of *Mortgaging the Earth*, writes, "More than any other entity on earth, the Bank shapes the worldview of proponents of big international development, and the Bank is its biggest funder."[2] Gayatri Chakravorty Spivak, perhaps the leading figure in the field of postcolonial studies, definitively asserts, "The main funding and co-ordinating agency of the great narrative of development is the World Bank."[3] I could go on. In fact, it would not be difficult to assemble a litany of equally direct, unambiguous statements by academics, activists, and politicians from across the political and intellectual spectrum, asserting the profound global impact of the International Bank for Reconstruction and Development (IBRD), the international financial institution typically referred to by a moniker at once more pithy and more profound: the World Bank. And yet cultural critics—scholars who have rigorously theorized other institutions of colonialism, postcolonialism, and globalization—have made only halting, ineffectual attempts to analyze and critique what is surely one of the most influential global institutions of the post–World War II era.

One of the central but relatively modest arguments of *Invested Interests*, then, is that scholars and teachers who work in literary and cultural studies have much to gain from, and much to contribute to, a careful, critical analysis of the World Bank and the sixty-year World Bank era, an era that dates its inception from the 1944 Bretton Woods Conference. This book moves from the central premise that the World Bank ought to be understood as a *cultural* as well as an economic institution. In part this is to reiterate what is by now something of a truism within cultural studies: that economics and economic systems are culturally constituted frameworks, both productive of and reproduced by complex networks of social relations. The ostensibly pure realms of accounting and finance function as rhetorics and mechanisms of control, inclusion, exclusion, and the like. As global economic forces seep into the practices and routines of everyday life in ways that are ever more diffuse, indirect, and invisible, *the market* is routinely subjectivized, not treated as a conceptual apparatus but, rather, personified as an active agent with its own capricious will and temperamental mood swings. A cultural critique that focuses on political economy rather than on economics or the market as such enables us to better understand how the mechanisms of finance and the rhetorical appeals to pure economics are marshaled in particular moments, for particular purposes, and in response to particular pressures— which is to say, ideologically. Beyond unveiling the politics of numbers, however, it is important to recognize that *the Bank* was never only, never even primarily, *a bank*. In its aspirations toward global management, and particularly in its stranglehold over *development* as both a theoretical principle of modernity and a set of lending practices that have effectively remapped the globe along an increasingly stark grid of economic coordinates, the World Bank has been, and remains today, one of the most influential global-cultural actors of the postwar era.

My contention that the Bank must be understood as a cultural institution, however, entails more than a simple recognition that the Bank affects and is affected by social forces. I suggest that the World Bank has been instrumental in shaping the very idea of culture as we have come to understand it today. Here I develop one aspect of Michael Denning's provocative thesis that the cultural turn in the humanities and social sciences, often associated with cultural studies, ought properly to be understood both as global in scope and historically specific to the age of three worlds.[4] According to Denning, the "concept of culture undergoes a sea-change at mid-century" when "suddenly, in the age of three worlds, everyone discover[ed] that culture had been mass produced like Ford's cars; the masses had culture and culture had a mass."[5] On the one hand, Denning contends that this turn is the product of a new density and global reach of the mass cultural commodity form coupled with technological advances in information, reproduction, and distribution—a global culture industry. On the other, he argues that historical antinomies within the age of three worlds, particularly the revolutionary nationalisms of the third world, put pressure on the category of *culture*, opening space for intellectuals across the globe to theorize cultural formations as active spheres of power, contest, and negotiation.

My book attempts to overlay the history of the World Bank onto this cultural turn, looking at the ways in which each informs, pressures, reinforces, and at times makes possible the other. The Bank, I argue, *traffics in culture*. In a very basic sense, this means that it engages in rhetorical acts of public persuasion that rely on cultural formations and that appeal to cultural values. But throughout the book I also explore several more precise instances of this cultural traffic. For example, I examine the Bank's role in the export of Fordism, analyzing the ways in which mass cultural commodities become the ideological tools of development by promising a "better way of life through cultural dialog and exchange." Further, I examine the Bank's investments in nationalisms and national culture (or, perhaps more accurately, nation-state culture), tracking the Bank's moves toward social lending projects in response to decolonization. I locate a final example of the Bank's cultural traffic in the institution's contemporary turn to *the literary* in the form of success stories that attempt to articulate the institution in relation to both global capital and global protest. In broad strokes, I contend that the Bank's cultural trafficking enables it to move beyond a narrow economism to construct an interventionist mission of development that is global in geographical scale and that claims infinite and eternal reach into the everyday processes of social life.

This book, then, endeavors to map the debates and lexicon of culture study onto a historical analysis of the World Bank as an imperial institution, and conversely to map the World Bank's institutional history onto the theoretical evolution of culture as a politicized sphere of radical anti-imperial contestation. In particular, I examine mid-twentieth-century anticolonial intellectuals such as Aimé Césaire, Frantz Fanon, and Richard Wright, tracing their burgeoning awareness of cultural struggle within the grip of global financial capital and institutions such as the Bank. Later in the book, I turn to contemporary public intellectual Arundhati Roy, who provides a useful link to present-day anti-imperialist social movements. I consider the revisions and reactions of each of these figures to Marxist cultural theory, specifically their attempts to trouble the base/superstructure model by exploring the ways that modes of production are generative not only of class formations but also of race formations, gender formations, national forma-tions, and the like. That is, my analysis pays special attention to production of collectivities, in particular the connection between mass culture and mass movements for democratic equity.

In many instances, these authors take direct aim at the Bank and we can consider them as specific antagonists. In other moments, I draw out more diffuse connections, locating the historical contra-dictions and antagonisms that condition the parallel ascendance of both the World Bankers and the third world cultural radicals. This double vision requires me at times to treat the Bank with historical specificity as an institutional actor (a subject), and at times to read or interpret the Bank as a social text, authored variously by its own agents (e.g., Bank presidents, employees, and affiliated agencies) and by those forces organized in opposition to both the institution itself and the historical forces of capitalist neoimperial expansion of which it plays such an important part. More, however, such a double vision insists that we interrogate both the limits and the necessity of such readings by examining the ways in which the World Bank has played a formative role in the development of pre-cisely those critical tools and critical categories upon which such a project must rely. Consider, as one small example of this sway, the enormous number of Left/progressive critiques of global inequity and exploitation (even critiques of the Bank itself) that rely heavily on statistical and ethnographic evidence collected, interpreted, and published by the World Bank. This speaks not only to the Bank's preeminence as *the* largest and most influential research institution for questions of development, but also to the way that the metrics, categories, processes, and methods of analysis identified and pio-neered by the Bank have conditioned the very manner in which we see and understand individual regions of the planet, as well as a particular notion of an integrated global whole.

I contend that an extended, exacting reading of the World Bank as a cultural institution is needed to develop a more nuanced and sophisticated critique of the Bank itself—its policies, practices, and philosophical underpinnings, past and present. Such an analysis demands that we move beyond the reductive tendency to circumscribe the World Bank solely within the historical period and the economic symptoms of globalization.[6] It is surely the case that the Bank has played an important role in producing and maintaining some conditions associated with globalization (most notably the ascendance of neoliberalism), and this book indeed attempts to theorize the present state of the Bank. I maintain, however, that it is politically irresponsible, indeed disabling, to treat the Bank and globalization as in any way coequal or coterminous. Bounded neither by standard periodizations of globalization, nor by a finite set of conditions associated with these periodizations, the Bank must be read in thicker, more layered historical and political contexts. In addition to a consideration of the contemporary moment, the emphasis of *Invested Interests* falls on the first quarter-century of the Bank's existence, in part to fill a historical gap left underexamined by most Bank critics, and in part to highlight the relationship between the Bank and the historical origins of culture and culture study as we now understand them, which I purposefully locate (extending Denning) in the emergence of the so-called third world and the radical political and intellectual challenges posed by the anticolonial and national liberation movements of the mid-twentieth century.

Attentive to the place of intellectual work in radical political movements, Denning proposes that the first urgent challenge for contemporary scholars is to develop a critical globalization studies capable of reading our own historical moment against the grain of the three-worlds era from which we have so recently emerged, the legacies of which remain indelibly inscribed on the living present. At "the heart of this project," he contends, lies

> the elaboration of a transnational history of the age of three worlds, that is to say a history that does not take the nation-state as its central actor. Not only are the social movements of the age of three worlds relatively absent, movements that live in a chronology of uprisings and massacres: Birmingham, Sharpville, Watts, Prague, Soweto, Kwangju. So too are the transnational corporations which seem to loom so large in popular imagination: IBM, ITT, United Fruit, the Seven Sisters of oil, Ford, Sony, and Nike. A central task

of transnational cultural studies is to narrate an account of globalization that speaks not just of an abstract market with buyers and
sellers, or even of an abstract commodification with producers and
consumers, but of actors: transnational corporations, social movements of students, market women, tenants, racialized and ethni-
cized migrants, labor unions, and so on.[7]

I understand this book to be a contribution toward just such a critical globalization studies history. Any transnational cultural studies
project committed to understanding, explaining, and presumably
ending the violence of imperialism must not only account for the
World Bank but also do so in a way that addresses the multifaceted
historical manifestations of this institution, which has cast such a
long shadow of influence over the age of three worlds and beyond.
Critical analysis of the World Bank as a cultural institution offers
one valuable thread by which we can unravel some of the continuities and disjunctures that mark the historical transformation of
imperial power during the twentieth century. This transformation
is often reduced in popular accounts to a schematic contrast between a finite era of direct European colonial rule and an equally
discernable era of U.S.- and corporate-led transnational financial
control. Never so simple or so clear, this historical fissure between
colonial rule and globalization can, I am suggesting, be variously
bridged or sutured by a critique of the World Bank, an institution
founded in 1944 arguably for the express purpose of negotiating
this historical transition.

The transnational cultural studies framework of *Invested
Interests* attempts to do just this. Methodologically, this critique
entails refolding the various analytical perspectives of literary, cultural, theoretical, rhetorical, and media studies into a critical project that takes aim at the World Bank. In broader historical and conceptual terms, however, it entails an attentiveness to the genealogy
of culture and cultural study, a lineage that relates the World Bank
to those anti-imperial social movements that arguably brought the
Bank into being and that certainly have shaped—and continue to
shape—its ever-evolving role in the global political economy. Such
a transnational cultural studies approach can develop a more accurate portrait of the Bank as a dynamic foe, fully capable of adapt-
ing to new threats, but also one by no means impervious to critique
and resistance.

Postcolonial Studies and the Bank

In a 1964 speech titled "The Development Century," George Woods, the Bank's fourth president, reminisced that "when we began this quest, we were like explorers setting foot on the shore of an unknown continent. The terrain proved to be vaster, the topography more rugged, the explorations more demanding than we dreamed [they] could be."[8] The imperialist genres of discovery narratives and adventure tales evoked in Woods's address will hardly be unfamiliar to students of postcolonial studies. Why, then, given both its weighty role in shaping the postwar globe and the Bank's self-announced imperial legacies, have postcolonial and cultural studies been so reluctant to examine the Bank in any detail?

It would be wrong to suggest that scholars in these disciplines have ignored the World Bank altogether. Over the past decade or so, postcolonial studies has indeed begun to call attention to the Bank, its sister Bretton Woods organization the International Monetary Fund (IMF), and their more distant relation, the World Trade Organization (WTO), which evolved from the General Agreement on Trade and Tariffs (GATT). Although not a primary concern in the early work of postcolonial studies' "big three"—Edward Said, Gayatri Chakravorty Spivak, and Homi Bhabha—or in the pioneering postcolonial research of Bill Ashcroft, Gareth Griffiths, Helen Tiffin, Robert Young, Mary Louise Pratt, Peter Hulme, among many others, the World Bank appears with increasing regularity as a reference within the postcolonial scholarship emerging during the early- to mid-1990s. One sees this shift most clearly in connection with a growing body of scholarship that began to reflect on the limits and possibilities of postcolonial studies both as a (bureaucratic and increasingly institutionalized) discipline and as a critical category; this work called into question aspects of both the *post* and the *colonial* in an attempt to draw connections between a history of colonialism and anticolonial movements, and the apparently new (or at least deepened or accelerated) manifestations of global capitalism (and related questions of postmodernity) that have since come to be referred to in shorthand as "globalization."[9] Early contributors to this shift include, among others, scholars such as Anne McClintock in her 1992 essay "The Angel of Progress: Pitfalls of the Term 'Post-Colonialism,'" Aijaz Ahmad in his 1992 book *In Theory,* Masao Miyoshi in his 1993 essay "A Borderless World?

From Colonialism to Transnationalism and the Decline of the Nation State," and Arif Dirlik in his 1994 essay "The Postcolonial Aura: Third World Criticism in the Age of Global Capitalism."[10] This scholarly trend deepened over the next few years,[11] paralleling the field's increased scrutiny of the seemingly new or accelerated phenomena of globalization, transnationalism, and (late) global capitalism. By the late 1990s and early 2000s, references to the Bank pepper much postcolonial scholarship—perhaps most notably, given her stature in the field, in Spivak's later writings, spanning both her translation work such as *Imaginary Maps* (1995) and her scholarship, including the seminal *A Critique of Postcolonial Reason* (1999).[12] The apex of this turn is likely found in Amitava Kumar's 2003 edited collection *World Bank Literature,* a book that explicitly and urgently asserts the need for postcolonial studies and cultural studies to engage with the practices and legacies of the World Bank.[13]

Without in any way trying to minimize the intellectual significance of this growing awareness within postcolonial studies about the Bank's pivotal role in shaping the phenomenon of globalization, I will argue that scholarship in the field remains structured by an academic division of labor that, when it comes to the World Bank, has severely limited its range and depth of analysis and critique.

McClintock's essay, though chronologically early in postcolonial studies' growing disciplinary awareness of the Bank (and perhaps *because* it is early) can be seen as emblematic of this academic division of labor. I turn to McClintock's piece as an example not because of any lapses or failures on her part; to the contrary, in her thoughtful remarks about the political and intellectual crises facing postcolonial studies in the early 1990s, McClintock pays more attention to the Bank than most postcolonial critics before and after. Moreover, the critiques she levels against World Bank policy, in the interest of her broader arguments about the "pitfalls of progress"— the pervasive legacies of Enlightenment narratives of history—are largely correct. Detailing the Bank's prominent role in structural adjustment and in the production of chronic indebtedness in Africa and elsewhere within the "underdeveloped" world, the Bank's numerous failed environmental projects, and the disproportionate burden that these and other Bank policies have placed on women, McClintock rightly calls into question the Bank's "vaunted technical neutrality and myth of expertise" (94) as part of her underlying arguments about the persistence of a (failed) capitalist notion of progress during the postcolonial era.

"The Angel of Progress" offers a useful departure point for this project, however, because of the manner in which it—and the bulk of subsequent postcolonial scholarship—engages critically with the World Bank as an institution. To open her essay, McClintock *reads* a New York City art installation, the Hybrid State Exhibit, carefully analyzing aspects of the gallery space and the pieces on view, as well as dissecting the paradox of linear historical progress evident in the exhibition brochure. The exhibition, the gallery, the art, the brochure all present themselves as available texts for McClintock's discerning scholarly eye, and she uses her analysis of the dual historical movements of progress and degeneracy to both frame and illustrate her argument that the "term 'post-colonial,' like the exhibit itself, is haunted by the very figure of linear development that it sets out to dismantle" (85). Although she *reads* development as figured by the exhibit, McClintock only *reports* on development as a paradigm and objective pursued by the World Bank as an institutional actor, relying almost exclusively on the (admittedly excellent) research of economist Susan George, political scientist Cheryl Payer, and sociologist Walden Bello for the force of her critique. Their scholarship provides her with a set of relevant statistical and historical data, enabling her to talk authoritatively about the devastating effects of Bank policies. However, this dependence on the research of social scientists means that the Bank is necessarily relegated to background *context*, in McClintock's analysis. Although her knowledge of particular Bank-sponsored development projects presumably enables her to better interrogate and expose the underlying narrative/historical assumptions of the Hybrid State Exhibit, the reverse cannot be said.

Of course, in the context of a single essay there is nothing wrong with an analytical focus that privileges a particular mode or object of reading. What is striking, however, is the relative failure of literary and cultural studies during the following decade to advance and develop McClintock's specific arguments about the World Bank in any significant way. In the years since "The Angel of Progress" was first published as part of the influential double issue of *Social Text* on third world and postcolonial issues, the virtual absence of postcolonial scholarship that attempts to *read* the World Bank and its textual archive as McClintock reads the art exhibit should give us pause—all the more so given postcolonial studies' rich history with colonial discourse analysis, in which a vast array of texts from colonial archives were examined and interpreted with great nuance and insight and to great political effect.

Perhaps the root of this pattern of reading colonial archives while only reporting on the institutional role of the Bank lies in a self-policed division of academic labor not entirely unlike the one that Carl Pletsch outlines in his famous analysis of the division of social scientific labor undergirding the three-worlds system.[14] As I suggested above, although postcolonial studies has become increasingly attuned to the substantial impact of the World Bank, virtually all detailed academic analysis of the Bank has been deferred to scholars in the social sciences. What this means is that, although references to the Bank in literary/cultural scholarship are more frequent, they take on a mantra-like quality, rehearsing the agreed-upon litany of Bank abuses, a list that often bears a striking resemblance to McClintock's (via George's, Payer's, and Bello's) concerns with structural adjustment, debt, environmental devastation, and the gendered nature of development programs. In many instances, references to the Bank forego even this degree of specificity and the institution is lumped in with the IMF, the WTO, and multinational or transnational corporations as a metonym or synecdoche for globalization, global capitalism, or neoimperialism. I argue later in the book that this metonymic representation has proved of great strategic value for anti- and alter-globalization movements; as a highly visible institution, the World Bank—not unlike Nike or Wal-Mart, each the object of massive consumer boycott campaigns—comes to stand conveniently as the infamous target of public outrage that arguably ought to be directed at the broader systemic processes of global capitalist exploitation that the Bank participates in but does not uniquely orchestrate. As a type of global brand, that is, the Bank has perhaps never been more relevant at the level of signs and signifying practices. Nevertheless, this period-bound association of the Bank with globalization undoubtedly reduces the historical complexity of the institution's role in the postwar transformations of imperial power, including its influence (uneven, though undoubtedly potent) over the shape of a postwar system of internationalism, the emerging nation states from the decolonizing global South, and the increasingly dominant role played by corporate and financial capital.

Somewhat surprisingly, even analyses about the implications of language have been left to social scientists. The excellent book *Encountering Development*, a Foucauldian analysis of development discourse by anthropologist Arturo Escobar, has received a fair share of attention from postcolonial scholars, as has to a lesser degree the collection, inspired by Foucault and Raymond Williams, *The Development Dictionary*, edited by Wolfgang Sachs, in which a number of major critics of development each contribute an essay about a development keyword.[15]

What we see as the result of this academic division of labor—cultural critics' almost complete reliance on the social sciences when it comes to forming conclusions about the World Bank—is a significant narrowing of the range of Bank projects and policies that can be discussed in literary and cultural scholarship, as well as a reluctance to engage in specific, substantive critique of either the broader implications of Bank policy or the ways those policies are characterized in the academic scholarship on development. I hope it is clear that my concern here is not with academic turf. My contention is merely that the tendency to paraphrase the findings of social scientific research, and the reluctance to pay close attention to the primary documents of the World Bank archive, have often led literary and cultural theorists to settle for a caricatured, reductive representation of this complex and tremendously influential institution, an institution that has produced a conceptual map of the world along the axis of developed/underdeveloped that arguably has proven as consequential as the three-worlds model interrogated by Pletsch.

Pletsch's work is significant here, not only because of its parallel focus on an academic division of labor, but also because of his claim that the "preposterous simplification entailed" (575) in the *academic* classificatory system of three conceptual worlds serves to reinforce both the broader hegemonic notion of capitalist modernity and the specific Cold War requests for vastly increased U.S. military budgets. That is, for Pletsch, the central role of academics in constructing and perpetuating the "astonishing simple-mindedness of the [three worlds] scheme" (574) raises important questions about both the division of academic disciplines and the division of the globe. Pletsch's arguments overlap with my concerns about the constricted nature of academic research on the World Bank in part because the Bank itself played a major role both in the maintenance

of the three-worlds system throughout the Cold War, as well as in
the transformation of that conceptual division of the globe during
the years since the demise of the second world. Moreover, we can
see in Pletsch's schema a logic that implicitly informs the division
of academic labor that I am identifying around the institution of
the World Bank, and that is suggestive of the broader implications
stemming from postcolonial studies' willingness to defer entirely to
social scientists in this regard. Pletsch argues that the three-worlds
system enforces a reductive characterization of the third world as
the site of tradition, culture, and religion, and therefore as the academic realm of anthropology, that "ideographic science par excellence" in which "theory has traditionally been secondary to the ex-
quisite description of otherness" (580). By contrast, the first world,
characterized by science, technology, rational thought, democracy,
and freedom, is understood as a "natural," fully "modern" society, and therefore becomes the academic terrain of economists,
sociologists, and political scientists authorized to make nomothetic
claims extrapolating the universal from the particular—theoretical
arguments about the "natural" laws governing social systems and
human behaviors.

It is my contention that the academic division of labor here described in relation to the Bank unwittingly maintains a similar
paradigm. Postcolonial studies finds itself relegated to making
localized, ideographic claims about third world tradition and culture, while deferentially heeding social scientific claims about the
institutions of international finance and their role in the economic
systems of the world economy, claims that, in the absence of critical scrutiny, begin to acquire the universal or eternal weight of
nomothetic edict. I am suggesting that the caricatured figure of the
Bank as a recurrent trope of postcolonial scholarship naturalizes
the institution, and by extension global capitalism, as permanent
and inevitable; it cloaks the Bank in a gauzy haze so as to render
it visible but ultimately inscrutable to scholars trained to analyze
the nuances of culture. And, as a paradigmatic figure of science,
technology, rationalism, modernity—those ideologically laden attributes of capitalism and first-world-ness that Pletsch identifies
as produced and reproduced by the classificatory system of three
worlds—the World Bank comes to be understood as a reified ab-
straction of global capitalism rather than as a powerful political
actor engaged in struggle over the modes of production, materi-

al resources, and axes of exploitation that define this particular world-historical system of capitalist imperialism—which is to say, hegemonic struggle over the very notion of *worlds* themselves.

Breaking Rules

Spivak quips, at the beginning of *A Critique of Postcolonial Reason*, "I am not erudite enough to be interdisciplinary, but I can break rules."[16] As a rule, postcolonial studies' critique of the Bank has been blunted by a disciplinary reluctance to read the institution with any degree of specificity. But rules, so it is said, are proven by their exception, and one must extend due credit to the rule breakers. In the collection *World Bank Literature* (edited by Kumar in 2003), and in Spivak's more recent work, I see two such exceptions addressing the concerns raised above.

"Can 'World Bank Literature' be a new name for postcolonial studies?" Kumar asks in his introduction. Of obvious importance to the present analysis, *World Bank Literature* spotlights, more explicitly than any previous scholarship in the field, the central role that the World Bank as institution has had in shaping the contemporary moment, and thus the inherent challenge it poses to literary and cultural studies. Identifying the nature of the collection's intervention, Kumar contends that the "focus on the World Bank, as an agent and as a metaphor, helps us concretize the 'wider context' of global capitalism," particularly when understood in relation to the "widespread and collective" opposition typified by protesters in Seattle, Washington, D.C., Quebec City, and elsewhere. Hence, he argues, the "analytic shift from the liberal-diversity model of 'World Literature' to the radical paradigm of 'World Bank Literature' signals a resolve not only to recognize and contest the dominance of the Bretton Woods institution but also to rigorously oppose those regimes of knowledge that would keep literature and culture sealed from the issues of economics and activism." This argument provides the intellectual force behind Kumar's collection, which does indeed take steps toward both an analysis of the Bank and an analytic mode refusing to segregate culture from political economy.[17]

I applaud numerous aspects of Kumar's collection (to which—full disclosure—I have contributed an essay). For one, *World Bank Literature* contains numerous examples of scholars who are attempting to read and interpret the complexities of specific World

Bank documents in ways that address the charges I made earlier about postcolonial studies' tendency to rely on a reductive caricature.[18] By paying attention to the motives and effects of rhetorical maneuvering, and identifying shifting, even contradictory, positions within Bank materials that undermine any notion of a monolithic, internally coherent World Bank discourse, the essays of Kumar's collection lay the foundation for a more accurate and politically responsive understanding of the institution. The collection as a whole is bound by a commitment to reading the World Bank in relation to, as Rosemary Hennessy puts it, "the layered analyses and creative mobilizing strategies that are emerging from movements that have targeted the World Bank and other agencies of corporate capitalism in the United States and internationally"[19]—a list that includes the antiglobalization[20] protesters in Seattle, the antisweatshop activists on campuses, the Zapatistas, the World Forum on Fish Harvesters and Fishworkers, and many other movements explored by the contributors. This attention to social movements illustrates another important aspect of Kumar's collection, which insists that we see the Bank not as an unassailable institution but rather as one engaged in an ongoing hegemonic struggle with democratic and popular movements across the globe. Finally, Hennessy's chapter, in concert with those by Doug Henwood and Richard Wolff, takes up Kumar's challenge to "concretize the 'wider context' of global capitalism."[21] In different ways, these three essays argue that capitalism and class relations ought to be, as they indeed have been in many cases, identified as the underlying problem, and that the force of any critique leveled against the World Bank will come from an analysis of its role in the broader system of capitalist production and the exploitation of surplus value from labor.

In these regards, I see Kumar's collection as a valuable corrective to the timidity of postcolonial scholarship in its limited treatment of the World Bank. Inherent in the nature of an edited collection, however, is the sacrifice of depth for breadth. Although the volume's chapters suggest important directions, they tend to offer first steps rather than substantive remappings. Despite its explicit challenge to the discipline of postcolonial studies, the collection shows little historical range and no attempt to wrestle with the fact that the postcolonial era (of course an impossible term to periodize with any finality, but which often at least implies the era following the 1947 decolonization of India) is also the World Bank era and might usefully be reperiodized as such. Precisely what such a reperiodization would mean, however, is far from clear in the context of this collection. That is, despite Kumar's expressed desire that the collection "focus on the World Bank, as an agent and as a metaphor,"[22] its dominant tendency is toward metaphoric or semiotic readings at the expense of historically specific analyses of the Bank as a potent force in postwar global political economy. As Bruce Robbins candidly points out in his afterword to the collection, figuring the Bank metaphorically leads to a pair of dangerous analytical conflations: first, imagining that global financial exchange can stand for the world economic system as a whole, and, second, imagining that "the World Bank can properly stand even for the domain of global finance." Robbins also correctly notes that, despite the contributors' sanguine assessments of the Seattle WTO protests, and despite contributors' arguments about emergent anticapitalist analyses and practices stemming from such movements, the collection as a whole makes only fitful efforts to "interpret Seattle a bit more strenuously. . . . It is pleasant to dwell on this moment of alignment between American unions and anti-sweatshop students," he writes, "but there is real analytic work to be done if the moment is to be made to last."[23] Although *World Bank Literature* should be applauded for its challenge to postcolonial studies and for the strides it makes toward a serious engagement with the institution of the World Bank, there remain significant gaps in its treatment of both the Bank and the social movements mobilized against it.

Spivak, of course, has been breaking rules for quite some time now. Although her work was published before Kumar's collection, I turn to it after Kumar's because I consider *A Critique of Postcolonial Reason* among the most sophisticated interrogations of the intellectual and political complexities facing transnational cultural studies. Spivak minces no words when it comes to her assessment of the Bank:

> The main funding and co-ordinating agency of the great narrative of development is the World Bank. The phrase "sustainable development" has entered the discourse of all the bodies that manage globality. Development to sustain what? The general ideology of global development is racist paternalism (and alas, increasingly, sororalism); its general economics capital-intensive investment; its broad politics the silencing of resistance and of the subaltern as the rhetoric of their protest is constantly appropriated.[24]

Far from rehearsing the standard list of grievances, Spivak's critique consistently probes for both complexities and complicities. Troubling is the persistent gender bias of Bank policies, but equally troubling is the Bank's newfound awareness of *gender* as an intellectual category, and its calculated shift from a discourse of Women in Development (WID) to Gender and Development (GAD) where "the Woman from the South is . . . the favored agent-as-instrument of transnational capital's globalizing reach."[25] Troubling are the Bank's environmental failures and the profound ecological loss that results, but equally troubling are the NGOs and International Civil Society groups who work in collaboration with the Bank to promote so-called sustainability and who "wheel now to the 'native informant' as such, increasingly appropriated into globalization," to discern the "true needs" of a people and to justify interventions based on this allegedly grassroots knowledge and expertise. Troubling are the close ties between local developers in the South and the forces of global capital, but equally troubling is the fact that "this complicity is, at best, unknown to the glib theorists of globality-talk or those who still whine on about old-style imperialism."[26]

While the Bank is by no means the central figure in *A Critique of Postcolonial Reason*, its recurring presence throughout the book, coupled with the repeated references to the historical proximity of the Bretton Woods conference in 1944 and Indian decolonization in 1947, suggests Spivak's keen awareness of the enormous role that the Bank has played in shaping the particular "History of the Vanishing Present" that she attempts to sketch. More than simply broadening the standard postcolonial critique of the Bank, or adding levels of nuance to the argument, Spivak's analysis is a useful corrective to previous work in postcolonial studies precisely because it compels us to see the Bank as a moving target. Far from a permanent and inscrutable feature of global capitalism, the Bank is properly understood in *A Critique of Postcolonial Reason* as a powerful but mutable agent, perpetually transforming itself in reaction to critique and crisis. To acknowledge that the Bank has consistently and effectively appropriated the language of critique from both activists and academics is to acknowledge the agency of social movements engaged in hegemonic struggle to contest development and global capitalism, as much as to acknowledge the Bank's role in both. In this sense, Spivak's critique of the Bank

remains sanguine about (or at least fully committed to supporting) the "impossible but necessary"[27] project facing the non-
Eurocentric "globe-girdling movements," to use Spivak's resonant
phrase, which struggle at the forefront of campaigns for ecological
justice and against population *control* (among other issues). In concert with these globe-girdling movements (or at least in attempting
not to subvert their actions), the academic project of learning to be
transnationally literate becomes the ethical and political imperative
for cultural studies, an imperative that plays out in the space and
time of classroom teaching as well as in a broader conception of
pedagogy: "From our academic or 'cultural work' niches, we can
supplement the globe-girdling movements with 'mainstreaming,'
somewhere between moonlighting and educating public opinion."[28]
Here, Spivak's intertwined notions about the value of transnational
cultural studies as a mode of academic labor—first, that various
forms of academic and cultural work might productively supplement[29] the transnational movements aligned against the Bank and
global capitalism, and, second, that such a thing as public opinion
still exists and therefore persuasion and communicability remain
essential political tactics for mobilizing such opinion—represent
important interventions into the ways in which postcolonial studies positions itself in relation to the Bank.

All of this, it seems to me, offers us a much more conceptually nuanced and politically sound platform from which to mount
a critique of the Bank than what is found in the vast majority of
postcolonial scholarship. However, although her argument offers a depth impossible to achieve in a collection such as Kumar's,
Spivak's principal project is not a detailed critique of the Bank itself.
Her profound erudition, despite feigned protestations to the contrary, spurs her to fry much bigger fish, as she attempts to track the
figures of the "Native Informant" and the "Postcolonial Subject"
through the intellectual categories and practices of philosophy, literature, history, and culture. The Bank remains for Spivak but one
thread of a much larger "text-ile."

Kumar, Spivak, and Denning all serve as important critical
models for this book in that each, to a greater and lesser degree,
insists upon the type of double vision that I called for earlier. Each
focuses our attention on the need to develop analytical frameworks
capable of adequately accounting for the mechanisms adapted by
the dominant capitalist and imperialist institutional actors such as

the World Bank while at the same time acknowledging the potent counterhegemonic social movements that serve as constitutive combatants. Kumar dedicates his collection to the students in Seattle. Spivak turns again and again to the globe-girdling movements that stand in radical opposition to the powerful forces of imperial globality. And Denning attempts to map a set of historical origins and ideological continuities that characterize today's so-called antiglobalization movements. My book follows suit, overlaying an analysis of the Bank's historical evolution with a genealogy of anti-imperial struggle by tracing continuities and disjunctures between today's alterglobalization movements and the mid-twentieth-century national liberation movements.

Overview of *Invested Interests*

An institution with global reach, capable of mobilizing vast resources and of exerting enormous coercive and persuasive power, the Bank is also an institution that has repeatedly refashioned itself over the past sixty years in response to specific historical pressures from events, individuals, and movements. It is by no means self-evident, then, to speak in any singular sense about *a* World Bank ideology or *a* World Bank political/economic legacy. The first three chapters of this book look at a sequence of the refashionings that have taken place during the Bank's first quarter-century of operation.

To explore the implications of these institutional shifts, *Invested Interests* develops a critical analysis of the public documents of the Bank, such as brochures, pamphlets, press releases, speeches, and electronic materials from the Bank's Website—documents that are typically aimed at nonspecialist audiences (often from the North), and that therefore represent a key site of hegemonic struggle over the principles and values of Bank-sponsored development, indeed over the questions of the Bank's continued relevance and existence.[30] In particular, I examine three historical moments: the Bretton Woods Conference in 1944; the Bank's early bond-selling years, from 1946 to 1949; and its internal *population crisis* spurred by the rising tide of postcolonial membership between 1959 and 1969. This history is necessarily partial and selective; the monumental task of compiling more than six decades of materials is beyond the scope of this project.[31] Any number of episodes in the Bank's history might be deemed of equal, or even greater, consequence. For instance, I only scratch the surface of the highly influential and transformative years of Robert McNamara's presidency, and provide few specifics about the Latin American debt crisis during the 1980s or the substantial changes that James Wolfensohn wrought during his ten-year term (which recently came to a close). My selections, however, are based on several organizing principles.

First, I eschew organizational schemes based on the terms or influence of individual Bank presidents, and instead focus on moments that show the Bank responding and reacting to historical, political, and social forces. This is not to deny the enormous influence of Bank presidents; on the whole, they have enjoyed considerably more autonomy, and have therefore wielded, considerably more authority for shaping policy and direction than have the heads of most (if not all) multilateral agencies. However, as I am hopeful my rhetorical analysis of archival documents can illuminate, the directives and directions being charted by individual presidents are themselves responses to a constantly changing set of pressures brought to bear by radically different constituents, all of which collectively constitute the social landscape in which the Bank operates in any given moment.

Second, though I engage with contemporary issues in the latter half of the book, the bulk of my analysis emphasizes the Bank's first decades. If I pay disproportionate attention to the earlier periods in the Bank's history, it is because I give credence to the notion that much can be learned about an institution by examining its origins. Michael Manley, the former prime minister of Jamaica, put this as well as anyone: "You ask 'whose interests?' I'll ask the question, 'who set it up?'"[32] Undoubtedly this holds true for the Bank, making its Bretton Woods inception essential knowledge. However, because the institution has been so malleable, and because the world in which the World Bank grew underwent such massive and rapid transitions during the era of decolonization, it is not so simple to trace an untroubled line between Bretton Woods and the modern World Bank. A recurrent pattern emerges in many of the best critical Bank histories, where authors examine the Bank's foundation and then skip ahead to the McNamara presidency twenty-five years later.[33] That oft-slighted quarter century is the subject of this book's first four chapters.

Although this heavy focus on the Bank's early years is designed in part to fill a gap in critical scholarship, several less academic rationales also inform my extended treatments of the 1940s and 1960s. For one, the significant institutional reinventions that take place during this era (in the simplest construction, the shift from 1940s fiscal conservatism to 1960s liberal interventionism) illustrate the Bank's capacity to remake itself in response to the pressures of the day, a pattern that is repeated throughout its history. Moreover, the first quarter century of Bank operations, which witnesses the breakup of the European empires and the rise of national liberation movements throughout Asia and Africa, is indispensable for any examination of the transformation of postwar imperial power. The early chapters of this project trace the Bank's contradictory and evolving positions in relation to British imperialism, the emerging nationalisms (and nation states) of the decolonizing world, and the remapping of the globe along a North–South axis of developed and underdeveloped regions. Finally, I devote such careful attention to the mid-twentieth-century decades in order to set up my argument, following Michael Denning's, that the World Bank is intimately involved with the origin of culture and culture study, a claim that is developed in chapter 4.

Chapter 1, in addition to developing a methodological overview for the rhetorical and archival analysis that forms the backbone of the first three chapters, examines the World Bank's inception at the 1944 Bretton Woods Conference. After sketching out the constricted conceptions of both *production* and *development* that underwrite the Bank's Charter of Principles, this chapter examines the political context in which the document was written and the audiences for which it was intended, arguing that the institution's founding is haunted by the specter of failing public confidence. Chapter 2 turns to the Bank's early years of operation. Tracing the initial steps of the Bank's evolution from a reconstruction bank into a development agency, the chapter suggests that the Bank forges its early conception of development primarily as a response to the fiscally conservative demands of U.S. investors; Wall Street aligns the Bank's priorities in the late 1940s. The third chapter concentrates on the Bank's transformations during the decade of the 1960s, a tumultuous period that finds the Bank scrambling to appease insistent demands from an exponentially expanding membership of decolonizing nation states without slighting its constituencies in the North. Here I contend that the Bank marshals the rhetorical dialectic of crisis and possibility to establish itself as a permanent fixture of the global landscape and to authorize a neoimperial interventionism with a scope and ambition that are virtually limitless.

It may be said that the central argument of *Invested Interests* is located in its central chapter, chapter 4. Here I take up Michael Denning's argument about the mid-twentieth-century sea change in the conception of culture, a change that stems from the contradictions and struggles of the historically specific age of three worlds. I develop my argument that the Bank traffics in culture, analyzing the institution's metamorphoses during its first quarter century as both symptoms of and responses to the global cultural turn. The chapter looks at the Bank's role in the global spread of Fordist-Keynesianism, analyzing the ideological and utopic function of mass culture under development. It goes on to examine the Bank's place within the anticolonial writings of midcentury cultural radicals such as Aimé Césaire and Frantz Fanon, before considering the Bank's pivotal role in absentia at the 1955 Asian-African conference in Bandung, Indonesia. In brief, I argue that the World Bank underwrites the global cultural turn. My argument is not that the Bank produces culture in any straightforward, determinative sense, but rather that it is an important institutional actor in the historical transformations that produce the conditions in which culture comes to be critically reevaluated and revalued by midcentury cultural theorists. Moreover, the Bank discovers culture and the social sphere as available spaces for development at roughly the same moment as do the anti-imperialist cultural radicals, suggesting that the two histories can be read in relation to each other as a means of examining the often contradictory cultural investments of the era.

Chapter 5 brings the study up to the present historical moment. Responding to Kumar's conception of World Bank literature in more detail, I examine the degree of critical specificity with which that title phrase may be used, keying on the idea of literature and *the literary*. Reading several World Bank documents, with a particular attention to the ICT (Information Communications Technology) Stories project, I argue that literary forms are increasingly prevalent in the Bank's self-representational strategies, and that a particular genre of Banking bildungsroman can be identified. In this chapter, I examine the increasingly mediated forms of authorship that emerge in response to intensified opposition throughout the long aftermath of the global debt crisis of the 1980s. I read *the literary* as a residual cultural form (based on Raymond Williams's distinction among dominant, emergent, and residual) that indicates a reactive position in relation to both global capital and global social movements. Extending my critique of the Bank as a paradigmatically liberal institution, I contend that World Bank literature authorizes development through an appeal to alternative residual values signified by *the literary*—values that circumscribe the individual through an appeal to humanism, and the social through an appeal to civil society, values that appear to be outside of and prior to the dominant logic of global capitalism but in fact serve to prop it up.

Through all the chapters runs an analytical thread that reads the transformations and maneuvers evident in Bank documents and projects as an ongoing reaction to critique from social movements. Far from showing an omnipotent, autonomous agent, managing the global economy from on high, *Invested Interests* paints a portrait of an institution perpetually engaged in hegemonic struggle, reacting to pressure and critique from Right and Left, from individuals, corporations, nations, and movements. These reactions, I argue, constitute strategic maneuvers, containments, and affirmative engagements in the struggle over the everyday normalcy of development and its supposedly natural role in the social sphere. The Bank's ability to contain critique with various degrees of accommodation and appropriation, often through an address to liberal inclusivity, has been vital to its institutional success and longevity.

In recent years, on the other hand, much has been made of the so-called antiglobalization movement and the increasingly potent critiques mounted against the Bank, the IMF, and the WTO. The final chapters of this book turn to these contemporary social movements, with a particular focus on the World Social Forum (WSF). Chapter 6 functions as a literary excursus, where I develop a reading of Arundhati Roy's novel *The God of Small Things*. Anticipating the analysis of the WSF, my argument in this chapter is that Roy's novel figures an impossible form of productive collectivity. That is, chapter 6 theorizes the politics of reading at the intersection of the World Bank, the World Social Forum, and *the literary*, suggesting that Roy's novel attempts to name a form of collective body that exists only as a political potentiality in our present moment. In particular, I examine the problem of literary politics—the crisis in representational acts of truth telling. This representational crisis raises broad questions about the aporias of signification, pointing to the near-inscrutable gaps that appear to exist between, for instance, rhetorical persuasiveness (or lack thereof) and the production of public consent or dissent. If I have no answer to the vexed questions of whether the Bank, through its rhetorical maneuvering, actually convinces people to believe in the project of development, I am no more certain about the prospects of social movements to generate collective action through literary texts. Beyond reading for political programs, then, this chapter asks, what value can be gained from theorizing figures of impossible collectivity?

I trace this same theme through chapter 7, where I discuss Roy's participation in the World Social Forum. Here I examine the WSF as a promising form of collectivity, but one marked with political fault lines that have much in common with the contradictions and legacies of Bandung. The World Bank, I suggest, is a constitutive antagonist for the WSF, and as such the Forum is particularly well suited to organize global opposition to the Bank and to advocate for immediate, comprehensive debt relief, among other demands. I take issue, however, with the Forum's embrace of global civil society, suggesting that the World Bank itself is eager to adapt to such a model. The chapter develops an argument about the political efficacy of the WSF using readings of Roy's Forum addresses from 2003 and 2004, arguing that they work in concert with her novel to imagine emergent political forms of collectivity. Among other things, mine is an argument that reaffirms the continued relevance of midcentury national-liberation cultural radicals for orienting contemporary anti-imperialist social movements. Following Roy, I argue for a dialectical politics of minimum agenda, an approach that hopes to account for the indispensable utopian imaginings of other possible worlds while still committing itself to the long, hard labor of organizing democratic movements for equity.

1. Imaginative Ventures: Cultivating Confidence at Bretton Woods

To most observers, the World Bank stands a paradigmatic symbol of contemporaneity, an institution on the leading edge of a historical wave of globalization, awash in the ongoing struggles of the day. In the popular public imaginary, the World Bank conjures images of, on the one hand, the ever-advancing financialization of the globe, and, on the other hand, the vibrant (and perhaps violent) social movements that resist such an advance; we locate the Bank somewhere within the present and pressing contradictions of e-commerce and eco-warriors, intellectual property and internet organizing, Wal-Mart and workers, profits and poverty, power and protest. The United Nations, by contrast, founded a few months *after* the Bank, labors under the public perception that it is an antiquated institutional relic, a black-and-white photograph from a history lesson about Wilson's League of Nations. As both have come under significant public scrutiny in recent years, the perceived contrast between the two institutions cannot be explained simply by notoriety or its escape. There is something about the Bank, it would seem, that resists historicization. Although there are surely many reasons for this curious distinction, two stand out: first, the institution's profoundly antidemocratic nature insulates it from public accountability, making it appear somehow outside the influence of both political and historical pressures; second, the institution's insistence that it operates according to strict economic laws and principles tacitly casts it as an actor not subject to the irrational tugs and tussles of history.

The early chapters of this book attempt to cut across this anti-historical facade by scrutinizing the archival record from the first decades of the Bank's operation, arguing that the institution has played an essential role, if not always a consistent or coherent one, in the transformations of imperial power and global capital during the postwar era. To trace this movement, I turn to the methods of rhetorical analysis. Through careful readings of a variety of public Bank documents, I explore specific historical moments of reaction in which we can see the Bank working to produce and maintain consent—"confidence," in the Bank's vernacular—among a presumed public, if not always a historically stable or homogenous one.[1] I understand *rhetoric* here not in the cynical, disparaging sense of obfuscation, mystification, and distraction, where language is artfully assembled to obscure underlying truth (though we certainly find more than a little of that sort of rhetoric in the Bank's documents); I read the Bank's rhetorical shifts over time not simply as attempts to paper over each new crack in the façade by using the fashionable, finely spun language of the day, but rather as substantive attempts to respond to and contain a sequence of powerful and typically unforeseen crises. I understand rhetoric, therefore, in both its productive and its interpretive contexts, as a means of examining the work of texts in the world: the social effects of texts, and how they produce these effects.

My work here draws on scholarly traditions in rhetorical critical discourse analysis (most notably the work of Norman Fairclough and Teun van Dijk), and on the work done in postcolonial studies under the rubric of *colonial discourse analysis* (a tradition that goes back at least as far as Aimé Césaire's *Discourse on Colonialism,* and that includes scholarship by the field's biggest name, including Spivak, Said, Bhabha, Young, Pratt, Hulme, McClintock and many others, albeit with decidedly varied understandings of *discourse*).[2] Rhetorical analysis in this sense intersects with a British cultural studies tradition in the work of such figures as Raymond Williams, Stuart Hall, and Terry Eagleton, who, in the conclusion of his *Literary Theory: An Introduction,* calls for a return to the analytical category of *rhetoric* as a means of understanding "speaking and writing . . . as forms of *activity* inseparable from the wider social relations between writers and readers, orators and audiences, and as largely unintelligible outside the social purposes and conditions in which they were embedded."[3] This dual understanding of rhetoric—both as a method of historicized interpretation and as an active intervention into the production of social relations—underpins these first chapters.

That said, it is important to acknowledge the valuable critiques of the textual turn within development studies[4]—the tendency of some scholars to privilege discourse and discursive analysis over the material affects of lending practices, institutional organization, and the lived experiences of lenders and borrowers, all of which can differ significantly from documentary or textual evidence.[5] Such work at times offers an exaggerated Foucault- or Said-inspired model of discourse, where language itself appears the dominant actor in the production of social reality. Take, for example, Escobar's argument, from his pioneering book *Encountering Development,* that "the 'Third World' *has been produced* by the discourses and practices of development since their inception in the early post–World War II period,"[6] or Gustavo Esteva's claim, regarding Harry Truman's 1949 inauguration speech featuring the terms *development* and *underdevelopment,* that "on that day, two billion people *became underdeveloped.* . . . Since then, development has connoted at least one thing: to escape from the undignified condition called underdevelopment"[7] (emphasis mine, in both quotations). Distancing himself from Marxist critiques of culture and economy, Escobar argues that "one should avoid falling back into the division between the 'ideal' (the theory) and 'the real' (the economy)" and instead "investigate the epistemological and cultural conditions of the production of discourses that command the power of truth, and the specific mode of articulation of these discourses upon a given historical setting."[8]

Many (myself included) would argue that Escobar's work at times errs toward an inversion of the base/superstructure model where the discursive "ideal" produces the material "real." Where the textual turn runs up against its most decisive limit, at least in *Encountering Development,* is in Escobar's hope that "the possibilities for transforming the politics of representation, that is for transforming social life itself," will emerge from the "postdevelopment" forms of "hybrid or minority cultures" and the politics of "cultural difference."[9] As I argue throughout this book, the politics of hybridity and difference are, in my estimation, likely to be ineffectual as a challenge to the World Bank. When faced with crisis from below, one of the Bank's most practiced responses has been an institutional swing toward liberal inclusivity; at these moments, the institution casts itself as a civil society actor, stressing the importance of debate and dialogue, accepting and even welcoming critique, and adopting the language of humanistic values. A politics of cultural difference, far from "subverting the axiomatics of capitalism and modernity in their hegemonic form,"[10] as Escobar suggests, is likely to find a warm welcome at an institution that throughout its history has proven adept at absorbing, containing, and appropriating liberal critique. As I will argue in the latter half of this book, a more promising model, both intellectually and politically, can be located in the critiques of radical social movements (especially from the South), including those from midcentury that contribute to the revisions of Marxist thought, that interrogate and complicate the base/superstructure model of economics and culture that Escobar tends to simply invert.

However much Escobar's work can, at time, err toward an exaggerated construction of discourse as power, it would be a mistake to extend a critique of the textual turn too far in the opposite direction. I prefer to see the differences between my own research and Escobar's theorizations of development discourse as a matter of emphasis rather than a matter of kind. His work, and the work of scholars like him, advances a critique of development and underdevelopment that contributes in profound ways to our understanding of the paradoxical manner in which aid, lending, investment, social projects, and the like have underwritten hegemonic forms of global exploitation and immiseration in the postwar era. In addition to its overarching arguments about the ways development discourse has worked to construct an ubiquitous and debilitating image of the third world and its relationship to modernity, *Encountering Development* helps us to understand that the Bank's rhetorical choices (as well as those of USAID and other development institutions) influence funding decisions, shape research and scholarship, focus oppositional resistance, and much more.

Escobar's work and the work of rhetorical/discursive analysis more broadly (including my own) help to illuminate the broader cultural apparatus of development. However, a rounded picture of the Bank and its global influence cannot be sketched solely by reading its *own* texts. Other methods of inquiry are necessary; perhaps most notable would be place-based analysis that attends to the particular effects of development as it articulates in specific locales and upon specific individuals and collectivities across the globe—attends, that is, to the movement of investment capital as it is lent, borrowed, disbursed, and, perhaps most importantly, to the many points along the way at which surplus is extracted and conflict produced. The ethnographic and economic analyses that examine the complexities of development through local case studies by scholars such as Julia Elyachar, James Ferguson, Naila Kabeer, Timothy Mitchell, and Vijayendra Rao and Michael Walton, ought to be understood as an indispensable complement to this book. Likewise, my understanding of the Bank is powerfully informed by the more activist scholarship of Walden Bello, Patrick Bond, Catherine Caufield, Kevin Danaher, Susan George, Teresa Hayter, Cheryl Payer, Bruce Rich, and others. And transnational feminist scholars including Cynthia Enloe, Rosemary Hennessy, Naila Kabeer, Maria Mies, Chandra Talpade Mohanty, Vandana Shiva, and Gayatri Chakravorty Spivak have provided invaluable theoretical frameworks and empirical data for understanding the dense and varied articulations of international finance.

My hope is that the limits of discursive or rhetorical analysis in general, and my present study in particular, can and will be read in the context of this larger body of scholarship.[11] But if the full complexity of the Bank and its policies cannot be located solely by *reading* its texts, neither can it be read distinct from its public rhetorical performances.[12] Washington, D.C., after all, is a *place* as much as are Cairo, Dhaka, Lusaka, or Manila; and its disproportionate global influence, indeed imperium, suggests that there remains an urgent necessity to examine the centers of ruling power in addition to those places where U.S./World Bank influence is exercised.

I understand rhetorical and discursive analysis, then, to be one among many necessary scholarly interventions into the field of development. I make no claims to any privileged status for rhetorical analysis; I see it as a methodological approach that affords a critical vantage that can complement and extend other modes of scholarship, investigation, and critique. Far from assuming that the official record of Bank documents matches up precisely with the experiences of those working and living with the effects of development on the ground (so to speak), my approach to rhetorical investigation in the following chapters reads Bank documents with an eye toward examining not just what the Bank says and how it says it, but also, more important, what is absent from the Bank's own public record: to whom the Bank is addressing its arguments, to what pressures the Bank is responding, about which alternatives the Bank hopes to forestall or encourage action, and in whose interest Bank decisions are made. My approach seeks to historicize the Bank's rhetorical maneuvers, reading them variously as symptom, reaction, contestation, and preemption—engagements in the hegemonic conflicts and struggles of specific historical moments.[13]

Faith in Confidence

The Bank's document archive provides a record through which we can trace the fundamental continuities and unchanging principles that have guided the Bank over its history. By extension, the record enables us to examine the Bank's other, more malleable and fluid, beliefs, those contextual and contingent positions that emerge in response to one crisis and are discarded in response to another. Edward Mason and Robert Asher, writing in their commissioned twenty-fifth anniversary history, *The World Bank since Bretton Woods,* contend that the researcher will "look in vain in the Bank files, both current and old, for any evidence of accepted theories of development or models of the development process."[14] Their argument goes on to suggest that a coherent World Bank *theory* of development can be located only in the patterns of its lending *practices,* particularly its predilection for large public infrastructural investments such as roads, railways, power plants, port installations, communication facilities, and so on, which the Bank had assumed necessary to entice private capital to a region. To this day, the Bank continues to exhibit an unhealthy fascination with big dams (particularly unhealthy for the millions who have been displaced because of them);[15] however, in response to several decades' worth of scathing critiques from environmentalists, indigenous rights groups, and others, the Bank has gradually diversified its lending and worked to distance itself from the large infrastructural lending practices that Mason and Asher believed the only discernable constant in the Bank's approach to development.

My own reading of the Bank's underlying theoretical continuity is better summed up in Mason and Asher's assessment of the Bank president John J. McCloy and his two vice presidents, Robert L. Garner and Eugene R. Black (who would succeed McCloy and become the first long-term Bank president, with a term stretching from 1949 to 1963). About the three men, who are credited with stabilizing and setting the future direction of the Bank, Mason and Asher comment, "faith of the new trio in private investment as a panacea for the economic ills of the world was almost boundless."[16] To locate any coherent theoretical principles that serve as a steady foundation for the Bank's institutional history, one must look not to its constantly shifting articulations of development but rather to its unshakable *faith* in capitalism and the power of the market. Although different Bank regimes have varied (sometimes substantially) in the degree to which they have believed markets should be regulated or left alone to correct themselves, or the degree to which redistributive policies or inducements to privatization might be necessary, a consistent belief in the steadfast bond between progress and capitalist economic growth has never waivered. The Bank's faith is so resolute that in its public assertions capitalism goes largely unspoken; the concept functions as common-sense logic and economic law, the coherent, foundational principle on which a flexible, responsive, contingent conception of development can be built and perpetually renovated.

This institutional belief goes hand in hand with an unwavering certainty from within the Bank, particularly early on, that, to function properly, capitalism requires the construction and maintenance of public faith. I am thinking of a related, though slightly different inflection of *faith* than the one advanced by Susan George and Fabrizio Sabelli in their important critique of the World Bank, *Faith and Credit*. Their metaphor figures the Bank as the shepherding church: "Why do we think we need the Bank? For the same reasons we think we need the Church. Frail, imperfect humanity needs constraints, guardrails, continual instruction in, and the interpretation of, the doctrine. Those who have not yet reached the full expression of market capitalism and consequent development, those who fall by the wayside, must be goaded along the path of salvation."[17] For George and Sabelli, faith becomes a way to explain the Bank's hermeneutic role as exegete, moral guide, and (disciplining) conscience; that is, they account for its authority by suggesting that the Bank functions as though it were the earthly, material instantiation of divine will, at once visible and stable, providing firm and consistent assurances to its members in times of crisis.

This rock-like stature is undoubtedly part of the role that the Bank plays for members of its flock. But of equal importance is the obverse side of faith: the ongoing effort to cast the "laws" of

capitalism as inevitable and eternal, thereby rendering them effectively invisible. My use of the term *faith* attempts to call attention
to the work of ideology, which only *works* when subjects *work* all
by themselves. "Amen—so be it" in Louis Althusser's phrasing.[18]
When ideological structures are challenged—when they are unmasked not as social truths, but as practices and ideas constructed
in the interests of some and to the detriment of others—they cease
to function as ideology. To historicize the Bank, then, is to work
against one of the recurrent tropes of the Bank archive, whereby
the institution insists that its practices and policies are nonhistori-
cal, nonpolitical, nonideological, and based on an objective reality
of economic facts and laws.

When we examine the Bank's early attempts at self-definition
and self-justification, then, we find that, as much as the institution
is a historical product of the Second World War, it is even more a
product of the Depression and of the worldwide economic crises
that followed World War I. As a levee against such economic un-
certainties as led to the worldwide capitalist crisis of the 1920s and
1930s, the Bank is keenly aware that its own institutional future
along with the broader world-capitalist system is entirely dependent upon the ability to build and maintain public confidence. "If a
bank's first building block is a hard cash investment," argue Devish
Kapur, John P. Lewis, and Richard Webb in their comprehensive
fiftieth-anniversary history of the Bank, *The World Bank: Its First
Half Century,* "all further additions to the structure are made out
of a less substantial material: confidence."[19] Or, in McCloy's calcu-
lations about the relative importance of the Bank's role as a provider of moral guidance and stability to reassure the investing public,
versus its role as a provider of capital, "[t]he moral is to the physical as 2 to 1."[20] Variations on this theme appear time and again in
the Bank archives. As we will see in more detail below, the Bank
found itself, particularly in its early years, having to demonstrate
its own bona fides as a secure, prudent financial institution, while at
the same time convincing reluctant constituencies that the financial
risks of international investment are both necessary and valuable.
From the beginning this has been a difficult case to make, largely
because the rationality of the former (prudent investment) relies
upon and simultaneously seeks to produce the irrationality of the
latter (the production of public confidence/faith in capitalism). It

is precisely this gap between persuasion and faith that a rhetorical analysis of the World Bank archive must address.

Selling confidence, then, becomes the Bank's first and ever-present task. To wit, George Martin, the director of the marketing department of the World Bank from 1950 through 1963 described Eugene Black, the Bank's third president, like this: "He's a master bond salesman, always has been, always will be. No matter what he does in the Bank, he's still going to be a bond salesman."[21] He goes on, however, to describe just how difficult it was to sell the idea of an International Bank to the public: "But I can assure you that many many people just wouldn't stand still long enough to let you tell them the story of the International Bank for Reconstruction and Development. It was an awkward name to begin with. It was a foreign situation in the minds of most people. And it took a lot of selling, a lot of doing, to convince these people."[22] In a 1961 oral history interview, Black, the "master bond salesman" himself, re-calls the massive investments that went into what would today be called the *branding* of the World Bank:

> Well, we made speeches all over the country to groups of finan-cial people. We invited groups to come to Washington, and we had what we called "information conferences," where people would come and spend two days or three days. We would have various officials of the Bank discuss with them how we planned to operate or how we were operating. In that way they became familiar with what we were trying to do, what our objectives and our policies were. That takes time. It's a lot of work. We just made speeches all the time, everywhere. That's been going on ever since.[23]

My point for the time being is simply that: the process of selling the idea of the World Bank and the idea of development *have been going on ever since*.[24] Moreover, the explicit, rational arguments that a salesman such as Black uses to persuade audiences about the merits of the Bank and of development, arguments that have undergone frequent and substantial revisions over the course of sixty years, also engage in the generally unspoken, but consistent and coherent, work of producing public confidence by naturalizing the irrationalities of capitalism, principal of which, tautologically, is public confidence itself. This work is not *supplemental* to the work of investment lending or technical assistance; it is integral to the very nature of the capitalist project at the heart of the Bank's mission.[25]

Mason and Asher sum up this essential aspect of the Bank's work nicely through a reference to John Maynard Keynes, the British economist who was among the driving conceptual and political forces behind the Bretton Woods Conference, and who helped draft the initial proposal for a World Bank:

> As Keynes once remarked, if capitalists foresaw all the uncertainties to which their investments would be subjected, they would probably not have invested in the first place. He attributed their behavior largely to the possession of an unusual endowment of "animal spirits." Since the Bank is using other people's money for the most part, so much animal spirit is not required to make an investment decision. What is required is a certain amount of faith in the development prospects of a country—a faith that transcends the expectations that can with certainty be associated with particular projects.[26]

More on Keynes's "animal spirits" in a moment. For now let me only reiterate that the work of producing confidence in the Bank and in development—and thereby producing faith in capitalism—has been one of the few constants for the Bank during its sixty-year existence. Certainly this work is not entirely rhetorical or discursive. Although there are unmistakable rhetorical and discursive elements within the Bank's operating policies, procedures, decisions, relationships, and so forth, all of which help determine public confidence or lack thereof, the full spectrum of the Bank's work cannot be accessed through a methodological approach restricted to rhetorical or discursive analysis of the Bank's archival documents. Nevertheless, the Bank's rhetorical performances ought not be disregarded, and rhetorical methods of analysis capable of developing materialist critiques (sometimes too hastily constructed in simple opposition to rhetoric or discourse) that illuminate the Bank's relation to class, production, surplus, and the like, have much to contribute to the scholarship on development and on capitalist imperialism during the postwar era.

In the following chapters, then, I rely on the disciplinary double-vision of rhetoric, concerned as it is with both production and interpretation. I take the Bank's rhetorical responses, particularly in moments of pressure and crisis, to constitute and be of themselves real, active interventions, not merely ornamental window dressing distinct from (or worse, a distraction from) the "real work" of development taking place in the field. Careful rhetorical analysis of the recurrent tropes, figures, and tendencies within the Bank archive (analysis that also attends to questions of audience, context, and persuasive purpose) affords us glimpses into the ways the Bank uses its public statements and documents to justify and authorize its role within a contested social sphere. By interpreting the specific rhetorical strategies that the Bank employs to produce and naturalize not only its own institutional work but also the broader world-capitalist system on which it depends, we can develop a clearer picture both of the Bank's interventions in the postwar transformation of imperial power, and of those oppositional energies and pressures—at times conservative, at times revolutionary—that constrain and compel the Bank, forcing it perpetually to react, respond, and reposition itself.

Bretton Woods Foundations

"[The International Bank for Reconstruction and Development] is one of the most imaginative ventures in the field of international cooperation that the world has ever seen and great hopes are built on its achievements."[27] So proclaimed J. W. Beyen, the Bank's executive director for Holland and the Union of South Africa, to the annual meeting of the Savings Bank Association of New York in October 1946, less than four months after the Bank had, so to speak, opened its doors for business. It must have seemed particularly imaginative—and particularly venturesome from Beyen's perspective, representing, as he purported to, both a European nation and its colonlial territories. Following Beyen's Bank-steeped language and jargon, I offer the following thesis: the financial institution *imagined* by delegates at the Bretton Woods Conference (and rather fancifully at that) effectively performs an *imagined* internationalism,[28] bridging the era of colonial ad*venturer* and the era of international *venture* capital.[29]

Few of the delegates at the United Nations Monetary and Finance Conference that took place between July 1 and July 22, 1944, in Bretton Woods, New Hampshire, would have thought the International Bank for Reconstruction and Development an institution capable of bringing about such significant transformations, and none would have conceived of the transition in such terms.

In fact, the World Bank, as it would soon become known (in no small part, as George Martin suggested, because the full name, International Bank for Reconstruction and Development, proved exceedingly cumbersome as a public relations slogan), was something of an afterthought at Bretton Woods. Although Harry D. White, the U.S. assistant secretary of the Treasury, initially conceived of and laid the early groundwork for an International Bank, support for the idea at Bretton Woods came primarily from Latin American countries and those European countries with economies severely damaged by the war, largely because they saw such a bank as a potential source of relatively inexpensive lending. Interestingly, one of the institution's early proponents, the Soviet Union (USSR), ultimately chose *not* to become a member of the Bank and the Fund because of what it saw as disproportionate U.S. influence: in 1947, as the Cold War was heating up, the Soviet representative to the UN called the Bretton Woods institutions "branches of Wall Street" and (rightly) complained that the Bank was "subordinated to the political purposes which made it the instrument of one great power."[30] Despite, or because of, support from the suspect quarters of Latin America and, initially, the Soviet Union, the Bank occupied very little of the delegates' attention at Bretton Woods, being officially added to the agenda only at the last minute. The International Monetary Fund was the primary topic of discussion at Bretton Woods and was presumed by most delegates to be by far the more consequential financial institution. Burke Knapp, who at the time of the conference was a member of the Federal Reserve and who later joined the Bank staff, remarked about just "how little attention was paid to the Bank in the pre–Bretton Woods planning or in the Bretton Woods Conference itself. I suppose if one measured the time spent during those fourteen days of work at the Bretton Woods Conference, the Bank probably didn't take more than a day and a half."[31]

The Treasury Department invitations sent out to the forty-four participating governments declared that the meeting was "for the purpose of formulating *definite* proposals for an International Monetary Fund, and *possibly* a Bank for Reconstruction and Development" (emphasis mine).[32] Even the Bank's title and purpose, "Reconstruction and Development," came about as an ad hoc pairing. Although we now think of the Bank as almost synonymous with development, it was originally conceived primarily as a lending vehicle for European reconstruction after the Second World War. Early drafts contained no mention of the word *development* and no hint of a mission that might focus on poorer or *underdeveloped* countries. Kapur, Lewis, and Webb recount the following conversation between White and his deputy Edward Bernstein during the planning meetings leading up to Bretton Woods: "When [Bernstein] asked what they would do with the bank once reconstruction was over, White threw the question back: 'What do you suggest?' 'Let's have it there for after,' Bernstein said. It could lend to other areas that needed development. The draft, when it was subsequently circulated to other governments in November 1943, arrived with the words 'and Development' appended to the institution's name" (57).

"Let's have it there for after"? Hardly the type of rigorous argumentation that one might expect. And yet in this abbreviated exchange lies the unlikely seed of what over the course of the next sixty years would become the institution most responsible for constructing and shaping the concept of *development* both intellectually and economically. Any contemporary connotations of social welfare, equity, or wealth redistribution that may adhere (however loosely) to the concept of World Bank development were entirely absent at Bretton Woods.

Keynes in an oft-quoted passage about the Bank's function comes closest to articulating the priorities spelled out in the Articles of Agreement.[33] In his opening remarks to the Bretton Woods Commission on the Bank he argued the following: "It is likely, in my judgment, that the field of reconstruction from the consequences of the war will mainly occupy the proposed Bank in its early days. But, as soon as possible, and with increasing emphasis as time goes on, there is a second duty laid upon it, namely to develop the resources and productive capacity of the world, with special attention to the less developed countries."[34]

The passage is cited in so many Bank histories because it appears to accurately predict the Bank's evolution. Any apparent correspondence, however, is more incidental than prophetic. Although the language he uses will sound familiar to today's reader, Keynes, like the other Bretton Woods delegates, was describing an institution that had little resemblance to the *development agency* that the contemporary Bank has become.

Perhaps most notably, for Keynes and the other delegates the term *development* referred solely to the exploitation of economic resources. Kapur, Lewis, and Webb illustrate the deeply embedded imperialist assumptions from which the Bretton Woods delegates conceived *development*:

> At Bretton Woods [development] more often meant physical output than human betterment, economic opportunity rather than social justice. The word still evoked an age of discovery and settlement of "underdeveloped territories," when overseas economic development could be cheerfully described as "the hacking down of the forest or the sheep rearing or the gold mining which made Canada, Australia, and South Africa into world factors," an age when, for the most part, it was the land, not the people, that was to be developed.[35]

It is land, not people, then, that Keynes has in mind when he points to the Bank's duty to "develop the resources and productive capacity of the world." His understanding of *production* is similarly restrictive. With none of the richness found in Marxist theorizations of production and reproduction, which endeavor to articulate the inextricable connections between the mode of production and the broader social relations of any historical era, Keynes's economistic usage essentially constricts its understanding of production to the commodification of resources and the generation of wealth. Production in this sense is roughly synonymous with industrialization; like development, the Keynesian conception of production applies to resources not people, commodities not labor. This conception posits an economic realm, largely distinct from broader social relations, that can be measured, manipulated, and modernized.

If the Bretton Woods delegates had been pressed to articulate a connection between the development of the world's productive capacity and the development of its peoples, their rationale likely would have been couched in terms similar to the slogan "a rising tide floats all boats"; if national economies develop their productive capacities, the logic goes, the benefits will (eventually) extend to all their citizens. Article I of the Bank's Charter comes closest to articulating development as a social phenomenon in this sense; it lists one of the Bank's purposes as "encouraging international investment for *the development of the productive resources of members, thereby assisting in raising productivity, the standard of living and conditions of labor in their territories*" (my emphasis).[36]

Years before Reagan/Thatcher–era conservatism, Keynes and the Bretton Woods delegates were conceiving of the Bank as an institution founded on the capitalist principles of trickle-down economics, whereby the generation of wealth in any sector or among any class was presumed beneficial to all sectors and all classes. Although different Bank presidents have believed more and less firmly in the specific virtues of trickle-down models, the underlying assumption, articulated at Bretton Woods, that development is wrought through economic growth (through, i.e., the production of wealth) has remained a foundational principle for the Bank throughout its sixty-year history.

Even within this narrow frame of *developing productive resources,* however, Keynes's statement about promptly turning the Bank's "special attention to the less developed countries" likely overstates his actual expectations for the institution. His private remarks indicate a much more Eurocentric understanding of the Bank's primary function. Again, Kapur, Lewis, and Webb recount a telling exchange: "In private, at the British Embassy in Washington [Keynes] put it more bluntly. While expounding on his vision that, with proper economic management, governments could have 'a boom that would raise the standard of living of all Europe to the levels of America today,' he was asked 'Does that apply to India and the rest of the Empire?' Keynes replied: 'That must wait until the reconstruction of Europe is much further advanced.'"[37] Keynes's public assessment that the Bank would turn its focus to the underdeveloped world "as soon as possible and with increasing emphasis"—the statement quoted in almost every recapitulation of the Bank's Bretton Woods inception—suggests an undercurrent of internationalism with at least some concern for global equity. However, his private comments about India's place at the back of the funding queue, uttered from the juridically sovereign space of the British national embassy, nestled within the capital city of the world's most powerful nation, provide a glimpse of the uneven geography that underpins Bretton Woods internationalism. In fact Keynes never wanted an international conference at all, preferring instead to work out the details of the IMF and the Bank at a bilateral Anglo–U.S. summit. Irked at having to consult with such a large number of nations, Keynes lashed out: "Twenty-one countries have been invited which clearly have nothing to contribute and will merely encumber the ground, namely,

Colombia, Costa Rica, Dominica, Ecuador, Salvador, Guatemala, Haiti, Honduras, Liberia, Nicaragua, Panama, Paraguay, Philippines, Venezuela, Peru, Uruguay, Ethiopia, Iceland, Iran, Iraq, Luxembourg. The most monstrous monkey-house assembled for years."[38] Contemporary critics of the Bank's capitalist rapaciousness often portray the protectionist Keynes, himself quite dismayed at the final administrative structure imposed upon the Bank by the U.S. delegates at Bretton Woods, with nostalgic fondness, if not heroic resistance. The legacies of Keynesian regulationism echo loudly in the work of a diverse array of Bank critics, from Stiglitz to Sen, who believe that the institution can be reformed to better protect the poor from the inequalities and excesses of unregulated capitalism. Keynes, then, is frequently cast as the spurned founder who campaigned fervently (perhaps even at the cost of his own life) for a more humane, more truly international institution. Reading against the grain, however, the Keynesian portrayal of Bretton Woods as a "monstrous monkey-house" throws fresh light on his belief that regulatory mechanisms and economic institutions form necessary bulwarks against the irrational "animal spirits" of capitalist investors. Although Keynes may have argued for a kinder, gentler Bank that might help to manage the irrationalism of individual capitalists by developing international systems of economic control and security, this argument should hardly be confused with a principled commitment to the welfare of the peoples living in what would soon come to be known as the third world. As his embassy comment suggests, Keynes's first thoughts are with protecting the "humane" national economies of the United Kingdom, the United States, and, secondarily, Continental Europe. Worrying about whether a few more spirited animals might be unleashed in the monkey-house—that is, the effects of unchecked and unregulated irrationalisms of capitalism on the barely consequential economies of the non-European world—was at best a minor concern for him at Bretton Woods.

In contrast to Keynes's dismissive approach to the Global South, Harry White and the U.S. delegation insisted that Bretton Woods maintain every appearance of a truly international summit. Not only did White prevail in his desire to include the delegates from forty-four nations, including the twenty-one in Keynes's "monkey-house," but White also went so far as to publicly announce—somewhat disingenuously, one imagines—that the Bank "must not be a rich man's club."[39] In taking this internationalist approach, the U.S. gestures toward a different interpretation of (or, more accurately, a different strategic approach to) the irrational "animal spirits" embedded within capitalism. The outward expansion of capitalism across the globe—developing new markets and gaining or enhancing access to new supplies of natural resources and labor—was essential if the worldwide recessions that followed the First World War were to be avoided. But as the viability and legitimacy of the European colonial models of direct territorial control, settler rule, corporate proxies, or corporate/state ruling coalitions began to crumble under mounting pressure from decolonizing movements, new frameworks for building or deepening a world capitalist system were urgently needed. If White and the United States had little more concern for the welfare of the monkey-house nations than Keynes, they perhaps better understood the value of cultivating a sense of mutual investment and participation in international systems of financial management, a sense that could serve for establishing a sustainable postcolonial framework for global capitalist expansion. Economic development for the monkey-house nations might end up aiding the animals behind the bars; whether it did or not, creating the perception that there existed among the Bretton Woods powers a sincere commitment to such development would go a long way to insure the economic health, security, and prosperity of the zookeepers.

Despite the appearance of inclusivity, then, the Bank that emerges from Bretton Woods is anything but a democratic, internationalist institution. Mason and Asher make this point emphatically, arguing that the Bank "was an Anglo-Saxon creation, with the United States very much the senior partner."[40] Kapur, Lewis, and Webb contend that the Bank's organizational structure, which vests "predominant ownership and control in the economically more powerful countries," legislates a governance model that is "rooted in *political realism*" (my emphasis); unlike the San Francisco proceedings that would formulate the United Nations General Assembly the following year, Bretton Woods made no pretense to "follow the juridical theory that all states, large and small, rich and poor, were equal."[41] The United Nations, hardly a model democratic institution with its veto-wielding Security Council, unelected "representatives," and many other layers of institutional checks on democratic process, adopted a "one nation, one vote" model;[42] the Bank's organizational structure takes a very different form. Bretton Woods member nations were constituted as *shareholders*; to become a member of the Bank and the IMF (only joint membership was permissible—a nation could not elect to join only one Bretton Woods' institution), nation states were required to purchase shares in the Bank's authorized capital, with the level of their buy-in based on the relative economic strength of the nation. Of a nation's subscription, 20 percent was to be paid in immediately (and subject to call by the Bank), while the other 80 percent would be called only if the Bank was forced to meet exceptional obligations. Institutional voting power was tied directly to the size of a nation's financial contribution, meaning that wealthy nations, the United States in particular, had overwhelming authority in the Bank's governance. The relevant Article of Agreement reads, "Each member shall have two hundred fifty votes plus one additional vote for each share of stock held."[43] This insured that the United States held over 35 percent of the voting power when the Bank opened, well in excess of the 20 percent needed to veto any changes to the Bank's Charter.[44] Despite White's insistence on the international character of the Bretton Woods institutions and his enjoinder that the Bank "not be a rich man's club," the Bank's bureaucratic structures forego even the appearance of democracy established by the UN model, choosing instead the political realism of a governance structure based on the principle of "one dollar, one vote."[45]

White's personal inclinations toward internationalism may or may not have been genuine. "One dollar, one vote," was a pragmatic, if not also strategic, decision on the part of the Bretton Woods delegates, especially the U.S. drafters. Because the United States had emerged from the war as the only nation capable of making a significant financial contribution to the Bank, and because the dollar was the only currency sufficiently stable for international lending, the Bank's very existence was predicated upon its ability to win the consent of Roosevelt, the U.S. Congress, and the U.S. public. The political realism behind the governance structure is evident in the Bank's 1945 booklet *Questions and Answers on the Fund and Bank* (one of a series of similar publications). Early versions of this booklet were published by the Treasury Department while the fledgling Bank set up shop, but *Questions and Answers,* even though printed out of house, was for all intents and purposes a World Bank publication. In fact, during this period the Bank's entire marketing office was housed in the Treasury building rather than at the Bank's headquarters, indicating just how little separation actually existed between the two agencies in 1945. Given their question/answer format, this series of publications (predecessors to Internet FAQ files) offers an interesting window into the kinds of pressures the Bank saw itself needing to address.

The articulation of the questions (as much as of the answers) offers valuable insight into the kinds of rhetorical maneuvering deemed necessary by the Bank at this nascent moment. Consider the following queries: "How can we be sure that the interests of the United States in the Fund will be fully protected?" or "In joining the Fund, will the United States surrender control over the value of the American dollar?" or "Instead of accepting the Bank proposal now, would it not be safer for the United States to wait until normal financial relationships have been re-established?"[46] The pamphlet makes every effort to assuage any fears from U.S. citizens about foreign control of the Bretton Woods institutions, clarifying that not even the combined voting power of the British Empire could threaten U.S. authority over the Bank: "The United States will control 32 percent of the total voting power. Its vote will be larger than any other single nation, and larger than that of the British countries taken as a whole."[47] It is worth noting that the Bank's *only* audience in 1945 (or at least the only audience it saw the need to address specifically in its publications) was that of U.S. public opinion and U.S. political representatives. And in this regard the Bank's primary message was that the structures of governance put in place to operate the Bank and IMF would ensure that U.S. dollars would not be "simply handed over" to foreign governments, and that potential voting blocs, such as the nations of the British Commonwealth, would not constitute a threat to U.S. authority and autonomy.

If the Bank's governance model was, in fact, an expression of political *realism,* then White's declaration that the institution "not be a rich man's club" functions as an example, par excellence, of the ways the Bank's ideological work of rhetorical inclusivity constitutes a form of realpolitik in the expansion of U.S. economic and political power. The system of internationalism that emerges from Bretton Woods is in fact a system of U.S. global hegemony cloaked in the sustainable (to use from the jargon of more recent Bank history) guise of a bureaucratic organizational structure that

maintains the appearance of offering seats at the table to constituents previously excluded from the sites of power. In 1944, prior
to the waves of Asian and then African decolonization, this appeal to internationalism was aimed primarily at Latin America and
Eastern Europe, areas hungry for capital investment and therefore
willing to accept symbolic gestures of inclusion in exchange for the
promise of borrowing opportunities in the future. It is unclear how
much, if at all, the internationalist gestures at Bretton Woods actually accomplished in the way of producing consent either from
the national governments or the national publics of those would-
be member states on the periphery of the world-capitalist system.
The principal aim of internationalist rhetoric, however, was never
to lure those peripheral states into participation; in most cases the
economic leverage of the United States was powerful enough on its
own to accomplish that task. Instead, I would argue, the primary
concern was U.S. public opinion. Although there was certainly a
strong current of isolationism within the United States, appeals
for an international regulatory system to ensure economic and political stability would have found much support in the aftermath
of U.S. wartime sacrifice. Perhaps more important, free access to
international markets previously restricted because of preferential
trading arrangements between Europe and its colonial territories
provided a powerful incentive to U.S. business interests. Moreover,
the liberalism of such an appeal helped establish early on an ethos
of inclusivity that the Bank has successfully exploited in its public relations efforts ever since Bretton Woods, both as a means to
argue that the United States as the dominant world power has a
responsibility to the welfare of mankind, and conversely to deflect
any critique that the Bank is acting in the imperialist interests of
the United States.

But the internationalist argument alone would likely not have
carried the day among the U.S. public. It is essential to clarify the
political context in which the Bretton Woods conference takes
place. First, while the delegates were meeting in July 1944 to develop frameworks for a *post*war international economic system,
the war was very much *in the present,* with an Allied victory an-
ticipated but far from certain.[48] Consider, too, that in the aftermath
of the Depression deep skepticism about the economic wisdom of
international lending existed within the financial community, and
deep skepticism about both the security of banking and the effi-

cacy of government intervention in the financial markets existed within the broader public. [49] After the First World War, a host of poorly conceived loans were made, many of which ended in default during the Depression. Bankers and investors thus had little appetite for international speculation. Further, a lingering isolationist tradition, coupled with widespread belief in *laissez-faire* economics within U.S. politics, made the Bank a very difficult sell to Roosevelt, the U.S. Congress, and the U.S. public. The *New York Times* denounced the Bretton Woods plan and Robert A. Taft complained on the Senate floor that supporting the Bank and the Fund was tantamount to "pouring money down a rat hole."[50] Foreshadowing present-day movements to boycott World Bank bonds, several states passed legislation specifically prohibiting the purchase of World Bank securities because, in the words of one Wisconsin banking official, the money was being guaranteed by foreign governments whose commitments weren't "worth a whoop in hell."[51] In this political climate, and with success dependent entirely on U.S. financial contributions, the foundation of an International Bank for Reconstruction and Development was an act requiring no small amount of hubris. Teetering on the razor edge of public confidence, the new Bank required an enormous act of faith from all its participants. White's liberal appeal to internationalism, with its New Deal undertones, may have helped persuade some that the United States ought to shoulder the burden for worldwide peace and prosperity. But in the early days of the Bank, as we shall see more clearly in the next chapter, garnering the confidence of the U.S. public, the U.S. politicians, and (perhaps most important) the U.S. financial community was by no means certain.

Perhaps the Bank's most important task in its early years was producing this trust. The inaugural *Questions and Answers* booklet (published in 1944, one year prior to the edition cited above) asserted that the "operations of the Bank may be expected to have a wholesome effect on international investment by restoring the confidence of private investors in foreign securities."[52] But stating that the Bank would have a "wholesome effect" on confidence and *producing* that effect were two different things. Confidence—or put another way, faith—was the air in which the Bank moved and breathed. Often this translated into a positive articulation of the Bank's many virtues (we see examples of such institutional sales pitches in the next chapter). At other times, however, we find the formula reversed. Consider for a moment a striking passage from McCloy's first speech as Bank president in 1947, in which he offers a *negative* articulation of confidence: that is, the effect produced by the absence of confidence, the metaphoric lack of air. To quote his narrative at length:

> It is not only political health, but economic health as well that we must seek if we are to avoid the disruptions and unholy practices which lead to wars. I recall on one of my somewhat frequent trips around the world—this was after Germany had surrendered—I was walking through the battered and demoralized city of Vienna and suddenly across the street I saw the offices of the Credit Anstalt. It brought back memories of 1931 and I experienced a strange feeling. For suddenly, across all of the terrible destruction of the intervening years, I recalled the uneasiness and foreboding which the announcement of the failure of that bank had caused in knowledgeable circles in the United States. Although I had been entirely remote from any transactions involved in the bank and though I could perhaps not trace any direct connection between its failure and the terrible events that had in the meantime occurred, the sense of their connection was present. The economic disease of which that failure was a symptom was clearly a contributing factor to the fears and pressures which ultimately generated the war.[53]

World Bank presidents are not prone to having "strange feelings." Or at least not to admitting so in public. The emotional nature of this peculiar narrative suggests the degree to which Credit Anstalt—or rather, its eerie absence, its abandoned offices, which somehow called attention to themselves among the other devastations of a "battered and demoralized" postwar Vienna—haunted the genesis of World Bank.

Much could be made here of the ways that McCloy's narrative works to produce a sense of mutual fate and responsibility among his audience at the Seventh Annual Forum of Social and Economic Trends. His reference to the stir caused in "knowledgeable circles" generates a sense of shared insider status. And, in addition to constructing the ethos of wisdom born from experience, his haughty phrase "one of my somewhat frequent trips around the world" carries the imperial resonance of privilege and its incumbent collective moral burden. The consistent medical language of economic disease, symptoms, and health that organizes this passage is a trope found in many early Bank materials (and one to which I devote specific attention in the next chapter). More than anything, however, it is the tone of "uneasiness and foreboding" that stands out from this passage, the "strange feeling" evoked in McCloy upon seeing the abandoned offices of Credit Anstalt. The strangeness of this feeling is structured not by effects of a derelict, war-ravaged environment—surely postwar Vienna was glutted with empty and ruined buildings—but rather by the analogous abandonment, several years earlier, of public confidence in the idea of banking. The failures of banks-past hover as the spectral presence that animates the genesis of Bank-present. McCloy's story, queerly narrated as though a noir war film, casts the social institution of the bank, doubly figured by the ghost of Credit Anstalt and the newborn World Bank, as the barometer of public health, the canary in the mine. Bank failure becomes a metonym for a larger, unholy social collapse; the failure of banks—or, more to the point, failure of public confidence in banks—is read as both the symptom and the precipitating cause of immiseration, desperation, and rage: the social chaos and violence associated with the war. The connection, McCloy posits, is not direct and causal, not something that will be born out in statistics or numbers. Nevertheless, it remains real and identifiable in the "strange feeling" of "unease and foreboding" evoked by the absence of Credit Anstalt. Among the many affirmative formulations of institutional strengths and opportunities that can be found within the Bank archive, this negative articulation from McCloy speaks to the fears and desires that underlay the founding of the Bank at Bretton Woods, and also maps out the institution's immediate ideological challenge of transforming public anxiety and crisis into faith and stability.

When today's alterglobalization protesters are criticized for not "having a specific platform" in mind with which to replace the system that they so emphatically critique, they need only point to the foundation of the World Bank, one of their principle adversaries, as a model. Mason and Asher get at this point when they reflect that, looking at the Bank's origins, "one is struck by both the magnificence of the achievement and the lack of prescience of the founding fathers."[54] The institution we know today as the World Bank bears little resemblance to the one imagined by the delegates at Bretton Woods. The "magnificence" of the achievement stems not from the foresight of its planning but rather from the hubris of its undertaking—a postwar economic framework (conceived before the war was over) that promised nothing less than to serve as the bridge between wartime and peacetime, between depression and prosperity. The audacity of the Bretton Woods venture, however, is proportionate to the deep-seated fears it masks. That is, for an institution haunted by failures of public confidence in the recent past, the public performance of resolute swagger was an acknowledgment not only of firm convictions and the newfound economic dominance of the United States, but also of the institution's most pressing rhetorical challenge: the production and maintenance of public faith. That a hollow appeal to liberal internationalism, undergirded by an organizational model that left no doubt about U.S. institutional control, was able to gain consent from forty-four original member nations and, most important, from the U.S. public and its representatives, speaks to the ways in which the juridical structure of the Bank was designed to function in part as a rhetorical gesture—a gesture elaborated upon and bolstered by its early documents. It is important to take a more detailed look at the Bank's public communications with an eye toward the specific rhetorical appeals used by the institution to garner and maintain public confidence during its first years of operation.

2. Imperial Burden: Selling Development to Wall Street

Audience is the thread that binds together the salient rhetorical tropes from the Bank archive for the institution's inaugural years. Documents from the era between 1946, when the Bank opened its doors for business, and the beginning of Eugene Black's presidency in 1949 constitute a monumental effort of persuasion, assurance, and appeasement (with a bit of snake-oil salesmanship thrown in) aimed at the Bank's most pressing constituency during this period: the U.S. banking and financial communities.

If the Bank emerged from Bretton Woods with bluster but also great uncertainty and many skeptics, its first few rocky years of operation only added to the sense of institutional vulnerability. Mason and Asher conclude that "under the most charitable of judgments, the early years of the World Bank would have to be characterized as inauspicious."[1] Eugene Meyer, the Bank's first president, took office in June 1946, only to resign abruptly in December after a tumultuous six-month term and before any capital had been raised or any loans disbursed. If there existed moderate levels of public support for liberal internationalism, they were not shared by the financial community, which was extremely wary of Meyer and reluctant to support what they believed the do-good, New Deal feel of the institution. Lending, almost exclusively devoted to European postwar reconstruction, was slow to start and meager in scale. The Bank's first loan—$250 million to the French public corporation Crédit National (which had requested twice that sum)[2]—was not disbursed until May 1947, two months into John McCloy's presidency. This was followed by even smaller loans to the Netherlands, Denmark, and Luxembourg. Almost immediately, it became evident to the U.S. government (among others) that the Bank was not equipped to handle the volume and speed of lending needed by postwar Europe. In June 1947, the United States announced the Marshall Plan, which immediately overshadowed the Bank and became the preferred mechanism for the vast majority of reconstruction financing. Almost as soon as the Bank began operations, then, the rug was pulled out from beneath it. The job it had been created for was unceremoniously handed to a better-funded U.S. agency, bypassing, ironically, the cumbersome inclusiveness insisted upon by Harry White's internationalism for a more Keynsian bilateral structure. Almost from day one, that is, the Bank's reconstruction mission vanished and the institution was left to figure out just what might be made of the "and Development" appended hastily and crouching inconspicuously as the latter half of its official title.

Although we often attribute the Bank's stature as the world's most influential development institution to the enormous scale of its lending, its own loans, even in its most aggressive periods of expansion, have never amounted to more than a few percent of the world's total foreign investment, smaller in volume than private commercial lenders or bilateral (governmental) lenders. In relative terms, the Bank is a minor lender. This was never more the case than during its first few years of operation, and part of its rocky start stems from its initial dearth of capital. Consider, after all, how the Bank funds its lending. Its member countries all contribute a certain amount of "callable" capital (20 percent of each nation's total guaranteed contribution, based on the relative size of its national economy). Although the Bank began operations with a guaranteed capital subscription that amounted to the equivalent of $8 billion dollars from the collective contributions of its member countries (actual subscriptions took the form of individual national currencies), the weak exchange rates for most national currencies in 1946 meant that only funds available in U.S. dollars or in gold reserves could be lent as international investment. In effect this meant that only the contribution from the United States was available for lending, making the Bank itself little more than a bilateral agency during its first years of operation. Of the apparent $8 billion, less than $730 million was actually available for lending, a point that Bank officials take pains to emphasize in almost every speech or document from those early years of operation.

Because of the relatively small amount of available capital from its member subscriptions, the Bank—and here we gain some clarity about its status as a *bank* rather than, or in addition to, an international governance body—supplements its pool of lending capital by raising private funds. This point is worth emphasizing. Although the Bank is a multilateral financial institution whose "shareholders" are member governments (i.e., nation states), it raises the majority of its investment capital from private investment in World Bank bonds and securities. McCloy, the Bank's second president, states this point unambiguously to a Canadian radio audience in 1948: "The Bank is, I believe, a rather unique institution in that, although it is an intergovernmental organization, it relies primarily on the private investment community and not upon its member governments for the major part of its loanable resources."[3] The oxymoronic qualifier "rather unique" hints at the larger contradiction at play here: the already tenuous connection between "inter-governmental" and *democracy* within Bretton Woods internationalism erodes considerably further with the unqualified acceptance of, and reliance upon, private lending capital. Given the source of the Bank's funding, it is not surprising that the institution devotes its primary attention (particularly, as we shall see, during its early years when it was desperately trying to raise capital) not to the populations of its member states, not even to the member states themselves, but rather to the needs and desires of the "private investment community."

Investing Publics

Struggling to remain relevant in the face of Marshall Plan reconstruction, the fledgling institution began courting the U.S. financial community. Wall Street's deep distrust of the Bank began to soften after Meyer's resignation and with the 1947 presidential appointment of John J. McCloy, who, though a lawyer by profession, maintained close relations with the banking community. As a condition of his accepting the job, McCloy insisted on assembling his own fiscally conservative management team of Eugene Black (vice president of the Chase National Bank of New York) and John Garner (vice president of the General Foods Corporation). In what amounted to an ideological victory over the New Deal leanings of

U.S. Secretary of Treasury Henry Morgenthau, the pro-business trio of McCloy, Black, and Garner devoted much of their energy over the first few years to assuring the financial community that any liberal internationalist elements within the Bank were firmly grounded in "sound," "prudent," fiscally conservative *banking* principles.

In the Bank's early speeches and documents, then, we find almost without fail that, when the Bank addresses "public interest," it is referring to the interest of its investors. Mason and Asher are direct about this point: the "IBRD might later aspire to be a development institution," they aver, "but first it had to become a bank, at least in the sense of an investment institution that the financial community would respect. And during its first years, this meant the U.S. financial community."[4] In a typical speech from 1947, Vice President Garner addressed the National Association of Mutual Savings Banks (indeed the vast majority of World Bank public addresses in its first few years were given to associations of bankers, investment groups, and other financial audiences) and announced the Bank's intentions plainly: "You in this audience control billions of dollars of the savings of millions of Americans. We in the International Bank look to you savings bankers as one of the principal sources from which we hope to secure funds to carry on the work for which the Bank was organized."[5] Selling the Bank became the institution's first priority.

As I discussed in the previous chapter, the Bank's Articles of Agreement drawn up at Bretton Woods were conceived and rhetorically constructed so as to allay concerns from private investment sources. Article I states in part that the Bank's purpose is to "*promote private foreign investment* by means of guarantees or participations in loans and other investments made by private investors; and *when private capital is not available* on reasonable terms, *to supplement* private investment" (emphases mine).[6] If it was going to be able to lend, the Bank needed to be able to borrow. And to convince investors to buy its bonds, it had to convince them that it was an ally, not a competitor.

William A. B. Iliff, director of McCloy's loan department, goes a step further, making it clear to U.S. investors that lending is a two-way street. He assures his audience that profit not philanthropy motivates foreign investment, arguing that direct economic benefits accrue to lenders as much if not more than to borrowers. Offering an argument for why the U.S. public ought to support a Bank funding foreign governments almost exclusively with U.S. dollars, Iliff explains the following "self-evident fact of international lending": A lending country passes along not just money, but national currency, meaning that the borrowing country has "immediate claim on the goods and services of the lending country. . . . $10 million lent to Ruritania means nothing more than this: Ruritania is given the immediate means of buying turbines or agricultural machinery or electrical equipment or some other goods and services which the United States is able to produce."[7] The Bank is not merely lending money, then. It is lending U.S. *dollars*. Dollars lent to foreign governments equate to foreign dollars spent in the U.S. economy. Ilif's argument has borne out over time and the financial sleight of hand that he identifies, in which the United States effectively lends to itself while collecting surplus interest from a middleman, reveals one aspect of the historically profitable partnership between the Bank and U.S. industry. Bank critic Catherine Caulfield cites a World Bank official who reiterates this argument nearly a half-century after Ilif's remarks: "Most of our money doesn't go to the South, it goes straight from Washington to Pennsylvania, where they manufacture the turbines, or Frankfurt, where they produce the dredging equipment." Caulfield reports that, by the early 1990s (when her book is written), the $1.94 billion that the United States had contributed to the IBRD had returned more than ten times that amount to U.S. businesses.[8] So although it is certainly true that in 1947 the Bank is being propped up almost singlehandedly by the U.S. contribution, Iliff can accurately assure his audience that international lending works in the interest, not at the expense, of profitability.

In the context of the 1940s, the Bank's decision to court U.S. investors meant that nearly all of its early speeches and publications worked to establish a rhetoric of fiscal conservatism, emphasizing sound lending practices, traceable and transparent accounting practices, and a supplementary, never adversarial, relationship to private capital. Even three years into operations, the Bank still feels the need to refute the lingering impression of any international WPA-type do-goodism; its Third Annual Report assures leery investors that the "Articles of Agreement created a Bank and not a 'give-away' agency."[9] Because investor scrutiny of Bank operations ensured that the institution was, in the words of Black, "operated

as in a goldfish bowl,"[10] Bank officers were keenly aware that relief loans, loans for political purposes, loans where there was any
concern about borrower default, and loans not attached to specific,
productive projects would have been unacceptable to the U.S. investing community. This "reliance upon the private investor," insists McCloy, is "not only the limitation of the Bank's activities, it
is also one of its great elements of strength."[11]

Several aspects of this explicit reliance upon, and address to,
private capital are worth elaborating. First, the aggressive campaign by Bank officials to sell bonds proved enormously successful.
McCloy, Black, and Garner, all with backgrounds in banking and
investment, were able to persuade investors that the Bank was in
fact a bank, not a relief organization. The World Bank bonds were
first released on July 15, 1947, sold very well, and were awarded a
AAA bond rating by 1959, a testament to the rhetorical effectiveness of the fiscal conservatism message consistently preached by
the Bank presidents during these early years.[12] In reading the Bank
archives, it is immediately apparent that an enormous sense of relief accompanied the successful initial release and sale of the bonds.
The Bank crowed about the success of its initial bond offering in
a cartoon published in its internal newsletter, *Bank Notes,* which
showed investors lining up to purchase bank bonds as though they
were hotcakes. Boasting that the bonds had all sold before noon
on the day of their release, the brief story that accompanied the
cartoon proclaimed, "All in all it was one of the most successful
marketing operations on record and everyone connected with the
Bank has reason to be proud of it."[13] But the cartoon itself warrants comment, as the visual lexicon it deployed would appear to
belie, or at least undercut, the tone of congratulatory assuredness
conveyed by the story.

Although the accompanying write-up boasts of "one of the
most successful marketing operations on record," the cartoon (un-
consciously?) alerts viewers to the underlying fears for which this
exaggerated praise attempts to compensate. Entirely paradoxical, an image purporting to celebrate the newly cemented financial stability of the World Bank is structured by visual echoes of
Depression-era social panic. In the down-and-out, brother-can-
you-spare-a-dime, upward tilt of the speaker's hat, in the lament-
ing twist of his eyebrows, in the exterior, public space of the street,
where the built architectural environment of Wall St. literally

"I thought they were selling hotcakes,
but it's International Bank Bonds."

Bond sales cartoon from the Bank's newsletter, *International Bank Notes,*
July 25, 1947.

walls those comparatively diminutive individuals penned beneath
the buildings' facades, and most notably in the line of bodies that
snakes backward into the horizon, the cartoon draws heavily upon
the visual lexicon of the post-Crash runs on both soup kitchens
and banks. As we saw in the earlier case of McCloy, whose mel-
ancholy account of the abandonment of Credit Anstalt produced a
feeling of deep unease in the Bank president, here again the slightly
strained performance of institutional confidence is stretched taut
over the haunting fear that public confidence may evaporate.

For the moment, the public that most concerned the Bank was
the investing public. The unacknowledged but ever-present fears
about the consequences of a loss of investor confidence, presumably felt as powerfully by the investing community as by the Bank,
served only to strengthen the relationship between the two, pressing

the Bank toward ever more buttoned-down versions of strict fiscal conservatism. As its third annual report acknowledges, the Bank's "continued success would depend upon the confidence that the public, and especially the investing public, has in it, and . . . such confidence is gained only by operating the Bank as a business institution."[14] Acting (and speaking) like a business institution undoubtedly becomes the Bank's preferred tactic to buoy investor confidence (and next we shall examine some of the specifics of this strategy). But, as the *Bank Notes* cartoon suggests, the partnership between the Bank and the investment community is buttressed by rhetorical appeals to fear—or rather to the *fear of fear*—as well as the obverse formulation, tacit appeals to the *confidence born of confidence.*

Transparency and Verifiability

One of the specific rhetorical maneuvers designed to convince private capital that the Bank was being operated "as a business institution" was its insistence that loans be made for productive purposes. As we saw in chapter 1, the severely limited conception of production that underpins the Bank's early fiscal conservatism parallels the constricted understanding of development at Bretton Woods. In both cases we find an extreme economism, a charge more frequently associated with the critiques of orthodox Marxism. When the Bank repeatedly assures its investors that its loans are awarded strictly for "productive purposes," it has in mind projects that directly, unambiguously, and quantifiably contribute to the production of wealth: transportation projects to increase exports, energy projects to increase manufacturing output, and so on. Taken at face value, the economic logic behind this insistence on production is plain: one protects against default by insuring that borrowing states invest in profitable ventures. States that have money can pay back loans; states without, cannot.

Beneath this surface logic of balanced account books, however, lies the ever-present drive to produce confidence. In this light, the Bank's insistence on productive loans should be read not so much as a desire for borrower profitability, but rather as a means to induce nervous capital into global circulation (i.e., to transform wealth into capital). Whether or not a particular Bank-funded transportation or energy project makes profits is, so to speak, immaterial—at very least, secondary. More important, productive projects remove risk to investors by financing requisite infrastructure as a hedge against the conservative impulse to withdraw capital from circulation where it threatens to "become petrified into a hoard."[15] In the convergence of Bank lending and Bank rhetoric, we find, paradoxically, appeals to fiscal conservatism employed to elicit the progressive, risky circulation of capital from otherwise reluctant lenders. Although McCloy, Black, and Garner would have balked at Marx's pejorative ascription of greed, the impulse behind many of their documents has much in common with his assessment that the "boundless greed after riches, this passionate chase after exchange-value, is common to the capitalist and the miser; but while the miser is merely a capitalist gone mad, the capitalist is a rational miser."[16]

Thus we find that the rhetorical appeals to conservatism in early Bank materials, crafted to generate investor confidence, exhibit a scrupulous aversion to anything that sniffs of economic complexity, ambiguity, or controversy. One expression of this aversion is illustrated by the Bank's strict adherence to so-called project lending—that is, funds lent for, and limited to, a specific, definable project, rather than for general development purposes that might be left up to the borrower to determine. This particular "piece of banking psychology"[17] is one of the grand fictions spun by the Bank in its early years. Funds lent for specific projects helped maintain the illusion of full accountability and transparency. As Kapur, Lewis, and Webb explain, "Visibility, verifiability, and apparent productivity were the touchstones for projecting an image of supervised, controlled, safe, 'quality' lending, and these criteria were best satisfied by the large-scale, import-intensive, long-lived investment project. Dams, power stations, and roads could be described, photographed, and trusted in ways that funds spent on intermediate goods or short-lived assets or salaries could not."[18] In a particularly acerbic World Bank oral history interview, Paul Rosenstein-Rodan, the influential economist who worked for the Bank from 1947 to 1952, lays bare the fiction that funds, when lent for a dam or a power station, remain confined to that particular project. Commenting on the fungibility or substitutability of funds, Rosenstein-Rodan explains that project lending is essentially a "subconscious . . . psychoanalytic problem" that "appeals to the business method" because, if a "project is certain and concrete," then the "risk appears much less." From an economist's perspective, however, project lending looks like one big shell game: "The economists, of course, say that maybe under the circumstances it is an optical illusion; . . . that the Bank may think it finances an electrical power station, but if this electrical power station would have been created anyway out of the local funds in the country and the additional capital that flew in was used, for instance, for the creation of a brothel, then the situation would be that the Bank thought it financed an electric power station but in fact it financed a brothel."[19] The Bank is not unaware of this accounting trick.[20] Rather, it self-consciously relies upon the persuasive force of empiricism and verifiability to convince the U.S. public that it is not a give-away organization and to convince the investing public that World Bank bonds are secure investments. In effect, project lending is the first in a long line of rhetorical manipulations of *transparency*. Black had suggested that the institution was "operated as in a goldfish bowl." Perhaps a better metaphor would be "house of glass," after Indonesian writer Pramoedya Ananta Toer's novel by that name, in which, despite his many assertions of omniscient surveillance, the native informant (police inspector) protagonist ultimately proves unable (and perhaps unwilling) to either read or control the emerging revolutionary forces and nationalist movements apparently taking shape in his full view. In the Bank's house of glass, we find the institution declaring with conviction to investors that its project lending is entirely transparent and verifiable, knowing all the while that money lent for a power station may as likely be spent to build a brothel.

At this point, however, the analogy to Pramoedya's novel breaks down. Although the Bank may make a show of its capacity to survey and control the disbursement and application of loaned funds within the "house of glass," it may hold a greater stake in maintaining the architectural illusion of transparent structures than in perfecting its models of surveillance. Certainly the Bank has wielded the technology of transparency in Foucauldian fashion to discipline the borrowing inhabitants of various glass-house national economies. The conditionality agreements of structural adjustment loans have ensured as much. But it is also the case, particularly in the historical moment of the late 1940s, that the Bank would adopt the rhetoric of transparency to manipulate and manage those who would appear to be outside peering in. Steadfastly insisting that loaned money was working for productive purposes, safely and in plain view, the Bank's elaborate house of glass has worked to embolden an investing public, activating the progressive function of capital by luring it into global circulation.

Nonpolitical Lending

The fiction of discrete project lending is bolstered and extended by the Bank's frequent appeals to another constitutionally determined fiction: nonpolitical lending. Article 3, Section 5, of the Bank's charter links the two notions: "The Bank shall make arrangements to ensure that the proceeds of any loan are used *only for the purposes for which the loan was granted,* with due attention to considerations of economy and efficiency and *without regard to political or other non-economic influences or considerations*" (emphasis mine).[21] This juridical attempt to segregate economics from politics is stated even more definitively in Article 4, Section 10, under the heading "Political Activity Prohibited." The article reads: "The Bank and its officers *shall not interfere in the political affairs of any member;* nor shall they be influenced in their decisions by the political character of the member or members concerned. *Only economic considerations shall be relevant to their decisions,* and these considerations shall be *weighed impartially* in order to achieve the purposes stated in Article 1" (emphasis mine).[22]

One of cultural studies' central contributions to Marxist thought has been a persistent effort to trouble any absolute distinction between base and superstructure; a case can be made that the Bank has spent sixty years wrestling with this distinction (though not in precisely these terms). The "Political Activity Prohibited" clause of the Bank's charter is a case in point. Fiercely committed to the notion that pure economic decisions can be made without political consideration, the Bank has been alternately hiding behind and working around the fraught language in this clause throughout its institutional history. The provision has enabled the Bank to maintain relative autonomy from the United Nations, whose "one country, one vote" system left it at risk to political pressure from its member states; conversely, the Bank tap-danced around accusations of excessive political influence stemming from the disproportionate U.S. voting privilege—the pink elephant ambling through the hallways of 1818 H Street.

In the early years of courting the investment community, however, no illusion of a firm separation between the Bank and the

United States was necessary. In fact, such a distinction might have been detrimental. When McCloy reaffirmed the nonpolitical lending provision in the Bank's charter, he brazenly defined this to mean the possibility of "loans inconsistent with American foreign policy."[23] As the Cold War came into focus during the final years of the 1940s, the Soviet Union garnered an increasingly important presence in Bank rhetoric; that is, the Soviet Union's conspicuous absence as a Bank member, and its looming presence as a polar counterbalance to the United States, contributed decisively to the Bank's efforts to define itself for the U.S. investing public. Paradoxically, the Soviet Union's absence from the roll of Bank membership (the charter only prohibited interference into "the political affairs of *any member*") enabled the Bank to construct a self-image as a crusader for political autonomy and independence, unmarred by the presumed ideological obstructionism of the USSR. A McCloy speech from early in 1948 describes the emerging bipolar world in the following terms:

> [T]here has emerged, from a hitherto relatively undeveloped area of Europe, a new power, with large material and human resources, a strong sense of mission, and a fanatical devotion to revolutionary ideology. Politically and militarily the Soviet Union has become a great world power, and it seems certainly the most powerful single nation in Europe. Intensely concerned with her own development, she has associated with her own welfare the widest dissemination and stimulation of her social and economic philosophies combined with an attack on all others.
>
> At the same time, the United States has also emerged as the other great world power—perhaps the greatest. Following an entirely different economic and political course from the Soviet Union, the United States has, in a century and a half, advanced from a wilderness with a fringe of eighteenth-century civilization to become the greatest producing and exporting nation in the world. Her production achievements border on the phenomenal. Her political and economic concepts are perhaps the furthest removed of any nation from contemporary Soviet political or economic doctrine.[24]

It is hardly necessary to point out the overtly political evaluations that structure McCloy's comparison of these two "great world power[s]." More interesting is the way the Bank, in this speech of McCloy's, is able to cast such overt U.S. nationalism as natural and nonpolitical, and to equate capitalist production with political health. This is to be expected, given that McCloy is addressing the Philadelphia Chamber of Commerce; however, the distinctive narrative of American exceptionalism, where hard work and long-suffering enable the United States to "become the greatest producing and exporting nation in the world," clearly functions as the model for economic growth that underwrites Bank lending policies.

Speaking in Detroit, the Irish director of the Bank's loan department, William Iliff, takes McCloy's nationalist argument a step further. In the zealous tones of a convert, he characterizes the U.S. contributions to international lending in the familiar imperial terms of a civilizing mission:

> In its vigorous support of the International lending institution to which I belong, your government is making a magnificent contribution to world reconstruction and development and in the Economic Cooperation Act [Marshall Plan], you have not merely displayed a statesmanlike approach to the cure of economic sickness from which the non-American world is suffering, but you have also given one more manifestation of the warm-hearted generosity of the American people. These are but two of the directions in which, if I may presume to say so, you have proved your capacity and willingness to fulfill the high destiny unto which it has pleased God to call you.[25]

McCloy's earlier remarks, which eschew the missionary zeal that characterizes so much Bank discourse, might be read in more classically ideological terms: Bank lending aims to peer through any false consciousness associated with "fanatical devotion to revolutionary ideology" in order to locate a pure economic productive base untainted by, or outside of, politics. Illif, here, embodying the position of outsider by virtue of his nationality, needs no such critical apparatus, opting instead for the metaphysical "high destiny unto which it has pleased God to call you."

Development as Pedagogy

The rhetorical trope of speaking from an alleged position beyond or outside of politics also facilitated the Bank's evolution from reconstruction to development. In the wake of the Marshall Plan, the Bank gradually crafted a new institutional role for itself: not only as a lender of capital, but as a lender of "technical assistance" to the so-called underdeveloped world. The fiction of nonpolitical lending enabled the Bank to trumpet its ability to offer objective, unfiltered instruction to its borrowers—instruction that, if at times unpopular, nevertheless was delivered, according to the Bank, "without suspicion of being influenced by political or commercial motives or of sponsoring unrealistic recommendations."[26] From early in its history, then, the Bank understood development as an inherently pedagogical venture. As a reconstruction institution, it was to have dispensed funds to Europe; as a development institution, it dispensed funds *and instruction* to the non-European World. By the close of the decade, the Bank asserted that, though lending remained its primary activity, its work designing technical assistance programs was "likely to be more profound, since they should contribute to the formation of a climate conducive to productive investment from all sources."[27]

This particular construction of nonpoliticized lending and technical advice bears the marks of pressure from multiple directions. First, in trumpeting the importance of technical assistance, the Bank is attempting to justify its conspicuously small volume of lending to that point. The Bank's assurances to investors about prudent lending practices offered some explanation, given the time-intensive scrutiny required to minimize risk prior to a loan's approval. But if Iliff's arguments about the economic benefits for lending nations were to be believed, then a steady stream of well-considered loans would presumably be persuasive to even the most conservative investing audiences.

Second, technical assistance, couched as it is in the language of aid, worked to diffuse the mounting demands from member nations of the South, who were beginning to assert the need for an increased speed and scale of Bank lending. Technical assistance in this sense serves as a mode of pedagogy that—following in a long line of infantilizing imperialist rhetoric—functions to discipline its borrowing members. We can find an illustration of this function in McCloy's 1948 speech to the National Foreign Trade Convention: "Although our underdeveloped member countries are impelled by a tremendous desire to improve their situation, they generally lack the technical knowledge as to how to go about it. Few of them, for example, have any well-formulated concept of the over-all lines along which their development is most likely to make progress.

The projects they present to the Bank are all too often inadequately planned or prepared, reflecting in large part the severe shortage of technical personnel."[28] Here, underdevelopment as a condition is defined almost exclusively in terms of lack—McCloy argues that the underdeveloped world lacks not only funds, but also technical knowledge, personnel, and, more broadly, a long-range vision of development. As a pedagogical program, technical assistance becomes one method to call attention to these perceived absences and, by extension, prescribe the means and conditions under which these needs will be met. The paradigm of development lending, then, far exceeds any transfer of capital for a particular project. Technical assistance disciplines borrowing countries by instructing them in what constitutes an acceptable loan application and a bankable project. Moreover, technical assistance becomes the vehicle through which the Bank makes interventions into the overall economic landscape of its borrowers. Under the banner of objective, nonpolitical advice, for example, the Bank can proscribe the nationalization of economic sectors in favor of their privatization.[29] Using the rhetoric of "technical assistance," the Bank casts such interventions as pedagogical instruction rather than political interference.

By this point in its history, the Bank had realized that it would likely never disburse enough capital for development lending on the scale of the Marshall Plan. Put simply, the institution did not have and never would have sufficient available funds to shape the nature of global development solely by wielding its ability to withhold or disburse capital. (Note, however, that this tactic was certainly tried on any number of occasions, sometimes successfully; "small lending volume" is a relative term, and the Bank's economic might should not be discounted.) Beyond the sledgehammer of money made available or denied, the Bank's relentless efforts to fashion itself as a global research institution capable of providing expert, nonpolitical technical assistance to the underdeveloped world—dispensing advice, that is, above and beyond capital—go far toward explaining the institution's enormous global influence over development, a level of influence that the scale of its lending would not otherwise warrant. In establishing its ethos as a development institution, the quantity of research and data compiled by the Bank—its countless country reports and economic analyses generated by the many (appropriately named) World Bank Missions that were sent around the world—came to substitute for the relative paucity of its lending. We can say, therefore, that the Bank's aura of knowledge and expertise—the intimate connection it has crafted between development and research—not only works to authorize pedagogical interventions but also helps to explain the enormous sway that the institution has held for sixty years. In the late 1940s, McCloy's newfound enthusiasm for technical assistance signaled the beginning of this global influence.

Finally, "technical assistance" is a tacit concession to the fiction of discrete, verifiable project lending. Although transparent accounting procedures and wary investors may require the imagined containment of a concrete project, the Bank's burgeoning conceptions of development show ambitions toward broader horizons— "the formation of a climate conducive to productive investment from all sources," in Black's words.[30] By casting itself in the role of technical advisor, the Bank is able to maintain the accounting fictions provided by discrete projects, while developing a pedagogical and missionary role as the objective technical advisor, affording it a much more significant role in defining and managing a "culture of development."[31]

Disease and Famine

Metaphors of health and disease permeate early Bank documents. Careful readers will have already picked up on this recurrent trope, which appears in some passages quoted so far. The metaphors take many forms: epidemics, diseases, medicine, vaccination, infestation, symptoms, cures, treatments, and so on. This section reads several of these metaphors, paying particular attention to the frequent overlap between the rhetoric of disease and the rhetoric of famine in the materials from this era.[32]

That the Bank's work would be framed in terms of disease control and prevention is clear from Franklin Roosevelt's opening remarks at the Bretton Woods conference, during which he argued that "economic diseases are highly communicable. It follows, therefore, that the economic health of every country is a proper matter of concern to all its neighbors, near and distant."[33] The metaphor of Bank-as-physician would be taken up by Eugene Meyer, the first Bank president, largely in the service of an argument against isolationism to a U.S. audience reluctant to embrace international investment. In a speech delivered just days before his resignation in December 1946,[34] Meyer develops Roosevelt's "economic disease" metaphor, arguing that no nation is immune to global epidemic; that ever-denser circuits of global capital render isolationist notions of quarantine obsolete, nostalgic fictions of a past era when the nation state could imagine its borders as a sanitary bubble. He states:

> If we want to enjoy the kind of economic security in which individual men can thrive and live comfortably, we cannot retreat into our own rich land and cease to care how the rest of the world lives. We cannot do that because there is no way of shutting ourselves up and keeping the rest of the world out. The spread of economic disease beyond our shores will eventually infect us. The deterioration of the economic conditions under which men live inevitably leads to political illness, which will surely involve us unless it is cured. In other words, we cannot be the only happy and prosperous country on the face of the earth.[35]

Some version of this newfound awareness of global interconnectivity, or rather the awareness that profound new implications stem from the density and saturation of global interconnectivity, binds the World Bank to the new theorizations and reconceptions of culture emerging at the same historical moment. Culture, too, was contagious in the immediate postwar era. For now, however, let us focus on the rhetorical effects produced by these images of disease and contagion.

Implicit in the disease metaphor is the notion that, if properly treated by a scientifically trained expert, infection can be stopped and patients can be cured. Meyer argues that no nation is immune, not that the disease is untreatable. Lending, in this metaphor, is likened to medicine: curative when properly prescribed and administered, ineffective or destructive when misused. Meyer raises precisely this dichotomy in an earlier speech, where he offers the arresting Manichean image of Bank-as-doctor/Bank-as-pusher. He begins by quoting himself, referencing an analogy that he purports to have stated frequently prior to the war:

> "[C]redit is a little like some drugs. In the hands of people who know its powers but also its dangers it is the most helpful, useful and healing thing in the world. But like those drugs, with misuse,

with carelessness and with habitual indulgence to excess, it can become the most demoralizing, disintegrating and destructive agency." I think this warning is no less pertinent and applicable today. The credit supplied by the International Bank must be credit that is put to work, credit that is employed to produce wealth.[36]

The rhetoric of economic disease allows the Bank to draw an analogy between economic and medical expertise, implying that like a doctor it is capable of administering treatments to the global economy that are reassuringly precise, scientific, and, most important, safe. More to the point, a successful cure requires not only sound advice and treatment (which the Bank believes itself capable of providing), but also that the borrower/patient heed this advice in all regards. The metaphor builds in its own cautionary qualifications: beware of misuse, and beware of addiction. Although this caution is meant in part to remind itself about the steep responsibilities in prescribing economic treatments, the caution is more pointedly a warning for potential patients about the dire consequences likely if the Bank's prescribed treatments are not followed.

The other noteworthy aspect of Meyer's comment is its final line, where he appears to mix his medicinal metaphor by switching to a labor analogy whereby credit must be "put to work" and "employed to produce wealth." However, in a surprising number of early Bank documents, we find the metaphors of medicine and labor yoked not toward wealth but, improbably, through the figure of famine. Take, for example, Meyer's brief press release published upon his acceptance of the Bank presidency in June 1946. Of the statement's three paragraphs, two are devoted to articulating the Bank's new role in terms of a connection between famine and industry:

> I feel honored by my election by the Executive Directors as President of the International Bank for Reconstruction and Development, but above all I feel a profound sense of responsibility. I shall devote my full energies to the task.
>
> The world is well aware today of the food famine. At the same time we must become equally aware that the world is starving for the products of industry.
>
> The Bank was organized to promote reconstruction and development in both of these essential activities.[37]

That Meyer's first statement as Bank president (indeed, the first statement by *any* Bank president) should be an occasion from which to argue that the newly founded International Bank for Reconstruction and Development would serve a dual role as provider of food and provider of industry to alleviate two, presumably overlapping, notions of world starvation is extraordinary. Even more so, this dual-famine metaphor serves as the statement's *only* indication of an institutional mission, and constitutes roughly two-thirds of the announcement.

A pair of analogies buttress the claim. The first equates famine and communicable "economic disease," metaphorically casting the Bank in the role of epidemiologist, tasked with preventing the infectious spread of such maladies throughout the global economic system. The second equates industrialization and modernization, implying that the global dissemination of U.S. industry and industrial products would provide both the means and the motivations by which the underdeveloped regions of the globe could march (or be dragged) into modernity. Industry is conceived not merely as a spur for economic growth, but as the global South's entry ticket into history. Hidden beneath these assumptions about famine, disease, and industry, however, is the Bank's blindness, or perhaps callousness, toward the non-European world in general and India in particular—a disregard reminiscent of the private comments made by Keynes, quoted in the previous chapter, about India's spot at the back of the postwar funding queue. The roughly three million people killed during the Great Bengal famine that devastated the country between 1943 and 1947 (i.e., throughout Meyer's term) would likely have seen the world's starvation for "the products of industry" as a rather less pressing matter.[38] Although the food shortages in Europe and Russia (especially in the Ukraine in 1946) were rightly of urgent concern, India and its famine barely registered, in 1946, on the radar of the reconstruction-focused Bank.

Embedded in Meyer's acceptance is also a barb at U.S. labor for failing to meet its global responsibilities. This attack is spelled out more clearly in a subsequent speech when Meyer bemoans the "unnecessary stoppages" (i.e., strikes) that restricted U.S. production and exports from the coal and copper industries and from General Motors (that most boat-floating, tide-rising of American corporations). The passage is worth quoting at length as it ties U.S. labor unrest to worldwide "famine" in both of the senses outlined in Meyer's statement above. He says:

> But there is a starvation now going on in the world concerning which leadership has been inarticulate. The starvation for the products of fields in the form of food has been succeeded by a starvation no less extensive and dangerous to the welfare of humanity. I refer to the starvation for the products of our mines and factories. . . . In depriving other peoples of the tools they need for reconstruction, we are threatening world recovery and condemning vast numbers of human beings to serious deprivations. . . . I say emphatically that the crucial importance of continuous full production for our own welfare and for that of mankind the world over cannot be exaggerated . . . we must find a way of settling our labor disputes without the disastrous strikes which bring about world starvation in a broader sense than the mere withholding of food. And as to food itself, the demands upon us will be heavier the longer we lack ingenuity and the sense of responsibility to the rest of the world for the use of our powers to help our fellow men. This sense of responsibility we felt in full measure during the war. Let us feel it now in the same degree and make good the debt to our heroic deed.[39]

Note first the nationalism in Meyer's layered remarks. The pronouns "we," "our," and "us" all work to produce a sense of shared national destiny at once separate from and connected to a broader world system. The "sense of responsibility" that Meyer evokes draws upon the rhetoric of sacrifice and call-to-arms as a means of soliciting public support for intervention on behalf of a perceived greater moral good. Articulating his point, appropriately, in the language of a borrower's fiscal responsibility to "make good the debt," Meyer suggests that keeping the national industrial base functioning at full capacity is an extension of the nation's earlier "heroic deed" of wartime sacrifice; "continuous full production" (i.e., ending workers' strikes) is not a matter of profitability, he insists, but rather a national responsibility that must be undertaken "for our own welfare and for that of mankind the world over." Meyer's audience, likely to be sympathetic to management's arguments in any case, can redouble its efforts to haul labor back to work, emboldened by arguments about patriotic duty.

Further, Meyer's urgent plea that industry not be allowed to lie fallow illustrates the Bank's role in the perpetuation and transformation of imperial power. Compare Meyer's comments, for instance, to one of the most famous statements from arch–British imperialist Cecil Rhodes. Rhodes, also discussing the relationship between labor unrest at home and imperialist expansion overseas, writes:

> I was in the east end of London yesterday and attended a meeting of the unemployed. I listened to the wild speeches, which were just a cry for "Bread, Bread," and on my way home I became more than ever convinced of the importance of imperialism. . . . We colonial statesmen must acquire new lands to settle the surplus population, to provide new markets for the goods produced in the factories and mines. The Empire, as I have always said, is a bread and butter question. If you want to avoid civil war, you must become imperialists.[40]

Development, which Meyer has so tightly hitched to the question of famine (in his dual sense of food and industry), is likewise a "bread and butter question." Parallels can be drawn, too, between Rhodes' address to "we colonial statesmen" and the interpolating "we" in Meyer's speech to the Academy of Political Science. Although the Bank is not immediately concerned with exporting surplus populations to settler colonies,[41] the emphasis on developing "new markets for the goods produced in the factories and mines" is a priority no less for Meyer than for Rhodes. Neither is the firm conviction that developing such markets is the way to prevent civil war at home (though in Meyer's case the fear of a third world war also weighs heavily in his considerations). Haunting the references to famine and "continuous full production" is the Bank's familiar specter: Depression-era bread lines in the United States sparked by the failure of public confidence. The recurrent references to economic disease and famine that pepper the early Bank archive argue in effect that the Bank will be capable of inoculating business from the dual contagions of, on the one side, the types of fascistic regimes that emerged from the economic crises following the first World War, and, on the other, labor unrest and popular social movements demanding more radical redistributive measures. Although the phrase, "you must become World Bankers" does not have quite the same ring as Rhodes's version, nevertheless, in the matter of avoiding civil war (as in many others) imperialism and development are conjoined.

The vaccine that the Bank will turn to, of course, is credit. Credit "inoculates" at home by creating new markets abroad—Rhodes's prescription. But it also "inoculates" by disciplining labor at home through a calculated rhetorical appeal both to fear of contagion, and to patriotic responsibility sounded in the tones of a wartime call to arms. Bolstering the Fordist social contract with labor (discussed further in chapter 4), credit helps establish what Lenin terms a "labor aristocracy," utilizing surplus profits gained abroad to buy labor's compliance at home and thus effectively dividing the shared class interests of working people in the developed and underdeveloped worlds.[42] Moreover, Meyer's Bank, as you will remember, promises to provide the world with credit that will be "put to work" and "employed to produce wealth." Credit, of course, "works" only for capital; it "produces" only for capital; it does not "work" or "produce" for labor. Marx describes this phenomenon in *Capital*, volume 1, as a particularly telling form of the commodity circuit—the formula for which he gives as "M—C—M'," (money transformed into commodities for the purpose of being retransformed into money). In the case of interest-bearing capital, Marx states, the commodity step is skipped, leaving a formula of "M—M'" or "money that is worth more than money, value that is greater than itself."[43] World Bank credit generates surplus value in the form of interest, further exploiting the labor power of workers from the underdeveloped (i.e., indebted) world, who are burdened with a doubling of surplus extractions, having to provide profit both to their employer and to their employer's lender. This credit is productive only in the sense that capital generates additional capital; that is to say, debt becomes a mechanism to discipline labor both at home and abroad, and in doing so works to reproduce a system based on the false premise that capital *labors,* a dark euphemism for the deepening and intensification of labor's exploitation by global financial capital.

Imperial Burdens

The inaugural years of the Bank's operation coincide with the transformative historical period when Britain's imperial hegemony, as manifested in its many colonial territorial possessions, gives way to U.S. imperial hegemony, as manifested both in its growing military supremacy and in its extensive economic reach. Although Bank staffer S. Raymond Cope would later recall what he perceived to be a "certain distaste for colonialism on the part of some in the Bank,"[44] the institution's documents give little indication of any such aversion. If anything, the Bank appears to have perceived its role as a continuation and an enhancement of European, particularly British, imperialism.

If the Bank helped shape postwar decolonization (as I argue in chapter 3), its contributions came in a form that insured imperial nations were well compensated and insulated from any potential political or economic turbulences accompanying the independence struggles in the colonial territories of its member states. For instance, a 1951 loan to the Belgian Congo—a loan that marks the first Bank lending to a colonial territory of one of its members—came in two parts: a disbursement to the Belgian Congo to cover the expenses of purchasing equipment from Belgium, and a disbursement to Belgium to "cover the impact on the Belgium foreign-exchange position of the additional exports which she will provide to the Congo under the program."[45] Similarly, a 1952 loan to Southern Rhodesia specifically stipulates that the loan is intended to provide "dollars for purchases in the United Kingdom." This is necessary, the Bank explains, because the "dollars will help offset the drain on the U.K.'s financial resources caused by the large-scale provision of capital—public and private—for Southern Rhodesia's general development program."[46] Never does the Bank question the assumption that the imperial relationship is mutually beneficial for colonial territory and imperial nation alike; in fact, it goes out of its way to highlight the financial sacrifices being made by Europe to support the development of its colonial territories during the gradual transition into independence. Even those early Bank loans purportedly designed for the development of the (eventually[47]) decolonizing world carefully build in buffering protections to help defer any financial burden shouldered by the Bank's European member states.

The Bank's lending practices are mirrored in its rhetoric, where references to British Imperialism typically bathe nostalgically in, to quote Conrad, the "august light of abiding memories."[48] As part of a detailed discussion of European history leading up to and following the war, for instance, McCloy lavished praise on "the toughness of British human values" and the "great cohesive influence of the British Empire,"[49] the disruption of which he bemoans as one of the most grievous consequences of the war. Analyzing the successes of Britain's imperialism, presumably as examples to be followed, McCloy's first address as Bank president sketches the following history of international investment:

> From 1815 to 1914 Great Britain took by far the most important position in international investment. From the middle of the nineteenth century onwards her foreign investments increased by about 300 million dollars annually. In terms of present day purchasing power the investment was much larger, and it was made against the background of a population and a productive plant very much smaller than that, say, of the United States today. Not all of Great Britain's investments were wise or fortunate, but on the whole they were of enormous benefit to Great Britain, enabling her to build up in the period of her greatest industrial supremacy new markets with which to trade and a source of income to support her standard of living when that supremacy was challenged. They were of enormous benefit to the rest of the world too; much of the development of industry in Europe, and of the industrial and agricultural development of both North and South America and of the Far East was made possible through the financing provided by Great Britain.[50]

Although couched in terms of British imperial history, McCloy's comments amount to an argument, championing the benefits of international credit, aimed at garnering support for the Bank. Nevertheless, his comments display not the slightest unease about, let alone criticism of, British imperialism. In fact, the British Empire here serves as the model of wise international investment, bestowing "enormous benefit" (repeated twice) to both Great Britain and "the rest of the world." Note, too, McCloy's ever-present concern to emphasize the management of economic risk, here pointing astutely to the security afforded by colonial revenues that sustained British "standards of living" long after the period of its industrial supremacy waned. That is, although Germany's industrial productive base had equaled or surpassed Britain by the time of the First World War, the continued outflow of surplus revenue from Britain's far vaster empire (the extractive violence of which is entirely erased) provided the economic safeguard that insured the smaller nation's continued preeminence. International investment in this account, far from being risky, appears to forestall risk by protecting against an imagined future uncertainty.

Because there is so much overlap between the United States and the Bank at the moment of his comments, McCloy can speak openly about the Bank's role as catalyst for international investment by drawing upon the entirely positive analogy of British Imperialism; that is, the United States (with the help of the Bank) is now in a position, much like Britain's in the nineteenth century, to assume the dominant role in international investment, thereby spreading the fruits of modernity to the world while vastly increasing its own national prosperity. McCloy continues:

> This position gives the United States an opportunity to contribute to the recovery of the world, and to its own prosperity, an opportunity perhaps unparalleled except by the experience of Great Britain in the nineteenth century. As Great Britain then enhanced its own economic position by financing industrial and agricultural development throughout the world—railroads in the Balkans, gold mining in South Africa, rubber plantations in the Far East, to pick but a few random examples—so the United States today has what appears to be a comparable opportunity to contribute to a prosperous and expanding world economy by assuming the large role in international investment which its favorable productive position makes possible.[51]

The phrase "financing industrial and agricultural development throughout the world" is surely a euphemism for imperialism. But the phrase is intended neither to hide nor to soften any of imperialism's rough semantic edges. To the contrary, McCloy's speech offers nothing but unvarnished praise for, and open emulation of, British imperialism, not a hint of the "distaste for colonialism" that Cope alleged. Coming from the president of an international institution composed of forty-four member states, several of which had firsthand historical experience with British colonialism, and spoken just four months before the watershed event of the so-called postcolonial era, India's independence and partition in 1947, the complete absence of critique illustrates the degree to which the Bank understands its role to be an extension and refinement of British imperialism. The railroads, gold mines, and rubber plantations of Empire—projects that, according to McCloy, brought civilization to the South and stability to the world, as well as wealth, power, and economic security to Britain (not to mention Rhodes's and Meyer's assertions about preventing [civil] war)—function as the organizational templates for the fledgling Bank as it looks toward funding a new round of "bankable development projects."

Mission is precisely the correct term to describe the Bank's lending expeditions. I have already quoted William Iliff's ardent praise for Americans' "capacity and willingness to fulfill the high destiny unto which it has pleased God to call you," just one of many Bank comments over the years that exhibit the institution's missionary zeal. Following the successes of the Bank's first "survey of Colombia's over-all economy"[52] in 1949, its *missions*—teams of economists, engineers, planners, diplomats, etc. dispatched to individual countries to do "comprehensive" economic assessments—would venture across the globe collecting data and proselytizing the gospel of development. (As a provocation of sorts, I suggest that the academic discipline of anthropology is to colonialism what the World Bank mission is to globalization, or, more accurately, to the postwar transformation of imperial power and its relation to capitalism.[53]) Rather than catalog examples of the Bank's missionary bent—a task admirably accomplished by other Bank critics[54]—I will mention but one particularly familiar rendition of the imperialist missionary legacy: Kiplingesque warnings that the noble burden of imperialism must be shouldered for principle rather than adulation, since, as Kipling reminds his readers, the noble efforts of those who "take up the white man's burden" will frequently be rewarded only by "the blame of those ye better, / The hate of those ye guard."[55] Iliff's remarks to a Detroit audience, extolling the principled if arduous task for international investment, makes much the same claim: "For the lender, virtue must be its own reward, let him not expect gratitude from the borrower! . . . After all, gratitude is but a soothing syrup; and it is a poor substitute for the mental and spiritual satisfaction that is earned from the sense of a job well done."[56]

With the world emerging from an era of nationalist pleas in support of the war effort, it is not surprising that this type of address to selfless sacrifice might be persuasive. This was all the more true, when appeals to the greater good and the reward of "satisfaction that is earned from the sense of a job well done" were buttressed, as in the case of Iliff's speech, with substantial argumentation about how such principled altruism would directly and significantly contribute to economic growth and to U.S. industry's bottom line. Reading Iliff's speech, one cannot help but think of another famous line from Rhodes, "Pure philanthropy is all very well in its way but philanthropy plus 5 percent is a good deal better."[57] With upper lips stiffened to ignore ungrateful protestations from the underdeveloped world ("the blame of those ye better"), the Bank would adopt Rhodes's model of venture philanthropy, fully aware that, 5 percent notwithstanding, the World Bank's burden of development was to be a thankless one.

The Shifting Gaze

The decolonizing world is conspicuous only by its enforced absence from the Bank's archive during Meyer's and McCloy's terms; the institution's entirely positive assessment of British imperialism left little room for understanding the increasingly loud protests emanating from the decolonizing world except as ungrateful (though not unexpected) expressions of ignorance, the failure of the global South to recognize the many gifts that imperial contact had bestowed upon it. As the Bank underwent its institutional transformation from a reconstruction lender into a development agency in the closing years of the decade, the certainty that marked its earlier assessment of imperialism gradually weakened. Eugene Black, McCloy's successor, enacted this institutional transformation in a 1949 speech, marking a significant departure from his predecessors' unqualified embrace of the imperial legacy and their steadfast exclusion of the developing world from the Bank's perceptual horizon.

"The country that I shall speak about is India," Black avowed, "because it is a vast country, newly independent, with many economic problems to resolve and yet it holds out great promise for the future. I can think of few more important or challenging tasks for the Bank than that of assisting the development of India."[58] The concept of development in this speech shows little mutation from the Bretton Woods sense of developing "productive facilities"; the address, however, exhibits an orientalist fascination with the Indian subcontinent coupled with an emerging awareness of the scope of poverty and deprivation in India (and throughout what would shortly be known as the third world) entirely absent from previous Bank documents.

Black's depiction of India, in which he endeavors to paint a "more vivid picture" that can "bring alive" some of the new lending

opportunities for the Bank is thoroughly grounded in a set of orientalist assumptions about Indian civilization. In true Thomas
Babington Macaulay fashion,[59] Black assesses India through the
classic imperialist binaries of science/religion, industry/culture,
materiality/spirituality, and so forth. He writes that the "Indian
people have inherited a rich civilization; it is no accident that this
peace-loving nation produced one of the great spiritual leaders of
our time. But they need to develop material wealth."[60] That he sees
Indian civilization as "inherited" speaks to Black's deep-seated assumptions about property and ownership. That Gandhi is referred
to as a great "spiritual" rather than *political* leader suggests an implicit distinction between moral courage (of which an Indian might
be capable) and something like national statesmanship (the administrative complexities and tactical subtleties of which might best be
left to a Churchill or Roosevelt). That India is said to be "peace-
loving," the inheritor of "a rich civilization," and a nation capable
of producing "one of the great spiritual leaders of our time" speaks
to a liberal openness in Black's assessment of the subcontinent;
however, the compliments also carry the sting of backhanded jabs,
setting up the expected "but" that inevitably follows. Even so soon
after the war, the term "peace-loving," when coupled with "civilization" or "spiritual," reinscribes the colonial trope of a feminized
sphere of cultural softness, a sphere juxtaposed to the one occupied
by the Bank, which relies upon the hard laws of science or economics, the hard edges of industry, and the hard-fought truths of war.

Paradoxically, then, the speech depicts India's great inheritance—an inheritance, in Black's mind, constituted principally by
the *metaphysical* richness of Indian culture—as lack or deficiency.
By contrast, the Bank assumes its role as provider of the means and
knowledge to produce material wealth. It should come as no surprise that, at this moment of the historical emergence of the soon-
to-be-labeled "third world," development and underdevelopment
are framed in terms of presence and lack, provision and want. A
far cry from Meyer's claim that the world was starving for the
products of U.S. industry, Black attempts to convey the severity
of actual famine conditions in India. The "concern over the food
shortage was more acute than it had been for 60 years," Black
states, adding emphatically that "when I say food, I mean the bare
necessities of existence, not meat, which we think of as a necessity,
but grains."[61] Dearth itself (lack of knowledge, lack of technology,

lack of industry, lack of food, lack of sanitation, lack of health, lack of medicine, and the like), rather than a relationship to capitalism or socialism, comes to be the enduring definitional characteristic of underdevelopment, paving the way for a substantial if uneven overlap with the imagined construction of a third world.

Although the binaries of provision/dearth and material/metaphysical have a familiar imperialist ring, Black, as the head of a Bank still beholden to a private investment community, deploys these paradigms in a manner unique to the Bank. Exoticism and poverty may appeal to the imagination, perhaps even to the heart, but they do not necessarily appeal to the bottom line. Prudent projects and firm guarantees of repayment are nonnegotiable prerequisites for the Bank and its audience of U.S. investors, including the annual convention of the Savings Banks Association of the state of New York, to whom Black's speech is addressed. Black, then, endeavoring to justify the Bank's transformation into a development institution, fashions the strained image of India as, on the one hand, the site of severe deprivation, and, on the other, a model of fiscal and social responsibility, even civility.

Based on the Bank mission's recommendations, Black reports, short-term financing has been extended to the Indian government to purchase two tractors that will help clear weed-choked fields and improve crop yields—hardly the scale of lending that will raise the standard of living across the expanding population of 340 million people. In part, this demonstration of the Bank's limited capacity for lending is a tacit request for additional bond investment from his audience of bankers. In part, it is a case for why such investment is fiscally prudent: despite dire needs in the newly independent nation, Black reassures the crowd, the Bank will only fund sound projects. And in part this report is a testament to, and an encouragement of, the fiscally responsible actions of Nehru's government: designed to build confidence in the investing community that money loaned will be protected, the report also sends an implicit message about the Bank's expectations for good behavior to Nehru and any decolonizing nation states that hope to attract development lending. As much as the case for lending relies upon constructions of exoticism and deprivation, India ensures its status as the exemplary borrower for the Bank's new commitment to development through its willingness to guarantee the protection of foreign investment. Damning national liberation struggles throughout the decolonizing world with faint praise, Black nevertheless applauds the Indian government's economic restraint and resolve: "Independence had been rather too optimistically identified with a sudden improvement in material welfare, but disappointment when this failed to happen did not degenerate into bitterness and recrimination."[62] Although the Bank and its audience may have judged public bitterness over the slow pace of change after independence unfortunate, they surely would have viewed recrimination as an irredeemable crime. Praising the Nehru administration's economic policies, Black attempts to assuage any uneasiness about default that his audience may feel: "It is noteworthy that there has been renewed British investment in India recently and no attempt has been made by the Indian government to penalize existing British interests by nationalization or other measures. On the contrary, the Prime Minister has given assurances for the protection of all foreign capital."[63] India's lack of industry and lack of food are essential to the Bank's case for its own relevance as an international development institution; even more, India's lack of recrimination—Nehru's decisions not to nationalize private industry and to protect foreign capital—enables Black to sell development as both ethical and profitable. In this vein, the speech goes on to detail a series of funding proposals that the Bank decided *not* to make in India, based upon the assessments of its 1949 mission.

The Bank has long been fond of saying that the loans not approved often turn out to be the most important. Money not lent protects credit ratings. It also opens space for pedagogical intervention, allowing the Bank to instruct borrowing nations in the types of projects it deems likely to succeed, and therefore the projects it is likely to fund. Development remains a macroeconomic venture in Black's 1949 address, still conceived primarily in terms of promoting productive facilities and economic growth. But in this speech, which begins to cast its gaze toward the decolonizing world rather than toward Europe, which begins to make visible certain aspects of hunger, poverty, and deprivation, which begins to claim epistemological access to the "'feel' of the country, not just the bare bones of accounts and statistics," and, most important, which begins to balance every ethical claim with an assurance of profit, we can locate the origins of the contemporary conception of development, and the simultaneous and necessary emergence of development's object of attention: the decolonizing world.

3. Uncomfortable Intimacies: Managing Third World Nationalisms

Forced in the late 1940s from the familiarity of European reconstruction into the bold new world of development lending, with only a tenuous rhetorical apparatus that declared an unbending commitment to fiscal conservatism and the model of British Empire as guides, the World Bank found itself, one decade later, responding to a set of crises and constituencies that neither its Bretton Woods founders nor its original Wall Street bond managers could ever have imagined. During the tumultuous ten years between 1959 and 1969, which included portions of three Bank presidencies—the closing years of Eugene Black's term (which ended in 1963), five years under George Woods, and the beginning of Robert McNamara's tenure in 1968—the World Bank dexterously crafted an institutional identity as the world's most influential development agency. Under relentless institutional duress, most notably from what Black termed the "attendant clamor of unreasoning nationalism, envy, and recurrent crises,"[1] the Bank radically refashioned itself, reconceiving the very notion of development in an effort to remain relevant in the era of decolonization.

Pledging to remain true to its Wall Street roots while also assuaging Cold War fears from Washington, the Bank of the 1960s was called upon to channel the seething rage and utopian longings of decolonization into forms more palatable to a world capitalist system. The institution assumed the contradictory roles of fiscal disciplinarian, U.S. proxy, and ideological defender of revolutionary nationalism. Faced with the "clamor" of liberation movements, the Bank lurched toward liberalism as it scrambled in Africa and elsewhere to shore up global economic stability and international political order. Faced with hawkish fears of communist expansion, the Bank dutifully played its part as a cold warrior, lending strategically along the rim of third world containment. Never willing to abandon completely its economistic notion of capitalist production and growth as the engines of development, the Bank of the 1960s was nevertheless compelled to see and engage the complexities of *the social,* and to reckon with the dialectical relationship between base and superstructure. The investment banker's preference for visible, low-risk, "bankable" projects—and the corresponding rhetoric of simplicity, verifiability, and transparency—gave way to a new, more expansive understanding of development as the institution wrestled, both intellectually and politically, with the imbroglio of revolutionary movements and untenable levels of global inequity, disaffection, and disenfranchisement.

An address by Black, delivered early in the decade, captures some sense of the Bank's tightrope act, delicately trying to reconcile a deep unease about global systemic crisis brought to a head by decolonization, with a corresponding mission, born of fear that *civilizations* lay in the balance and based upon an unswerving faith in development and progress:

> To temper the excesses of nationalism is a pressing task for this decade. Vast and complex continents cannot be left alone to sort themselves out into nations through war and revolution, as Europe did throughout the nineteenth and into the twentieth century. Today we all know that every revolutionary shot is heard "round the world." Nor can we simply dismiss the new nations from afar because some are as yet unable to govern themselves. The combination of Jefferson's ideals and the spread of technology have brought us into an uncomfortable intimacy with the world which is as inescapable as the cycle of the seasons. We cannot repeal the impact of our civilization; we can either observe its repudiation or work for its vindication.[2]

This chapter will look to untangle the many interwoven threads of Black's passage: his expressed desire to "temper the excesses of nationalism," articulated through the self-consciously nationalist appeal to Jeffersonian ideals and the vindication of "our civilization"; his concern about the communicability of revolution in a world shrunken by communications technologies; his juxtaposition of constructivism and naturalism—culture and nature—used to advocate for calculated interventions in parts of the world that "cannot be left alone to sort themselves out into nations through war and revolution" despite, or rather because of, a newfound global interdependence as "inescapable as the cycle of the seasons"; and finally, underpinning all of these issues, Black's guarded assessment that by choice and by necessity the Bank's current and foreseeable relationship with the decolonizing world would be one of "uncomfortable intimacy."

This *intimacy* was alternately coerced and cultivated. Born in part from social transformations associated with the phenomenon of a "shrinking world," the insistent demands for independence and self-determination throughout the decolonizing world left the Bank with little choice in the matter. Nevertheless, this newfound global intimacy was sought out and welcomed by the Bank, which found new rhetorical purchase in a return to the posture of liberal internationalism. It welcomed its new members with open arms, frequently speaking in a decidedly third worldist idiom that gradually elevated "poverty alleviation" to the central institutional objective.[3] The *discomfort,* on the other hand, was felt acutely by the Bank as it worked to incorporate newly independent states into a global capitalist world system, not least because its strict economic faith in production and growth was severely tested by the scope of deprivation it encountered in the decolonizing world and by the vehement demands for retribution and redistribution that issued from national liberation movements and newly independent states. But the Bank would turn around and use that sense of discomfort for its own purposes as well, cementing the apparatuses of development and ensuring its own leadership in that field by sounding increasingly dire warnings about the inherent instability created by enormous (and still widening) economic and political inequities between North and South. Throughout the decade, the rhetoric of global crisis was marshaled in increasingly urgent tones, ascending to a near-apocalyptic shriek by decade's close under the missionary fervor of McNamara's presidency. Negotiating this "uncomfortable intimacy," then, became the principal challenge of the decade, as the Bank contritely sought to disavow its European imperial legacy while proclaiming with conviction its new civilizational mission to eradicate poverty and deliver the progress of modernity to those once-colonized, now underdeveloped parts of the globe.

This chapter explores several components of the Bank's evolution during the 1960s. I look first at the creation of the International Development Agency (IDA), arguing that it represents the Bank's bureaucratic concession and response to international pressures from newly independent states. Foreshadowing arguments about the origins of culture that will be developed in the next chapter, I pay particular attention to the ways the IDA has enabled/compelled the Bank to discover the social sphere, vastly expanding the potential scope of Bank activities. Next, I sketch what I term the dialectic of crisis and possibility that underpins the Bank's rhetorical case for development throughout the decade. Within the context of this dialectic, I interpret the Bank's conceptual investments in the nation state and the system of internationalism, by examining the contradictory position the Bank crafts in response to the phenomena of decolonizing nationalisms. I conclude by arguing that a neoimperialist belief in perpetual interventionism provides the underlying principle upon which the Bank justifies its work throughout the decade and beyond.

Dictates of the Heart: Bureaucratic Reform and the IDA

The Bank could scarcely ignore the radical transformations taking place in the decolonizing world, if for no other reason than the way they were reflected in the Bank's own membership.[4] By the end of the 1960s the World Bank—or, properly, the *International Bank for Reconstruction and Development*, whose member countries constituted its "shareholders"—had metamorphosed into an institution that its Bretton Woods founders would scarcely have recognized. In 1947, the Bank had 44 member countries, only 2 of which were African (Ethiopia and South Africa). A decade later, in 1957, the number of African members remained unchanged. That number, however, quadrupled to 8 by 1962, when Black addressed his board, more than quadrupled again to 34 by 1967, and climbed to 40 African member states by 1971. During the same period, the number of Asian members rose from 3 to 18. All told, the Bank's membership skyrocketed during the era of decolonization, swelling from 44 to 116 between the years of 1947 and 1971. It is worth reiterating that voting rights within the Bank are proportioned not on the basis of simple membership but according to the size of a member's capital contribution. Therefore, despite the exponential rise in African membership from 2 to 40—totaling well over one-third of the Bank's total membership in 1971—the cumulative weight of African voting power rose from 1.64 percent to a still-paltry 8.58 percent. By comparison, in 1971 the 58 Asian and African member states—half the Bank's total membership by nation, a much larger majority by population size—held less combined voting power (24.73 percent) than the 2 North American members (26.86 percent).[5]

Despite the rapidly changing membership rolls, however, the legacy of fiscal conservatism from the Bank's early years held fast. Black, whose tenure with the Bank stretched back to the era of the Wall Street reformers in the 1940s, was particularly reluctant to relinquish the investment banker's principles of low-risk, "nonpolitical," market-rate lending for transparent, visible projects, to countries with reasonable balance of payments, where there was little chance of default. As we have seen, these principles, if comforting to investors, were largely illusory from an economic perspective. But pressure from the decolonizing world made even the illusion of comfort difficult to maintain. The newly independent states of Asia and Africa, often perceived as high-risk investments because of their political and economic instability—not to mention their increasingly pointed anti-imperialist critique, which argued that the decolonizing world was impoverished and economically dependent *because* of colonial exploitation, not despite it—began to demand no- or low-interest grants or loans, to be repaid over longer periods, for a broader array of projects, and with fewer conditions attached. As the number of new nation states swelled, their influence within the (one flag, one vote) United Nations grew to the point where it seemed likely that the United Nations, rather than the Bank, would serve as the primary vehicle for development assistance. Faced with that prospect (reminiscent of its usurpation by the Marshall Plan), the Bank opted for institutional reform so as to remain relevant during the era of national liberation; its bureaucratic response to decolonization was the IDA.

By the time the IDA was created, the World Bank had already become officially known as the World Bank *Group,* having added in 1956 the International Finance Corporation (IFC), an organization designed to foster investment in private enterprises without requiring governmental guarantees. The IDA became the third member of the World Bank Group in 1960. Designed to provide the poorest countries with greater access to development investment, it divided borrowing countries into two groups—the richer Tier I and the poorer Tier II—and offered below-market interest rates and long-term loans to Tier II nations who would otherwise have been unable to borrow either from private capital or from the IBRD. Further, as I discuss in greater detail below, the IDA expanded the types of projects that qualified for lending, acquiescing to Southern demands that monies be made available to fund education, health care, agriculture, housing, and the like, rather than the roads, dams, and infrastructural projects that the Bank had restricted itself to until this point.

The IDA's new lending schema, as Mason and Asher astutely note, meant that the Bank's previous emphasis on creditworthiness "was more or less stood on its head." Prior to the advent of the IDA, they point out, "economists wrote their economic reports to demonstrate that countries *were* creditworthy and thus qualified for Bank loans"; under IDA guidelines, the objective was "to show that countries were *not* creditworthy and thus they qualified for IDA credits."[6] This reversal may be read, in the vein of Arturo Escobar or Gustavo Esteva, as an instance where the discourse of underdevelopment produces the condition of underdevelopment—poor nations performing and perpetuating their poverty to receive money. Interpreted differently, one may locate a mild form of resistance or subversion in their strategic malleability, as those nations trying to qualify for IDA loans remake their national public images to highlight their lack of creditworthiness, in an effort to avoid more onerous forms of debt. Although neither reading captures the entire dynamic of the IDA's influence, both point to the fact that the IDA's creation marks a radically transformed rhetorical context for the practices of international borrowing and lending.

To be clear, the IDA's creation *does not* radically upend the Bank's lending practices. The funding patterns and philosophies of the 1940s remain largely unaltered under the new regime. IDA lending amounts to only a fraction of the Bank's total outlays; Caufield cites the figure that, under McNamara, "less than 10 percent of Bank funds went to education, health, family planning, water supply, and other programs that help the poor directly."[7] Industrialization, infrastructure, energy, and the like would continue to receive the lion's share of Bank funds. Caufield and other critics, then, are right to see the IDA and what I am calling the Bank's "discovery of the social" as rhetorical ploys, a public relations effort that does not materially alter the nature of World Bank global economic practice.

Nevertheless, since the 1960s the World Bank has hitched its institutional image to IDA lending practices, associating itself first and foremost with the practice of innovative lending strategies that announce as their central objective the reduction of poverty and global inequity in the world's poorest countries. Prior to the 1960s, terms like *poverty* and *inequity* appear nowhere in the Bank archive; after the creation of the IDA, *poverty alleviation* defines the Bank's principal stated mission. The IDA is the vehicle that makes possible the institutional transformation from international bank to international development agency. Although we must not ignore the still-dominant banking side of this transformation, the IDA nonetheless provides an essential site through which to read the historical contradictions and conflicts of the era from which it emerges. A response to the decolonizing world's newfound persuasiveness—in the forms of rancorous crowds, polished statespersons, armed insurgencies, or novel and effective forms of social protest—the IDA's ideological (if not financial) prominence signals a strategic reactive intervention by the Bank. As a maneuver of containment, the constitution of the IDA substantially alters the manner in which the Bank addresses the world. However (as we see in later chapters), even as the IDA, with the Bank's rhetorical embrace of a social mission, forecloses certain avenues of opposition, it opens others.

Tellingly, Black and the Bank never wanted anything to do with the IDA; the agency was reluctantly created as a rearguard action to protect the interests of its Northern members (the United States most of all), to forestall pressure from decolonizing nations, and to ensure the Bank's position as the leading institution of international development. Most specifically, it was a "lesser of two evils" alternative to the proposed Special United Nations Fund for Economic Development (SUNFED). Burke Knapp, a senior Bank official who held top posts almost from the Bank's inception, recounts in a 1961 oral history the political considerations that went into the Bank's decision to found the IDA. The passage has enough substance to warrant quoting at length.

The issue, therefore, between SUNFED and IDA became rather acute at one time, and it was the United States government primarily that decided to go for an agency under the management of the World Bank rather than one under the management of the United Nations. The considerations were twofold: one, that an agency administered under the United Nations would presumably be dominated by the underdeveloped countries if the voting was on a unit basis, complicated by the fact that in the United Nations the Soviet Union and the rest of the iron curtain countries would be members and participate in the management. And for rather obvious political reasons, the United States felt that it would rather contribute its money to something under sounder professional and technical management than could be expected under United Nations administration.

Now, of course, the under-developed countries themselves tend to favor SUNFED for the simple reason that they want to escape some of the rigorous administration and management of these funds, or, as they would put it, they would like to have a much larger voice in policies of the institution and the administration of funds.[8]

Several things from Knapp's remarks stand out. First, Knapp exposes the thin veneer of separation between the U.S. government and the Bank. The IDA was a U.S. project from the beginning, conceived as a way for Washington to maintain direct control over development funds. Because of the UN's voting mechanism, such control would be much more difficult to achieve if these funds were administered under the aegis of SUNFED. The Bank, then, had become Washington's preferred vehicle of internationalism, largely because of its constitutional immunity from the influence of both the Soviets and the clamorous nationalisms of the developing world.

Second, Knapp endeavors to force intellectual and economic "rigor" into a strained opposition with democracy.[9] Confronted for the first time by demands from peoples of color—no matter that, for the most part, the Bank's contact was limited to the cosmopolitan representatives of the national elites—Knapp seemingly filters their collective demand for a figurative seat at the negotiating table through the racist stereotype of the lazy native, hoping to shirk work and responsibility, who needs to be told what is best for her or him. Disbelieving that decolonizing nations may actually want "a much larger voice in policies of the institution and the administration of funds," Knapp presumes to attribute the decolonizing nations' support for SUNFED to "the simple reason" that the emerging nations of the South, like petulant schoolchildren who refuse to do their Latin homework, are doing their best to find ways of avoiding the Bank's "rigorous administration and management." Faced with a threat to its international authority, the U.S., using the Bank as spokesperson, portrays the democratic longings of the decolonizing world as simplistic and simple-minded, the fantasies of a collection of nascent states unable, from lack of training and lack of resolve, to match the standards of economic rigor set by the Bank.

In reviewing this history, Mason and Asher accurately summarize the pressures and demands that led to the establishment of the IDA, but they come to a conclusion that seems hardly borne out by the facts that they sketch. They concede that the IDA "is not under UN control, it does not make grants, and it operates by weighted voting" (i.e., that it fails to meet the central objectives proposed by the decolonizing nations). Nevertheless, they argue that the IDA "stands as historic proof that the 'international power structure' is responsive to persistent peaceful pressure. The IDA confirms one's faith in the ability of bureaucracies to remain afloat, to unfurl fresh sail, and to benefit from prevailing winds."[10] Much wind here, to be sure, but before we unfurl any fresh sail in a salute to bureaucracy, we should be clear about the internal resistance that the IDA faced, the institutional form it ultimately took, and the effects produced by that form for both North and South. It is worth reiterating that the IDA is at root a reactionary agency; the Bank and many of its member nations agreed to the IDA with only grudging reluctance. The German government opted for an unfortunate if revealing phrase, arguing that the IDA was "a woolly-headed idea."[11] The Bank itself under Black's leadership had finally achieved the coveted AAA bond rating in 1959, making its bond offerings extremely desirable for inclusion in investment portfolios and thereby assuring steady and substantial funding income for the IBRD. Kapur, Lewis, and Webb capture the sense of deflation that accompanied the roughly concurrent creation of the IDA: "After striving for fifteen years to achieve Wall Street respectability, the Bank watched as the IDA suddenly materialized and conjured up the 1940s' augury that the Bank would grow up to be a soup kitchen."[12] The idea of lending money for balance of payments, disaster relief, or so-called soft sectors like health, education, housing, agriculture, and so on was anathema to Black's fiscal conservatism. Rejecting the idea of lending practices that had the slightest whiff of social welfare, Black provided blunt assurances to the closing session of the 1959 Bank–IMF meetings that "This pledge I give you . . . IDA will not be a 'soft lender.'"[13] Two years later, with the writing beginning to appear on the wall, he defensively restated this position to his board, reaffirming the emphasis on sound lending that defined the Bank's approach in the 1940s: "And that brings me to an important point. Several Governors have urged that IDA be administered in accordance with the dictates of our hearts. If what is meant by that, in using IDA resources, we must constantly have in mind the ultimate objective of improving the standards of life of the peoples of the underdeveloped world, I am in full agreement. But if the meaning is that we should substitute our hearts for our heads in investing IDA resources, I could not disagree more completely."[14] Here we see a Bank president asserting his executive authority over his board, reproaching those presumably Southern members agitating for more lenient borrowing terms and conditions. Nevertheless, the degree of discomfort evident in a phrase like "dictates of the heart" suggests that the Bank, in conceding to the demands of the United States and to the "clamor" from the South, creates the IDA against its own better judgment; in fact, only when India, the Bank's showcase borrower, began to have balance of payment problems that left it dangerously close to the limit that could be lent under IBRD standards, did Black agree to the IDA. In such an official venue as this address to the board, Black is making it clear that, although he begrudgingly agreed to found the new lending institution, he will not allow it to compromise the Bank's scrupulous reputation for economic integrity. To this end, Black insists that the IDA be placed under the managerial control of the World Bank Group, answering directly to its president and top staff.

As the decade wore on, however, and Black was replaced by Woods, who was in turn replaced by McNamara, the IDA gradually became the focal point of Bank public relations. Freed somewhat from IBRD restrictions, the Bank's work with the IDA allowed it to craft itself as a much more activist—some might say crusading—agency, with poverty alleviation as its new centerpiece. As such, the IDA is perfectly suited for the interventionist rhetoric of *crisis and possibility* that becomes the dominant thematic of the era (more on this trope later). But the publicness of the IDA stems from institutional reasons as well, most notably the fact that the agency is funded only through capital contributions from member governments. Unlike the IBRD, which borrows money on the private bond markets to fund the majority of its lending, the IDA's lending capital needs to be replenished every three years or so, meaning that it is under much more direct influence from member governments, who control the agency's purse strings. Consequently, its pool of lending funds is considerably smaller than the Bank's, meaning that the poorer countries are forced to compete for scarce resources. Additionally (as we will see when we look more closely at some of the speeches from the 1960s), this shift in the source of funding manifests itself in a rhetorical address no longer primarily geared toward private investors, but instead toward national parliamentary publics; that is, underlying almost every Bank speech from this era is an argument about the world's dire need for the IDA, and a plea for larger allocations from member governments. Once again the Bank finds itself in a perpetual sales pitch; with IDA, however, the primary audience is politicians and their constituencies who want to ensure that the institution works in their national interests rather than (or in addition to) financiers who want to ensure a profitable return on investment.

At best, this shift in the source of funding should be seen as a double-edged sword.

On the one hand, direct member funding makes the non-democratic Bank slightly more accountable to citizens around the world. On several occasions social movements, most notably Northern environmental groups during the late 1980s and early 1990s, have successfully pressured elected officials to, in turn, pressure the Bank into making policy changes. Although campaigns to reform the Bank through legislative action can at times have a strategic value that warrants the support of activists on the Left, the limits of such intervention are clear. In effect, the threat to halt IDA replenishment funds has served to increase (the already vast) U.S. influence over Bank policy. Given the U.S. Congress's reluctance to replenish IDA funds (often spearheaded by the far Right rather than by what passes for the Congressional Left), the United

States has wielded even more leverage than that already assured by its disproportionately large voting power. As Kapur, Lewis, and Webb put it, even though "the United States by no means has been IDA's whole political story, it has been the protagonist around which other plots thickened."[15] Even discounting the tenuous connection between actual democracy and the façade of representative politics that masquerades as such within the United States, the strategy of wielding pressure through legislatures affords disproportionate access to social movements (or, more likely, to well-funded NGOs) from the North, and overlooks those people most affected by the Bank's policies and those movements that have articulated the most radical critiques of Bank practice.[16] At best, additional parliamentary leverage over the Bank has led to isolated cases in which mild reforms were pressed through. More frequently, the power of the purse has tended to exaggerate the influence of the nation already most powerful, meaning that more than ever the Bank has operated in the national interests of the United States.

IDA and the Discovery of the Social

Perhaps the most significant shift accompanying the creation of the IDA is that this new bureaucratic venture marks the Bank's discovery of the social. As with all discovery myths, the object being sought has been there all along. The act of unveiling, however, confers upon it an analytical or categorical weightiness far in excess of its previous significance. The IDA proves to be the lens that makes visible to the Bank the complex interactions between economy and society, and the vehicle through which the now self-aware Bank attempts to intervene in the social sphere. Black, though a reluctant convert to the notion that Bank funds might be lent for social projects, had little choice in the matter; as Richard Demuth acknowledged during an internal meeting, "If IDA did nothing but Bank projects, there would be a revival of support for the establishment of SUNFED."[17] If Black was initially hesitant about social lending, his successors had no such qualms. Woods, and especially McNamara, launched an era of Bank operations that would shift the conception of development away from a strict economistic notion of *productive resources* into a more fluid, complex set of lending practices focused on *human resources*.

The Bank's new focus on education, for example, illustrates this shift toward investing in social production. As we have already seen, the pedagogical (or more accurately, *pedantic*) impulse within development was evident in the Bank's earlier focus on technical assistance. As Woods explained to a UN audience in 1966, "The very idea of preparing 'bankable' projects in education wasn't taken seriously until a few years ago."[18] But, as it became clearer to the Bank that social relationships and so-called human resources played a productive role in developing economies, the institution began to actively pursue "the idea of investing money, according to bankable standards, in the accumulation of intellectual capital."[19] Woods became an avid supporter of what he termed "imaginative forms of technical assistance, particularly in primary, secondary, and technical education and in agriculture."[20] And McNamara, true to his business roots at Ford and his managerial obsession with efficiency, argued that "we must make teachers more productive,"[21] tripling education lending between 1968 and 1973. Interestingly, both Woods and McNamara were early proponents of distance education and of various forms of mediatized teaching and learning, in part because the technologies involved provided concrete bankable projects to which the funds might be lent. In 1973, Mason and Asher, choosing their metaphors with some precision, aptly suggested, "In the parlance of the U.S. stock market, education is one of the Bank's 'growth industries.' The Bank expects to become, if it is not already, the largest outside financer of education assistance to less developed countries."[22]

The speed with which the Bank came to embrace social lending indicated both the intensity of the pressure from below and the malleability of the Bank as an institution. Kapur, Lewis, and Webb recount a 1952 discussion between Black and Lauchlin Currie, director of the Bank's mission to Colombia, in which Black rejected the principle of social overhead projects in no uncertain terms: "Damn it, Lauch. We can't go messing around with education and health. We're a *bank*!"[23] A decade later, Black's tune had changed dramatically: "We are forced by our circumstances into trying to fashion a whole new orchestra of financial instruments designed specifically . . . to implant and cultivate in the underdeveloped world the many factors that make a society productive."[24]

As Raymond Williams and many since have reminded us, the Latin verb *colere*, from which *culture* derives etymologically, denotes the act of inhabiting and cultivating, tending to the development of crops or livestock.[25] The sense of inhabitation carries over into the related words *colony* and *colonize,* and the term *culture* extends the metaphor of cultivation to human society. Black's argument that the Bank, and specifically the IDA, will "implant and cultivate" the "many factors that make society productive," marks a decisive break from the institutional role envisioned in previous decades. His acknowledgement of unnamed "circumstances" speaks to the pressure from below that calls this turn into being. The social irrupted into the Bank's field of vision—as Woods put it, "a sudden bursting into our consciousness"[26]—taking the irrepressible forms of liberation struggles, food riots, and increasingly obstreperous demands from nationalist leaders, intellectuals, and social movement actors across the decolonizing world. Still, the shift is not only a reaction. No longer convinced that infrastructure alone will lead to productivity, the Bank turns willingly (after a few years, eagerly) to superstructure—to *culture,* one might say. What needs to be stressed in this chapter is the Bank's *willingness and capacity to contain such an irruption through its own institutional cultural turn.*

I use the phrase *cultural turn* quite purposefully. This is not the Bank's language. Indeed, a case could be made that it is only within the past few years, largely at the prompting of political philosopher Amartya Sen, that the Bank has specifically recognized, labeled, and engaged with something called *culture.* To wit, Vijayendra Roa and Michael Walton, prefacing their 2004 collection *Culture and Public Action,* feel the need to justify the very premise that Bank staffers might venture into such murky waters: "Some may find it incongruous that two economists who work for the World Bank are editing a book about culture. It reflects an increasing recognition of the centrality of cultural process to the reproduction of inequality and human ill-being among development policy makers and economists. However, we are well aware that economists are newcomers to this field and that anthropology and sociology have made seminal contributions to it for over two centuries."[27]

Rao and Walton understand *culture* from an anthropological fieldwork model of ethnographic investigation—the study of local beliefs, values, customs, kinship structures, division of labor, and the like. Their inquiry into "'why' and 'how' culture matters for development,"[28] is a call to place global and local into a dialectical relationship—to understand the ways in which lending practices cannot be conceived as universal, but rather need to be crafted with attention to the local beliefs and practices of particular peoples. There is great value in this approach to the study of culture; some of the best writing about the Bank and development moves from a similar methodological practice, allowing for a nuanced understanding of the impact that lending decisions made in Washington have "on the ground."[29] Such work can call attention to the ways in which questions of gender, race, ethnicity, sexuality, class, nationality, and the like cannot be thought in the abstract, but rather must be understood as articulating variability and reflecting specific geographical pressures and histories. This work is indispensable for anyone trying to understand the material effects of Bank policy. It is no surprise, then, that the Bank—an institution sensitive to critique and (at present) highly invested in broadening both the number of shareholders in development and their contributions to participatory development—would move to evaluate its lending practices with a self-reflective turn toward cultural analysis.

When I talk about the Bank's cultural turn in the 1960s, however, my contention is not that the institution was engaged in this sort of ethnographic accounting of local difference (though I will argue that it does rely at times on an older anthropological conception of *culture* as a complex whole). Rather, I am suggesting that the Bank actively participates in what Michael Denning terms the "global cultural turn" long before it self-consciously recognizes that *culture* (in the sense implied by Rao and Walton) may represent a sphere of engagement or concern for development lending. That is, although the Bank does not discover the term *culture* until much later, its "discovery of the social" in the 1960s parallels a vast range of roughly contemporaneous intellectual projects from across the globe in which social processes come to be theorized as actively constitutive, rather than merely reflective, of subjectivities, collectivities, and material social relations. Denning links this global cultural turn to the historical struggles of "the age of three worlds" (the following chapter takes up his argument and the Bank's historical role in the global retheorizing of culture in greater detail). For now, let me simply make clear that, when I speak of the social or cultural turn in this chapter, I have in mind a certain conceptual collapsing of distinctions between economy and social relations, processes and apparatus—base and superstructure—that would not have been possible for the Bank of the 1940s (which, as we have seen, clung tenaciously to a narrow definition of productive, verifiable, transparent lending). Under Woods and McNamara, dams, energy projects, roads, ports, and the like still constitute the bulk of the Bank's lending portfolio, but this era also sees investments in education, water, housing, health, sanitation, family planning, and other social sectors, conceived not as welfare or aid handouts, but instead as *productive* aspects of national economies, indispensable to the long-term development prospects of any borrowing country. Some will scoff, suggesting that the Bank's small percentage of social lending amounts to little more than token handouts for the poor, designed to mollify demanding borrowers or, worse, to sweeten the pot just enough to coax borrowing nations into contractual obligations of indebtedness. Although there may be a kernel of truth to such an indictment, it does not adequately convey the substance of this conceptual shift. My claim is not that the cultural turn originates with the World Bank; rather, I am suggesting that the Bank is a product of its historical era, an era that sees radically heterogeneous intellectual movements with little direct contact or influence simultaneously turning toward culture as a productive sphere of investment and contestation. I read the Bank as a product of and a participant in this global cultural turn, and I read the IDA as both symptom and response.

In its discovery and cultivation of the social during the decade of the 1960s, the Bank begins to construct an interventionist model of development predicated upon the newly perceived complexities of orchestrating the relationship between economy and the totality of human and societal production. Woods would argue, a few years later, that the problems of economic development were "widely recognized" to be "part of a world-wide complex of problems" that "cannot be treated in isolation."[30] Indeed, much more than a new set of financial instruments at the IDA's disposal, the discovery of the social extends vastly the Bank's scope of action and influence. Once the direct link between the project and verifiable economic production has been exploded, the Bank is free to conceive of infrastructure and superstructure in a dialectical relationship: that is, where both can be thought of as potentially productive, and where infrastructure is no longer presumed to organically generate superstructure; rather, both need cultivation. Within the logic of this cultural turn, then, the potential scope and duration of Bank-sponsored development telescopes toward a horizon that promises to be infinite and eternal.

Yawning Gulfs in a Shrinking World

"Today the people of the underdeveloped world are on the march," Black assured the Bank's board of governors in 1962. "To actually look on the grim face of poverty," he continued, shifting into a rather more foreboding register, "is to get an overpowering impression of why the peoples of the underdeveloped world can so easily be cast into the lethargy of despair or roused to furies of envy, hatred and malice."[31] If the IDA represents the Bank's bureaucratic response to decolonization, this dialectic between crisis and possibility structures the Bank's rhetorical case for development in the 1960s.

Throughout the course of the decade, the Bank sounds ever more urgent warnings about the widening disparity between the developed and underdeveloped worlds. Woods picks up where Black left off, frequently admonishing his audiences with dire predictions about the untenable and growing gap between the world's rich and poor: "A world divided by such a yawning gulf in living standards would be a world headed on a straight road for some kind of catastrophe," he told an audience of Canadians in 1964.[32] Two years later, in an address to UNESCO, he sounded a similar note: "Today, the disparity between the living standards of a prosperous fraction of mankind and the rest of humanity is a gulf that separates the two; but tomorrow it may swallow up both rich and poor in political strife and economic chaos."[33] Robert McNamara, in his evangelist style, whipped the rhetoric of crisis toward apocalyptic frenzy by linking global inequity to the "population explosion,"[34] arguing in 1968 that "human dignity is severely threatened by the population explosion—more severely, more completely, more certainly threatened than it has been by any catastrophe the world has yet endured."[35]

Warnings about the potentially catastrophic North/South divide find their necessary counterpart in the rhetoric of a shrinking world.[36] That is, as the gap between rich and poor grows, so, cautions the Bank, does global interdependence and interpenetrability. Raising the specter of communicability and contagion once again, the Bank presidents throughout the decade argue that global inequity in a shrinking world leaves the populations of rich nations more vulnerable to social unrest and makes the populations in poor nations aware of, and therefore covetous of, standards of living that have been denied to them. This notion of interconnectivity likewise underpins the global cultural turn; planetary flows of bodies, commodities, media, contaminants, and more position local difference and global standardization into apparently antagonistic but in fact mutually constitutive relations. Black, for instance, argues that "[m]odern communications—the radio, the motion picture, the airplane, ever-increasing contacts among nations—have shown the people of the underdeveloped world what they are prepared to regard as a better way of life than their own."[37] Woods in turn highlights the systemic instability produced by this new visibility; in a shrunken world, vast global inequality can no longer be masked. "It is unrealistic," Woods avers, "to think that this global state of affairs can persist."[38] Extrapolating from the political model of the democratic nation-state, he examines the new implications for world governance within the "small neighborhood" of the "community of nations," a metaphor that shares much with later Marshall McLuhan–derived discussions of the "global village": "Surely any government, if half or more of its people lived in poverty, either would make strenuous efforts to help them or would itself fail to survive. Through changes in communications and transportation, the world each year becomes a smaller neighborhood, and what is intolerable in a single nation inevitably—and quickly—will become intolerable in the community of nations."[39] The metaphor emphasizes the responsibility of governance institutions, including the Bank, to remedy the global disparities in wealth. The rough logic is as follows: no population within the bounded, finite political system of a sovereign nation will tolerate severe and chronic inequality. The nation-state, as a bureaucratic institution, functions because it is collectively understood to be constituted by, and therefore beholden to, the "will of the people." In a political formation of this sort, any system perceived to work in the interest of the few and at the expense of the many will inevitably be replaced by a different system, whether by bullet or by ballot. As the community of nations becomes more finite and visible—more nation-like—it will increasingly be held accountable to the will of the people, meaning that it too will face the crisis of representative legitimacy.

The contradictions entailed in extrapolating a national structure to a model of world governance are myriad; most notably, the passage's appeal to an imagined democratic public intolerant of inequity only underscores the constitutively antidemocratic nature of the Bank as a supposedly representative institution. As national politics are analogized to the system of internationalism, the mediating mechanism of representation—in the sense of "speaking for"—reveals itself to be ever more hollow, ever more removed from actual democracy. Already we have examined the ways in which the Bank deploys "representational" structures to ensure a system where dollars rather than nations or individual subjects "vote." In this regard, Black's analogy prefigures more contemporary debates about various forms of global citizenship displacing the sovereignty of the nation state. As with Black's, such claims are often based precisely on the phenomenon of a shrinking world. Globalization pundits such as Walter Wriston, former CEO of CitiBank and an influential figure in the debt crisis in which private banks successfully and steadfastly refused to forgive any Latin American debt, contend that the market functions in effect as the new global *polis,* "a giant vote-counting machine," in Wriston's words, that takes "constant referendums" on the policies of nation states and "discipline[s] imprudent sovereigns" whose fiscal or social policies are not to the global citizen's liking.[40] Black's own analogy, though perhaps not quite so blunt as Wriston's, promises much the same type of international "neighborhood," where representation is determined by dollars not peoples.[41] However, though Wriston sees global citizenship as the product of declining national sovereignty, Black grounds his analogy firmly in a conception of the autonomous nation state as the locus of political representation (i.e., the nation state as bureaucratic representation of the people and as the representative political form upon which to model global governance). This distinction (as we see in the following section) speaks to the era's, and the institution's, "uncomfortable intimacy" with nationalism.

Our Heritage: Nationalist Longings

For an institution founded, in great measure, to prevent the conditions that produced European fascism, the upsurge in nationalist liberation movements—especially in the perceived context of an ever-shrinking world—was cause for enormous concern. On the other hand, as a constitutionally inter*national* body—that is, an institution predicated upon the nation state as the hegemonic form of bureaucratic and political organization, an institution whose membership comprised nation states and whose charter only authorized the transfer of monies between and among nation states—the Bank found in the sweeping nationalism of the decolonizing world a *raison d'être* for its own reincarnation as a development agency. Not only did the emerging nationalisms provide a source of new borrowers and new lenders, the nation state and the system of internationalism would prove to be among the Bank's most effective tools for managing the revolutionary movements of the age. Dangling carrots and wielding sticks, the Bank used development lending as a wedge to divide potential regional or third world-ist blocs (a tactic it would later use with great success during the 1980s Latin American debt crisis).

It would be an exaggeration to claim that the Bank was solely, or even largely, responsible for insuring the continued hegemony of the nation state as a political form. Likewise, it overstates the case to say that the Bank's divide-and-rule tactics brought about the demise of an international third worldist revolutionary program; the internal divisions between and among national liberation leaders and movements were quite real and any number of historical factors helped undo the promise of the third world. Nevertheless, it is certainly the case that the Bank helped to prop up the institution of the nation state in a moment of potential crisis (often in collaboration with national elites from the decolonizing world) by codifying the state as the only legitimate solicitor and recipient of international development funds. Nationalism and the nation state emerge as central preoccupations of the decade, then, and the Bank finds itself delicately treading a fine line: encouraging what it would identify as the "progressive force"[42] of nationalism (i.e., where "progress" is expressed through the political form of the nation state), while trying to contain and manage the "form of nationalism, sometimes racialism, often of the narrowest and most violent sort,"[43] that threatens to undermine the nation state and the interstate system upon which the Bank's existence is predicated.

Although the documents of the decade are rife with allusions to nationalism, perhaps the topic's most elaborate treatment comes in Black's 1962 Founder's Day address at the University of Virginia (the university established by Thomas Jefferson). Although Black speaks here in his official capacity as president of the IBRD, this is not a policy speech per se. Nor is it executive in the sense of his address to the board. Rather, in speeches such as this (which Black and other Bank presidents delivered with some regularity), we encounter a different rhetorical context in which to read *the Bank*. This particular address offers a more intimate sense of Black as an individual and an intellectual. Prompted by the occasion to examine Jefferson's intellectual legacy, Black addresses the question of nationalism and its relation to an American political history in considerable detail. In his extended, even leisurely, analysis, Black develops a detailed argument about what he understands to be among the most pressing challenges facing the Bank and the world. In doing so, this speech affords an opportunity to see the Bank president engaging a broader public in the pressing debates of the era. No longer constricted to selling bonds to portfolio managers, Black endeavors to convince a national public of its international responsibilities. Although such an address is not technically a Bank statement, it provides a rich intellectual and rhetorical context from which to understand the values and assumptions within which the Bank president operates.

Sounding the alarm of crisis, Black outlines the dangers posed by what he characterizes as virulent forms of "ultra-nationalism." With allusions to the fascist regimes of Europe, Black portrays the emerging nationalisms as products of poverty and powerlessness, where desperate populations express their rage through acts of "racialism" and violence. Specifically, he argues that "two poisons" have "polluted" the "stream of nationalism": the first "is a kind of isolationism, a tendency to reject outside participation in the national life; the other is the tendency to exalt the national state and the powers of the state."[44] Black characterizes the first "pollutant" in the following manner:

> To shut out the rest of the world because of actual or imagined grievances in the past, and to turn away foreign technology, foreign advice and foreign capital, seems to me to be self-defeating and suicidal. This kind of nationalism can keep oil underneath the ground, for instance, instead of getting it out of the ground and putting it to work. Nationalism can chase the foreigners out, instead of permitting them to use their special skills in cooperation with local people in the making of a modern nation. Nationalism can make foreign aid impossible, or make it a waste of time and money.[45]

The form of nationalism that the Bank can least countenance is the form of nationalism that wants nothing to do with the Bank. How could a nation be so "self-defeating" as to reject foreign capital and leave oil in the ground rather than "putting it to work"? How could a nation not see the value in cooperating with foreigners to forge a "modern nation"? In the phrase, "actual or imagined grievances"—a recurrent refrain in Bank documents of the era—the "or" works to undermine the validity of anti-imperialist critique. Further, Black's example of unextracted oil dredges up the Bank's longstanding belief that noncommodified resources are without value. Arguing that "freedom has largely been won, and colonialism is sounding its death rattle,"[46] Black urges decolonizing nations to let bygones be bygones, move beyond the emotional responses of anger or retribution, and embrace the rational principles of a modern economy, which cannot be achieved without the financial support of international lending as well as technical assistance and industrial capital from their former colonial rulers in Europe.

Analyzing the second "poison," in effect an extension of the first, Black also cautions against "the exaltation of the state," code for the nationalization of industries and/or the broader socialization of economies. In this regard, Black's critique of nationalism is actually a defense of foreign capitalist interests in former, or soon to be former, colonial territories: "Nationalists are likely to argue that a dominant role of the state in the economy is justified, for one thing because government is more moral than business—or, to paraphrase the argument somewhat ungenerously, because they think that politics are more virtuous than profits. But the possibility is that in the end, the combination of both political and economic power in government may destroy the individual rights that government is supposed to protect."[47]

That Black is advocating for a separation between state and market is clear. Bank lending patterns stretching back into the 1940s and forward to the present day suggest a decisive, longstanding preference for economies that feature private ownership of key industries and a punitive reluctance (bordering on prohibition) to fund state-owned industrial projects. The overwhelming preference for private industry weakens somewhat during the later 1960s and, particularly, the 1970s under the liberal tenure of McNamara, only to have the encouragement of "privatization" reaffirmed in the mid-1980s as an official part of the Bank's role within the Washington Consensus response to the debt crisis.[48]

Perhaps the more interesting aspect of Black's passage, however, lies in his effort to overlay this distinction between private- and state-run economies with a second distinction between "individual rights" and "morality" or "virtue." The nation state, by this account, ought to stay out of the way of the market and concern itself with the protection of individual rights. A right to *private* property is affirmed, therefore, because the locus of its authority is the individual, the human subject. When the grounds for authority move from the individual to the collective, the discourse of rights (the proper realm of the state) shifts to the more metaphysical register of morality and virtue (the realm of religion). In this formulation, economic decisions enacted in the name of such ideals as equity, the greater good, the people, or in fact the nation (as distinct from the state) operate within the residual logic of morality and virtue rather than the modern logic of efficiency and productivity. Implicitly, then, the argument associates state-run economies, especially those in the allegedly premodern, not-yet-developed South, with the irrational dictates of ritual and tradition. Although we may be tempted today to use the term *progressive* in describing regimes committed to principles of equity and the collective good over the protection of individual rights such as to property, Black and the Bank argue in epochal terms that such nationalisms represent a regression—a de-development—backward from the humanist revolutionary ideals of the "rights of man" and toward, paradoxically, a form of oriental despotism: "If it follows this road," Black opined, "nationalism will end by substituting a new tyranny for the ancient tyrannies that Jefferson worked so hard to destroy, and the new tyranny will be more tenacious and powerful than any since the Dark Ages."[49]

Of course it is hardly astonishing that the Bank, working to ensure global economic stability and to shore up financial confidence in its nervous constituencies from the North, would attempt to critique and contain those forms of nationalism that it perceived to be hostile. Predictably, nationalist movements that are anti-development, anti-imperialist, anti-American or -European, and/or anticapitalist draw a certain amount of ire from the Bank. More interesting is the timorous, equivocal manner in which this critique is presented. In part, this is evidence of a shift in audience, where for the first time in its history the Bank finds itself having to address both North and South, meaning that the Bank must be diplomatic in how it characterizes decolonization movements. Indeed, we find throughout the documents of the 1960s a consistent appeal to the principles of liberal inclusion and openness. Black describes the IDA as combining "a banker's glass eye with a philanthropist's tender heart."[50] Woods speaks of the need for patience and understanding, encouraging dialogue with the new nations of the decolonizing world. And McNamara preaches "mutual *respect* and *tolerance* between the countries giving aid and those receiving it."[51] All told, the Bank makes a consistent and concerted rhetorical effort throughout the decade to acknowledge and appease the decolonizing world. It would have been a notable departure had a Bank president unconditionally condemned nationalism during the zenith of national liberation movements.

Further, the Bank needs nationalism even as it disparages certain forms of nationalist expression. It needs nationalism to the extent that it needs the state; that is, because the Bank regards the nation state and the interstate system as the most promising apparatuses through which to manage the disaffections of impoverished and exploited populations around the globe, it understands nationalism to represent both the expression of that disaffection and the first steps toward its resolution. Poverty and inequality themselves come to be cast as opportunity rather than burden. The same energy that gives rise to racialism and violence can be channeled into development, which in turn, according to Black's formulation, converts the energy of nationalism into productive labor, constructing both the state and the sense of national belonging that he terms *nationhood*:

> In the very poverty of those parts of the world where nationalism today is strong lies the best hope for channeling nationalist energies in a direction compatible with the security and well-being of the world community. Nationalism stirs up people; it creates energies. Economic development converts that energy into work; it sets people to building things. If enough people can be set at constructive jobs, there is hope that a real sense of nationhood will emerge, and that resentments will become less sharp and frustrations less agonizing in those parts of the world.[52]

Here, Black attempts to articulate the possibility latent within nationalism. He argues that development harnesses the energy of nationalism and "converts that energy into work" in order to produce a working nation—in other words, a nation with full employment and a polity in which a "real sense of nationhood" works to blunt the "resentments" and "frustrations" that stem from poverty.

If Black celebrates a form of nationalism issuing from the desperations of poverty, this is in great part because he has in mind an ideal of American nationalism in stark contrast to the seemingly more analogous example of fascist regimes of Europe. Making the most of the Founder's Day occasion, Black trumpets the Jeffersonian legacy (absent any reference to the slave labor upon which it is built, of course) within the nationalist movements of the era. "An American businessman asserting his right to be free of government intervention, and an African political leader asserting his right to be free of a colonial master," Black told his Charlottesville audience, "both owe something to the eighteenth-century ideal of liberty which Mr. Jefferson pursued during the whole of his political life."[53] This is a striking comparison. For the U.S. audience it suggests, of course, the deeply persuasive appeal of "free" markets, where a businessman's "freedom" from "government intervention" (from taxes, from labor laws, from monopoly prohibitions, etc.) presumably does not extend to the myriad of protections and subsidies that the U.S. government provides for capital and capitalists. The comparison must be read either as a hyperbolic elevation in the stature of business owners' freedom to pay fewer taxes or lower wages, or an equally extreme trivialization of the anticolonial liberation struggles taking place in Africa and elsewhere. Or, perhaps, both. That is, while trying to minimize the revolutionary import of nationalist movements in the South—the struggle of former colonial subjects against grievances "real or imagined"—Black is simultaneously laying the groundwork for a model of the working nation that has as its highest priority the protection of business freedoms. By constricting the Enlightenment's "ideal of liberty" into an argument about the freedom of business, Black is able to figure both the Bank and the decolonizing world as the intellectual co-inheritors of a specifically American revolutionary tradition.

The specifically American valence of his Virginia address provides a valuable context from which to read his addresses to the Bank's board of directors a few months prior:

> For this development business is *our* game and our heritage. . . .
>
> It is *our* heritage which has demonstrated to the peoples of the underdeveloped world that there is an alternative to abject poverty.

It is *our* heritage which introduced the radical idea of self-determination and national independence.

It is *our* heritage which has shown the way to mass consumption and to the widest participation in the fruits of economic progress.

It is *our* heritage which, by giving impetus to this whole revolutionary business of development, has carried a message of hope to human beings the world over. [54]

Given the international makeup of the board, one might be tempted to read *our heritage* in reference to *Western civilization* or modernity at large. Certainly the phrase casts the Bank's mission in world-historical terms. But Black's Virginia address allows us to see that *our heritage* assumes a decidedly American inflection, one that mixes a national lore of revolutionary exceptionalism with a contemporary identification forged through mass industrial production and consumption. An equivocal phrase, *our heritage* invokes the authority and the intellectual lineage of an Enlightenment discourse of rights (property, foremost), even as it lays claim to a U.S. anticolonial revolutionary legacy. With a knowing wink to the Bank's European partners, the phrase endeavors to distance that institution from a dying colonialism, linking national independence to "the revolutionary business of development": the American notion that business is revolutionary.

This connection has consequences for Black's U.S. audience as well. For instance, in another of Black's addresses, the simple fact that Americans are conscious of nationalist movements across the decolonizing world bears more significance than the precise form that such nationalisms take. Tapping into the era's end-of-Empire zeitgeist, Black suggests that romanticized associations of colonialism (typified by the literary forms of adventure tales and travel stories) have given way to a postimperial realism where fantasy is replaced by the immediacy of daily life, and in which the emerging nations of the South come to be seen as sovereign political actors in their own right. "The American who today knows the names and something of the personalities of leaders in every continent, who can put a face or policy to a Sukarno, a Betancourt, an Nkrumah or an Ayub, would in 1916 have known little of individuals outside the countries of North America and Western Europe. The rest of the world belonged to geography books or travelers' tales; now, like it or not, it is part of our daily lives. The concerns of other nations are ours also, and ours are theirs."[55] Less interested in lauding the "good" nationalisms and condemning the "bad," Black cavalierly couples the strange bedfellows of pro-American, prodevelopment figures such as Cuban dissident Ernesto Bentacourt and Pakistani head of state Mohammed Ayub Khan in the same list as the socialist nationalists Sukarno and Kwame Nkrumah. By doing so he throws a spotlight not on the ways that nationalist movements are storming into state houses across the global South, but rather on how they are muscling their way into the everyday consciousness of America.

In this regard, the Bank's treatment of nationalism dovetails with the Bank's growing focus on social lending; taken together, a coherent intellectual project begins to emerge, whereby the paradigm of development is understood to seep down into virtually every aspect of everyday life in both North and South. Woods expresses the horizontal, geographical version of this logic, arguing that,"when economic history is written by future generations, . . . the chief attribute of the period will be seen to be the extension of the notion of 'progress' to the entire surface of the planet earth."[56] Black's argument about "our daily lives" represents the corresponding vertical movement, in which the Bank works to produce and naturalize a capitalist culture of development that permeates all aspects of the everyday social lives of individuals, regardless of where on the planet they reside. In other words, "the revolutionary business of development" works to make nationalism an extension of "our heritage." The possibility latent within the radical American legacy of self-determination is the obverse of the crisis posed by the "ultranationalism" of a Sukarno or a Nkrumah. Working dialectically, the Bank marshals both the fear of violent racialism and the opportunity of seeming independence (effectively muffled by the apparatus of the nation state) in the service of a neoimperialist project.

Imperial Transformations and Interventionist Imperatives

This chapter has examined several of the competing forces pressuring the Bank during the 1960s, arguing that the era is characterized by a newfound "uncomfortable intimacy" between the Bank and the decolonizing nations of the South. We have seen how the IDA, created as a response to Southern demands for more favorable borrowing conditions, effectively extended U.S. control over development funding and, perhaps more important, extended the scope and reach of development funding by exploding the notion of "productive projects," via its "discovery of the social." The chapter has spotlighted the rhetorical swings between crisis and possibility, perhaps best exemplified in the Bank's conflicted position regarding emerging nationalisms, at once condemning the fascistic tendencies of poverty-induced violence, and praising the Jeffersonian heritage within decolonization, whereby the energies of nationalism are put to work by and for the nation state. This final section attempts to weave together these threads, arguing that collectively they authorize a project of neoimperial interventionism.[57]

Part of the chapter's argument has also been to demonstrate that the Bank's message and practice shift in response to new audiences. In contrast to the documents from the 1940s, invariably targeted toward an investing public interested principally in securing the bottom line, the documents of the 1960s addressed a new constituency: *national publics,* both the emerging nations of the decolonizing world and the richer, industrialized nations of the North. While the decolonizing nations continued to wield only minimal voting power, their very existence provided a raison d'être for the Bank: in order to exist, a development agency cannot do without an "underdeveloped world." Some effort to appease and acknowledge this constituency was imperative if the Bank held any hope of currying favor with its would-be new members from Asia and Africa. On the other hand, given that the national parliaments of richer, Northern nations (especially the United States) controlled the IDA's purse strings, the Bank tailored its arguments toward audiences in Europe and North America, a constituency deeply concerned about "contagious" violence, nationalizations, and expropriations of property, and that in many cases was suffering from a bruised ego as the result of "ungrateful" anticolonial critiques being hurled in its direction. The Bank's strategic response was to acknowledge, and at times stoke, the perception of global upheaval, turning crisis into exigency. Proposing solutions that would have induced a fiscal panic from the button-downed bankers and investors who constituted the Bank's primary audience in the late 1940s, the Bank gambled that it could best gain consent from Northern national publics by articulating a sense of institutional mission in terms of sweeping scope and vast ambition.

As should be clear by now, the playing field between these two constituencies was hardly level. The Bank's primary audience remained confined to the North, even if that audience now included a public beyond Wall Street that demanded a broader, more comprehensive set of institutional rationales. Still, although the Bank was scarcely apt to adopt the tone of Fanon or Cabral, neither was it willing to depict the British empire in the honey-drenched language encountered in the early Bank archives. If the Bank hoped to gain access and influence in the decolonizing world, either a full-throated defense of empire or an entirely dismissive critique of anticolonial struggle would have amounted to institutional suicide. Instead, the Bank opted for a not-quite-middle-ground public position that amounted to a patronizing acknowledgement of colonial trauma and a Pollyannaish declaration that the sun had set on the age of imperialism. Here is Black, again from his Founder's Day speech:

> We all know that there are reasons for the hostile view which some of the new nations take of the world outside. Their contact with the countries of the West was a profoundly disturbing experience, overthrowing their time-honored traditions and shattering their ways of life. It was natural enough for them to rally their revolutions with the slogans of anti-colonialism and anti-imperialism. But today, freedom has largely been won, and colonialism is sounding its death rattle. To go on using these slogans as the support of nationalism, when there is a new world to build, is to turn nationalism from a constructive into a destructive force.[58]

Black's comments typify the Bank's attitude toward imperialism in the 1960s. He acknowledges "reasons" behind anticolonial hostilities, allowing that the colonial encounter between West and East proved a "profoundly disturbing experience" for the latter. This, however, is as much as he is willing to concede. What makes the experience "disturbing," according to the passage, is not the history of slavery, the plunder of wealth, or any of the countless other forms of violence inflicted upon non-European peoples under colonialism; Black depicts colonialism not as a military occupation, but as an epistemological encounter where the jarring forces of Western modernity call into question the fundamental(ist) assumptions underpinning the "time-honored traditions" and "ways of life" of more primitive civilizations. Applying an anthropological notion of culture as a way of life—the "complex whole," as the influential anthropologist E. B. Tylor termed it—Black locates the source of colonial trauma in the hermetic insularity of traditional peoples. As many others have noted, this anthropological concept of culture typically presumes an imperial vantage; that is, within the Tylorian conception of *the complex whole* collectively constituted by a people's habits, customs, social structures, belief systems, rituals, and so forth, *culture* is always *Other*. Anthropologists—or in this case World Bankers—scrutinize the traditions and customs of so-called primitive cultures, seemingly blind to the fact that they themselves are *encultured*; Black would hardly have considered the practice of compounding interest on a loan to be a local *custom*, or the principle of economic growth to be part of a *belief system*. Unlike the immediate association with primitive peoples implied by the phrases *time-honored tradition* and *ways of life*, the Bank's phrase "our culture" connotes something close to Matthew Arnold's conception of the "best that is known and thought in the world," the highest civilizational values and expressions of a people. In contrast to its upholding of the universality of "our culture," the Bank exhibits little more than a glancing, primitivist nostalgia for preserving intact the anthropological specimen of any authentic "ways of life." (The following chapter takes up the Tylorian and Arnoldian conceptions of culture in more detail.)

Black's dismissive acknowledgment that the pain and trauma of civilizational contact may have been real enough, even if many of the grievances were likely imagined, aims to mollify former colonial masters as much as to empathize with the decolonizing nations. Preaching patience and mutual understanding, the Bank endeavors to turn the page on both the era of colonialism and the era of revolutionary liberation movements. With colonialism "sounding its death rattle," the Bank sees an opportunity to link the symbolic moment of national independence with the historical demise of imperialism. It hopes that the emergence of territorially sovereign nation states can mark the end (both the close, and the final objective) of liberation movements. In this formulation, national independence and the institution of the nation state come to stand as surrogates for national liberation movements and their more radical, far-reaching critique of imperialism in its many guises. Banking on the soporific effect of national independence, Black avers that, through the institution of the sovereign nation state, the anger and resentment that fueled nationalisms can be "put to work" building "a new world." With the gentlest possible critique of colonialism, then, and the calculated endorsement of national independence and the territorial sovereignty of the decolonizing nation states, the Bank heralds the emergence of a new postcolonial, postimperial era.

However, even in its anti-imperial posturing, the Bank refuses to relinquish the broader reach and ambition of imperialism. Consider, for example, Black's 1959 speech to an audience of London Pilgrims,[59] in which he makes a case that the "noble venture" of development represents the best possibility for the survival of "our own culture" or "our civilization":

> If our own culture is to survive, we must show that we can help them, too, to create an alternative to poverty. At stake is the hope of peace in a world in which order of a kind is chiefly maintained by what Sir Winston Churchill has called the "balance of terror." The task we undertake will not be complete in our generation, nor even in the generation that succeeds us. But with a realistic and constructive approach—the hardness of head and bigness of heart that any noble venture demands—the work can be well begun. We can undertake the task, I think, in the belief that it is one of the most important of our time, and that there is no better way of signaling our determination to see our civilization survive.[60]

Ten years later, addressing the Bank's board of governors, McNamara echoes Black's sentiment in similarly world-historical tones, insisting that the Bank has a civilizational responsibility:

> I believe that you and I—and all of us in this effort—could ask for no more significant a responsibility than the one we share.
>
> It is an endeavor demanding the very best that is in us.
>
> Its reward is the very best, too: the satisfaction of demonstrating that though man's ancient limitations in nature may be perennial, his ancient deprivations of dignity need not be permanent.
>
> Our disappointment is about man's past.
>
> Our dissatisfaction is over man's present.
>
> Our dedication is to man's future.[61]

The decade, then, is bookended by grand claims about the Bank's historical "responsibility," and indeed volumes of documents from the intervening years make a similar case.

As I see it, this term *responsibility* functions as a hinge that allows us to connect the Bank's imperial legacy to its role in an allegedly postimperial age. *Responsibility*, in Bank parlance, inevitably signifies a future-looking project, never a means of accounting for the past. It carries no admission of wrongdoing, no acknowledgment, for instance, that the wealth of Europe and the United States was built in large part through the imperial exploitation of labor and resources. The Bank takes no responsibility, then, for the conditions of impoverishment or their many symptoms—the crisis—that it "discovers" in the decolonizing world. Nor is it likely to admit any responsibility for the continued exploitation of the South. Its lack of democratic accountability buffers the Bank from angry claims that it may be responsible for perpetuating the imperialist process of transferring surplus wealth from South to North.

Instead, responsibility speaks to a future-looking condition of moral desirability. The presumption seems to be that, having discovered inequity and impoverishment, the Bank and the nations of the North have the moral obligation to address and help rectify the worst forms of deprivation and suffering—an obligation grounded as fully in the shared values of humanism as in the self-interested fears about international security and desires for new markets. However, because this moral *responsibility toward* a harmonious, humane future remains divorced from any discomforting *responsibility for* past injustices, the project of development can be constituted in a manner that foregoes any commitment to retribution or redistribution of wealth, in favor of one designed to achieve "mutually beneficial" economic growth. McNamara puts it concisely: "there is no sense in simply redistributing the same pie."[62] Development's responsibility is to expansion, not equity. Once the Bank has foreclosed on the paradigm of equity as an organizing principle—which is to say, once it has defaulted on its historical indebtedness to the global South—the paradigm of *poverty alleviation* can proceed apace. Once the historical balance sheet has been erased, the contemporary loan agreements can be drafted—drafted in the name of "responsibility," "human dignity," and "man's future."

In this context, the ominous rhetoric portending systemic collapse—the growing disparity between rich and poor, the rising tide of ultranationalism, the fears of Cold War aggression or economic instability—provide not just political rationale but also ethical imperative to act. Claims of moral responsibility justify the neoimperialist interventionism of the Bank. Woods, for instance, argues that growing global inequity "would not only put our security in dire peril; it would be deeply offensive to our conscience."[63] And, though the Bank presidents throughout the decade make consistent and unabashed appeals for fiscal interventionism, it is McNamara—the Cold War hawk who, paradoxically, was probably the Bank's most liberal president—who marshals the rhetorical urgency of moral imperative most decisively. Consider this passage from a 1968 address on population control to UNESCO:

> There is time—just barely time—to escape that threat [the "population explosion"].
> We can, and we must, act.
> . . . Our only fundamental option is whether [the threat] is to be solved rationally and humanely—or irrationally and inhumanely. Are we to solve it by famine? Are we to solve it by riot, by insurrection, by the violence that desperately starving men can be driven to? Are we to solve it by wars of expansion and aggression? Or are we to solve it rationally, humanely—in accord with man's dignity?
> . . . Providence has placed you and me—and all of us—at that fulcrum-point in history where a rational, responsible, moral solution . . . must be found.
> You and I—and all of us—share the responsibility, to find and apply that solution.
> If we shirk that responsibility, we will have committed the crime.
> But it will be those who come after us who will pay the undeserved . . . and unspeakable . . . penalties.[64]

The irony of hearing one of the principal architects of the conflict in Vietnam condemn "wars of expansion and aggression" should not go unnoted. More to the point, however, McNamara's evangelical/ liberal hawkishness—with its unique mix of appeals to rationalism, humanism, and providential design—presents the case for moral intervention, insisting "You and I—and all of us—share the responsibility," and "We can, and we must, act." As we have seen, for the Bank, and for McNamara in particular, this interventionist imperative increasingly takes the form of social lending, relying on the IDA to attack poverty through programs in health, education, agriculture, housing, water, and family planning or population control (the principal topic of this particular address, and an issue about which McNamara was fervent). McNamara, who, unlike Black, frequently used his public addresses as occasions to make policy announcements, directs these remarks about the Bank's institutional directions to the UN's Economic and Social Council, the same group whose calls for better borrowing terms and a broader conception of development aid had played such an important part in the IDA's inception. The irony here lies in the fact that anti-imperialist pressure leads to the founding of what, in McNamara's hands, functioned as a neoimperialist missionary par excellence.[65]

More recently, this role has been taken up by NGOs, which Hardt and Negri refer to as "some of the most powerful pacific weapons of the new world order—the charitable campaigns and the mendicant orders of Empire."[66] They contend further that "moral intervention has become a frontline force of imperial intervention,"[67] the pretext and the catalyst for Empire's *bellum justum,* or "just wars." One would be hard pressed to find a more apt figure for mendicant militarism than McNamara. Indeed, I am suggesting that the Bank's own "just war" (codified by the Kennedy/Johnson "War on Poverty") employs the rhetoric of crisis to cement the Bank as a fixture of the postwar global landscape in perpetuity. Again, Hardt and Negri make a similar claim about what they term "Global War," arguing that under empire the "*state of exception has become permanent and general*; the exception has become the rule."[68] My contention is that the Bank's persistent warnings about "a yawning gulf" between North and South, the violence of decolonizing nationalisms, and the shrinking world in which these and other exceptional crises are taking place, likewise work to cast the state of underdevelopment as permanent. Black, you will remember, predicts that the project of development "will not be complete in our generation, nor even in the generation that succeeds us."[69] Woods, dissatisfied with the United Nation's announcement that the 1960s would be known as the "development decade," insists that the whole planet should be thinking in terms of a "development century,"[70] where it is not "merely desirable," but "inevitable" that Bank lending "should go on, and on an increased scale."[71] By decade's close, then, the bank has installed itself as an institution that, far from its vulnerable early years, appears inevitable and eternal. Under the banner of moral responsibility it pledges permanent intervention against the state of permanent crisis (including the crisis of exceptional states), intervention that promises to span the "entire surface of the planet earth" and to burrow down to all levels of everyday life.

4. Culture Underwritten: Radical Critique and the Bank's Cultural Turn

Michael Denning's *Culture in the Age of Three Worlds* provocatively contends that our contemporary conception of culture is the product of, and therefore historically bounded by, the era in which the globe was conceptually divided into three so-called worlds: the "short half-century"[1] from 1945 to 1989 in which global histories and territories were figuratively mapped and ordered into the distinct (if not entirely stable) spheres of capitalist first, Communist second, and decolonizing third "worlds." Denning asserts that, amidst this emerging imagined tripartite geography, the concept of culture "undergoes a sea-change at mid-century,"[2] marking a "global cultural turn" in the humanities and social sciences. As he puts it, "suddenly in the age of three worlds everyone discovered that culture had been mass produced like Ford's cars; the masses had a culture and culture had a mass."[3]

What is the nature of this sea change? Denning advances the familiar argument that understandings of *culture* at the turn of the twentieth century were principally dominated by a pair of related intellectual paradigms, perhaps best illustrated by two landmark texts of the Victorian era, Matthew Arnold's *Culture and Anarchy* of 1869, and E. B. Tylor's *Primitive Culture* of 1871.

Cosmopolitan in its address and eschewing the xenophobic provincialism of any narrow conception of national culture, the Arnoldian tradition understood culture as "the best that has been thought and known in the world," arguing that the finest examples of human thought and expression do not seek to teach the "inferior classes," but rather to "do away with classes" altogether and "make all men live in an atmosphere of sweetness and light." Culture, then, aspires to "the study and pursuit of perfection."[4] Arnold brackets the sphere of culture from the "rush and roar of practical life";[5] he insists in his essay "The Function of Criticism" that any critical engagement with culture must be characterized by "disinterestedness," assessing the intellectual and aesthetic merits of culture "irrespective of practice, politics and everything of the kind [and] without the intrusion of any other considerations whatever."[6] For the first half of the twentieth century, this apolitical, ahistorical conception of universal culture[7] reigned as the dominant humanist paradigm, effectively bounding culture within a particular bourgeois artistic and intellectual tradition that would later be labeled "high culture,"[8] and removing it entirely from the sordid consideration of politics, economy, and the mundane concerns of everyday life.[9]

The Tylorian conception, on the other hand, understands *culture* as a "complex whole which includes knowledge, belief, art, morals, custom, and any other capabilities and habits acquired by man as a member of society."[10] As we saw in the previous chapter, this anthropological tradition is intimately connected to imperial expansion and the study of non-European peoples. The study of the "complex whole" links culture to "primitive peoples," or rather to the supposedly primitive cultures of present-day peoples. Within the Tylorian tradition, then, the category of culture can be thought of as an abstract whole—as opposed to being divided into to an infinite number of local microcultures, with variations of custom, habit, value, expression, and so forth—only to the extent that culture is tied to the premodern state of "primitiveness." Tylor writes that the "hypothetical primitive condition corresponds in considerable degree to that of modern savage tribes, who, in spite of difference and distance, have in common certain elements of civilization, which seem remains of an early state of the human race at large."[11] Culture in this sense inheres to conceptions of development; in effect, it signifies the particular condition of *undevelopment*. Likewise it is tied to the colonial Other, presuming ethnographic contact between the modern and premodern subject.

Although the Arnoldian and Tylorian traditions adopt radically different conceptions of *culture* as a theoretical category of inquiry, Denning argues persuasively that these two dominant paradigms complement one another in their shared construction of *culture* as a space constituted by, though allegedly outside of, capitalism:

> Thus, culture, one might say, emerges only under capitalism. Though there appears to be culture in precapitalist societies, the concept is invented by Tylorians and Arnoldians alike to name those places where the commodity does not yet rule: the arts, leisure, and unproductive luxury consumption of revenues by accumulators; and the ways of life of so-called primitive peoples. The world dominated by capital—the working day, the labor process, the factory and office, machines and technology, and science itself—is thus outside culture.[12]

Around midcentury, Denning argues, this too-easy segregation of capital from culture, base from superstructure, begins to break down under the weight of historical and intellectual pressures. On the one hand, the density and global reach of the mass cultural commodity form, coupled with technological advances in information, reproduction, and distribution (usefully theorized as the means of communication), made it increasingly difficult to identify a distinct sphere of culture beyond the reach of capital. As those "primitive peoples" of the world began clamoring rather loudly and persistently about liberation, modernization, redistribution, and the like, constructions of a "complex whole" circumscribed by premodern custom and tradition began to appear increasingly anachronistic. At roughly the same time, disparate sets of intellectuals from across the globe who came to be associated with the New Left collectively (if not always collaboratively) began to accord a new weightiness to culture. Interrogating culture not as a sphere outside of capitalism, nor as a *mere* superstructural projection from a determinative economic base, but rather as a sphere of power, contest, and negotiation, the theoretical innovations of the midcentury, often created by intellectuals affiliated with social movements and national liberation struggles, represented a renovation of radical and Marxist thought and marked the beginnings of cultural study in its contemporary sense.

Unlike other accounts of cultural studies, which tend to focus either on the British Birmingham School tradition, along the way perhaps pointing to diasporic variants in the United States or Australia, or on a European (predominantly German) history of ideas that trace the roots of *Kulturkritik*, Denning reads cultural studies as a movement at once more geographically expansive and more chronologically restrictive than as read by other histories.[13] Denning argues that an intellectually coherent concern for the social and political implications of culture and cultural analysis becomes evident in the work of a heterogeneous group of artists and thinkers across the globe at roughly the same historical moment. This work may not have always taken place under the heading of *culture* or *cultural studies*; even for those who reject these labels, Denning argues that "the choice of 'sign,' 'ideology,' 'discourse,' 'communication,' 'consumption,' 'everyday life,' or 'habitus' as one's name for the region others call 'culture' is itself part of the debate that constitutes the cultural turn."[14] Despite such idiomatic differences, however, Denning convincingly demonstrates that a critical mass of shared concerns, methods, and innovations—the global cultural turn—emerges out of the historical and ideological struggles of the age of three worlds; this shift fundamentally reconfigures the disciplinary structures of the university and reshapes radical thought through engagements with New Left social movements. Denning maps a cultural studies movement, global in scope, and not only at work in the academic setting of Northern universities but also informing, and informed by, social movements from across all three worlds during the second half of the twentieth century. To my mind, this transnational intellectual history offers the most richly nuanced and politically responsive account of the field to date.

Perhaps the more controversial claim of *Culture in the Age of Three Worlds* rests in its narrower reading of cultural studies, tethering these to the historically finite age of three worlds, an era that closed with the dissolution of the Communist second world in 1989. If cultural studies is understood to be a product of, and a response to, the struggles of three worlds, as Denning asserts, such a strict periodization "also suggests that the moment of cultural studies is a moment that has in some sense passed. Indeed I would suggest that the academic triumph of cultural studies in the 1990s came as the age that generated it was disappearing. So this book is an attempt to reckon with that break, that line between our moment—the moment of 'globalization'—and the period that now appears to have ended, the age of three worlds."[15] On the face of it, this apparent declaration of a postcultural studies era—a moment after culture—will strike many as a tired rehashing of debates about the newness of globalization. Indeed, Denning's arguments about the coup de grace of 1989 and the clean break between the age of three worlds and the age of globalization are developed only haltingly throughout the book, and Denning's evidence of an epochal shift is often unsatisfying. For instance, in giving heavy weight to the rapid speed with which the term *globalization* came to be commonplace in both academic and popular discourse he declares: "My background in the rhetorical sciences makes me curious about the emergence of new words. A new word may not signify a new world, but it points to some change. And if globalization claims to be a new world process, a new world order, it also gestures to a new kind of 'interdiscipline,' to use the older vocabulary, a new way of looking at the world."[16] Following an argument so adept at seeing beyond idiomatic differences to locate the deep commonalities between disparate intellectual and artistic movements in the mid-century global cultural turn, Denning's reliance on the emergence of the neologism "globalization" as evidence of an epochal break rings hollow.

An alternate, more plausible historicization of the contemporary moment of globalization might logically follow from Denning's own schematic periodization of the age of three worlds into three distinct moments, emblematized by the emergence of a New Left in the 1950s spurred by decolonizing movements, the uprisings and insurgencies of 1968, and the retreat of the New Left during the 1980s. Rather than a new, postcultural world, globalization may productively be read as a *fourth* moment in the global cultural turn. As Denning argues at points throughout the book, the contemporary moment of globalization is seemingly marked by a further erosion of any clear distinction between base and superstructure as capitalism and mass culture saturate the globe. Further, our contemporary moment is witnessing the emergence of a new wave of oppositional social movements that self-consciously blur simple distinctions among political, economic, and cultural interventions. One is tempted, then, to dismiss Denning's proclamation that cultural studies met its demise in 1989 as a familiar kind of theoretical grandstanding in which the contemporary moment, and therefore the contemporary critical project, inevitably is cast as radically new.

Although there is certainly an element of truth to this, my over-all assessment of Denning's book is more generous. Any attempt at periodization or categorization, after all, is a theoretical fiction that relies upon the apparent certainties of classification to make visible certain trends or tendencies. Theory is always polemical; it is boldly declarative, with the intent not only of describing an empirical condition but rather of calling conditions into being by naming potentialities. Instead of quibbling over precise dates, scouring the record for exceptional examples, or debating ad nauseum about degree or kind (as many debates about globalization tend to do), it is surely more useful to address what analytical clarity may be gained and lost by advancing a theoretical and historical distinction of this sort. Despite his claims that the moment of cultural studies has in some sense ended, Denning develops throughout his book a multifaceted address to the future *ends* of cultural studies as much as to its demise.

That is, even though Denning acknowledges the validity of the disciplinary arguments made by critics such as Meaghan Morris, who has pointed to the banality and complicity of pop-culture critique,[17] or Bill Readings, who claims that "Cultural studies arises at a point when the notion of culture ceases to mean anything vital for the University as a whole,"[18] Denning's argument ultimately moves in a very different direction. A staunch defender rather than detractor of cultural studies, Denning likewise takes a different tack than does Terry Eagleton, who claims that culture has become overvalued in recent theoretical work: "The primary problems which we confront in the new millennium—war, famine, poverty, disease, debt, drugs, environmental pollution, the displacement of peoples—are not especially 'cultural' at all. . . . Cultural theorists *qua* cultural theorists have precious little to contribute to their resolution."[19] By contrast, the intellectual category of *cultural studies* remains a potent signifier for Denning throughout *Culture in the Age of Three Worlds,* both as a slogan under which important academic work continues to be carried out, and as a rich intellectual and political legacy that continues to have great relevance for understanding the contemporary moment. Far from dismissing cultural studies as without relevance in a post–three world era—a dereferentialized absence, or a symptom of capitalist consumerism, as others have suggested—Denning time and again holds up the future-focused ideal of an "emancipatory cultural studies," an "emancipatory transnational cultural studies," a "critical emancipatory cultural studies," or a "cultural studies worthy of the name."[20]

Denning's broader argument that the age of culture and cultural study properly comes to a close in 1989 ought to be read, then, as a challenge to find ways of better theorizing the contemporary moment. That is, his provocation about the end of cultural studies is entirely consistent with one of the tradition's central tenets: theorize cultural formations as they function and evolve in the living present. What is gained by marking the year 1989? Among other things, the category of three worlds no longer holds analytical purchase. In particular, the idea of a collective, unified "Third World," an imagined geopolitical space that at midcentury seemed laden with revolutionary, destabilizing potential, a resistant "outside" that might throw into crisis the world capitalist system, holds little promise either as a theoretical category or as an agent of change in the contemporary moment.[21] Likewise, Denning declares "the end of mass culture," arguing, "the fact is that mass culture has won. . . . All culture is mass culture under capitalism."[22] Mass culture's end takes place at the moment of its ubiquity, its zenith, when the theoretical category of *mass*—in opposition to once-meaningful distinctions such as *popular* or *working-class*—loses its relevance.

If some of the inherited critical categories from the age of three worlds no longer seem entirely adequate to address the forces and contradictions of the present, history is not among them. That is, in declaring the age of culture over, Denning does not argue that its legacy is irrelevant. Quite the contrary. "Our moment is not the moment where liberation and culture are the key words," he argues, "but we have much to learn from a left for whom they were." If the goal of the present is "to build a newer left, a global left, we would do well to keep alive the promise and problems of a half-century of radical cultural analysis, for which our impoverished name remains, for the moment, cultural studies."[23]

The present chapter (and indeed this book) follows both Denning's periodization of the midcentury global cultural turn and his insistence that, although the demands and contradictions of the present moment may require new theoretical categories and new strategies for radical insurrection, today's "emancipatory transnational cultural studies" has much to gain by reflecting back on the age of three worlds and its legacy of radical cultural critique. Among the most pressing legacies that Denning identifies, and that underpin the remainder of this book, are the relationships among movements—the production of collectivities, peoples, masses, multitudes—and the struggle for equity and democracy. Historicizing the age of three worlds can and should take many forms. The contribution of this book is to suggest that the World Bank ought to be considered as an important historical actor in the global transformations taking place during that age. Looking back to the origins of culture in the age of three worlds, I argue in this chapter that *World Bank funding underwrites the midcentury global cultural turn.*

In spite of having just made the case for valuing theoretical provocation, I want to clarify the nature of this argument. I am not suggesting that the Bank is the precipitating force behind this turn; contemporary theorizations of culture do not originate with the World Bank. Nor is the institution primarily responsible for producing the conditions under which culture emerged as a newly visible and newly potent sphere of action during the age of three worlds. Likewise, my claims about the Bank's role in the cultural turn are not intended to damn the complicity or the hollowness of cultural studies as an intellectual enterprise or a field of academic study. Although I will argue that the Bank's role in this cultural turn throws into sharp relief certain fissures and antagonisms within the intellectual and political projects carried out under the name *cultural studies*, this chapter ought not to be read as any kind of straightforward indictment of cultural studies as the bankrupt intellectual progeny of a World Bank management scheme.

When I say that the Bank underwrites the midcentury cultural turn, I have several things in mind. First, I mean to suggest that the Bank is one of the actors involved in the postwar global expansion of a Fordist-Keynesian economic paradigm, which effectively if uneasily linked a particular mode of mass industrial production to an interventionist role for the nation state, a Taylorized management of labor, and patterns of mass consumption.[24] World Bank development, then, contributes to the internationalization of Fordism, a system of production in which "the new methods of work," as Antonio Gramsci, an early theorist of Fordism, noted, "are inseparable from a specific mode of living and of thinking and feeling life."[25] Both a response to, and a symptom of, the historical forces shaping the cultural turn, the Bank's postwar conception of development, as we will see shortly, is imagined through the lens of global mass cultural production and consumption.

Second, I will suggest that a number of radical anticolonial intellectuals were aware of, and defining their theoretical work in opposition to, both the Bank and the broader global expansion of Fordist-Keynesianism. That is, "aid" and the neocolonial project of development come into focus in the work of midcentury anticolonial thinkers who collectively have produced one of the richest and most varied bodies of scholarship in the cultural studies intellectual tradition. Because this corpus is too vast and heterogeneous to analyze adequately in such a short space, this section focuses briefly on the writings of Aimé Césaire and Frantz Fanon, teacher and student, who were publishing just before and after the landmark Bandung Conference of 1955. In both of these thinkers, though particularly in Fanon, we can find the lineaments of a conception of culture and cultural study grounded in movements, in masses, and in Marxism—even if a revised Marxism.

Finally, to connect the arguments about Fordist-Keynesianism and anticolonial cultural radicalism, as well as the previous chapter's claims regarding the Bank's contradictory positions on decolonizing nationalisms and the postcolonial nation state, this chapter analyzes the Bank's role in sponsoring a third world nationalist bourgeoisie that, more frequently than not, emerged as the abortive culmination of national liberation movements. Looking specifically at the fault lines crisscrossing the Asian-African conference at Bandung, a historical marker frequently used to signify the broader epoch of third world nationalism, I will argue that culture became the common, if contested, ground through which the conference attendees attempted to resolve fundamental economic and political divisions. This section pays particular attention to the work of Richard Wright, whose coverage of the Bandung conference triangulates the Bank, nationalists such as Nehru and Sukarno, and radicals such as Fanon. I suggest that the third worldist ideal of nonalignment, wrongly ascribed to Bandung in many accounts, is made possible—*underwritten*—by World Bank sponsorship. Further, the Bank's presence enables a postcolonial national elite to defer some of Bandung's contradictions by providing the cultural idiom of development through which a gathering of antagonistically *aligned* nations can still imagine themselves within some shared third worldist collective.

Impatient Imaginings of Detroit

If Wall Street was the metaphorical location to which the Bank's appeals were addressed in the immediate postwar era, Detroit was the metaphorical location upon which those appeals were based. The Bank sold Detroit to Wall Street and to the world. Put differently, the Bank sold to Wall Street the twin concepts of Fordism as a global export and Detroit as the prime beneficiary of Fordism's global spread. The Bank sold to the world the *idea of Detroit*, marketing development as an unquestioned faith in industrialization and modernization, and the corresponding utopic image of wealth and plenty.

Both Fordism as a mode of production, and the Ford Motor Company (or U.S. industry more broadly), occupy a central place in the midcentury social imaginary of the Bank.[26] David Harvey, in his assessment of Fordism, describes a "tense but nevertheless firm balance of power that prevailed between organized labour, large corporate capital, and the nation state," and that was "not arrived at by accident" but rather was the "outcome of years of struggle."[27] The archival materials examined in previous chapters offer much evidence to support the contention that the Bank actively involved itself in forging and maintaining this uneasy tripartite relationship among labor, capital, and the nation state (both established and newly emerging). Recall Eugene Meyer's early addresses where he argued that the world was "starving for the products of our mines and factories."[28] Meyer and the Bank responded to this starvation with the prototypical Fordist negotiated compromise to insure "continuous full production" from U.S. industry, striking a tone of mediation in the name of economic expansion. "For our present disastrous labor relations I have no disposition to allocate blame," he asserts. "But I do say this with every conviction that is within me—we must find a way of settling our labor disputes without the disastrous strikes which bring about world starvation in a broader sense than the mere withholding of food."[29] No great friend to organized labor, Meyer nevertheless is willing to compromise in the interest of systemic growth. He wagers that capitalist expansion, activated by international investment financing, will enable U.S.

industry to remain highly profitable. By displacing the extraction of surplus value onto the hyperexploitative labor markets of the underdeveloped world—not to mention reaping profits from the sale of U.S. industrial products purchased directly with borrowed World Bank dollars, as well as from the permanent income generated by interest payments on those loans—U.S. industry can afford to negotiate with U.S. labor over wage levels and working conditions. Surplus extracted from the South pays for labor peace in Detroit, dividing global class interests through the creation of what Lenin terms "the labor lieutenants of the capitalist class."[30]

The role of the state as facilitator of capital is part of the bargain, as well. Recall the mid-1940s *Questions and Answers* booklets published by the U.S. Treasury, which provided explicit rationales about why it was in the U.S. interest to subsidize the International Bank even if this meant footing the entire bill. A similar case was made by William Iliff, who insisted that international lending in U.S. dollars was a boon, not a burden, for the national economy. because it ensured that borrowers would be "buying turbines or agricultural machinery or electrical equipment or some other goods and services which the United States is able to produce."[31] Indeed, the Bank's mission as established in its charter—to "supplement private investment" by lending to nation states in order to fund infrastructural projects otherwise too risky for private capital— amounts to precisely the export of the Fordist compromise, or, more accurately, the merger of Fordism and Keynesian internationalism. This compromise, *another name for which is development*, worked in the broader interests of producing new markets for U.S. industry, displacing the extraction of surplus onto the developing world, and activating capital by removing risks for international investment. It accomplished this by negotiating loan agreements with the leaders of newly emerging states, most of which were crippled by the economic legacies of colonial exploitation. In lending directly and exclusively to states, the Bank helped prop up struggling regimes—some admirable, some odious—throughout the underdeveloped world. In the process, it assured that Northern capital would continue to have access to the labor and resources of the South. Moreover, it cemented the network of inter*nationalism*, placing nation states in competition with one another, especially for the more favorable soft money available from the IDA.

Detroit, then, becomes an American locale freighted with symbolic weight. For Iliff, the Irish émigré who manages the Bank's investments during the institution's early years, the opportunity to speak to the World Trade Week Convention in Detroit is treated as a pilgrimage to the shrine of U.S. industry. Witness the following exuberant response:

> I have, therefore, looked forward to my visit to Detroit not only with pleasure but also for the opportunity afforded me of seeing something of the real America. For us Europeans, the very mention of the name of your city raises up in our minds a picture . . . the picture of a pulsating hive of busy efficiency, of hundreds of thousands of working men and women tending tens of thousands of complicated machines in thousands of vast factories, and of the fruits of all this human toil and ingenuity rolling off the assembly lines in quantities only to be measured in astronomical arithmetic. To us, Detroit represents the zenith of North American industrial civilization.[32]

In contrast to the urban dreamscapes of New York or Washington, D.C., the two cities Iliff cites as constituting his U.S. experience prior to this journey to the heartland, Detroit is cast as "the real America"—this, in spite of its fanciful depiction as a "pulsating hive of busy efficiency," calculable only with "astronomical arithmetic." Iliff's implicit juxtaposition, however, is a familiar one, even today: Detroit's manufacturing and industrial base represents *real* economic production, frequently contrasted with the *hyperreal* finance of Wall Street or the political machinations of D.C. The logic pairs perfectly with the Bank's dogged insistence on funding sound, productive, verifiable projects—i.e., real economy. Pressed even slightly, however, the logic founders against the Bank's complete institutional dependence on the unreality of Wall Street financing and Capitol Hill's political backing, without which, as we have seen, the Bank would not have survived.

It founders, too, against the *time* of development and the *time* of mass culture. Detroit, the "zenith of North American industrial civilization," is inextricably tied to industrial manufacturing. Therefore, when the idea of Detroit is held out as a model to the rest of the world, its promise implicitly demands the patient time frame that necessarily accompanies large-scale industrial modernization. Borrowing countries, according to Iliff, need to realize that "Pittsburgh and Detroit were not built in a day," and that

industrialization requires "prudent, orderly and modest foundations."[33] But exporting the idea of Detroit implies more than merely the developing world's gradual acquisition of industrial *means
of production*; it also contains a promise about both the *means
and the ends of mass consumption*. Eugene Black, you will remember, proudly asserted, "It is *our* heritage which has shown the way
to mass consumption and to the widest participation in the fruits
of economic progress."[34] For Black, that is, one of the ends of development is to export the means of mass consumption; development in this sense may be measured by the underdeveloped world's
ability to purchase commodities (or, as seen from the perspective
of U.S. industry, to serve as new markets). Beyond dollars, this entails the production of new forms of subjectivity, precisely what
Gramsci was pointing out when he argued that Fordism represented the "biggest collective effort to date to create, with unprecedented speed, and with a consciousness of purpose unmatched in
history, a new type of worker and of man."[35] Exporting the idea of
Detroit means that workers in the South are asked to wait patient-
ly for industrial modernization to spread across the globe so that
they can sell their Taylorized labor to Fordist industry so that, in
turn, they can purchase Ford cars. The "fruits of economic progress" are manifested in the capacity for mass cultural consumption
practices—the "culture ideology of consumption," to apply Leslie
Sklair's useful term.[36]

But mass cultural consumption cuts in several directions, often
against the grain of Bank edicts of patience. This concern, and the
attempt to counteract it, forms the subtext of the following rich
passage from Iliff's Detroit speech:

> But today with the coming of the aircraft, the radio, and above all
> the movie, the Occidental way of life has become known in every
> corner of the globe . . . to the worker in the Chilean Copper Mine,
> to the coolie in the Chinese rice fields, to the peasant in the moun-
> tains of Iran. They hear about, and they see, a standard of life far
> exceeding anything that they themselves have ever known, or be-
> lieved to exist. They cannot be blamed for imagining that what
> others have achieved, they themselves can achieve. But it is the dif-
> ficult task of their leaders to educate them in the hard creed that
> Occidental standards have come about only through a process of
> accumulation of capital and of technical skills which must go on

not merely over five years or ten years but over generations. . . . It is only by a slow process of patient and unremitting effort in the less spectacular fields of building-up a country's basic resources that the foundations can be laid for economic security and progress, and for social betterment and contentment.[37]

Disregarding for the moment Iliff's "Occidental" mapping of underdevelopment, I would like to focus on the *impatient imaginings* of the developing world that he attributes to the spread of mass culture. Iliff again preaches patience, arguing that it is the responsibility of state *leaders* (more on this shortly) to instruct the peoples of the developing world about the generational time frames that will be required to build up the "less spectacular" industrial base and in turn raise standards of living. But this instruction takes place in the face of a new comparative or relational visibility—made possible by the spread of mass culture and the communications technologies through which this culture circulates—whereby the peoples of the underdeveloped world see that which they purportedly lack. The instruction is meant to quell popular desire, produced by the global circulation of mass culture, for standards of living that, depending on one's vantage, *have not yet been achieved* or, conversely, *have been purposefully denied.*

A complex tangle of analyses and expectations thus adhere to the mass cultural commodity exchange, understood not merely as economic but also as communicative. Marx's theorization of fetishism and value in the first volume of *Capital* hones in on precisely this communicative aspect of commodity exchange. At one point in his argument, Marx uses language as metaphor to clarify that exchange value bears no relation to utility or to any natural qualities inherent within a commodity; like the seemingly transparent qualities of language, which masks but cannot entirely conceal its human origins as a social system of exchange, value is the product of social construction: "for to stamp an object of utility as a value, is just as much a social product as language." But Marx extends his discursive metaphor far beyond a simple parallel between two constructed systems. Commodities are "queer" or "mysterious" things, according to Marx, because their exchange, which appears based on the relative value inherent within distinct objects, effectively obscures the material social relationships between producers; in his words, "There is a definite social relation between men, that assumes, in their eyes, the fantastic form of a relation between things." Value, he argues, "converts every product into a social hieroglyphic." Only by deciphering this signifier can we understand how a transaction that appears to exchange one commodity for another of equivalent value (or, even more opaque, to exchange money, the universal abstract form of commodity value, for another commodity), should in fact be understood as a social exchange between persons, who, because of the elaborate division of labor under capitalism, have no physical correspondence or interaction between themselves. Under capitalism, the "specific character of each producer's labor" acquires voice through commodity exchange—that is, through the congealed human labor power that is the source of value. Dramatizing this communicative aspect of commodity exchange, Marx goes so far as to anthropomorphize a commodity a few pages later, writing "Could commodities themselves speak, they would say: Our use-value may be a thing that interests men. It is no part of us as objects. What, however, does belong to us as objects is our value."[38]

Marx's playful insights regarding the social character and communicative nature of commodity exchange prove illuminating when considered in relation to the Bank's earnest depictions of international trade as a form of cultural dialogue. Marx's recurrent trope throughout *Capital,* whereby he personifies things, concepts, or processes—for example, variously giving voice and agency to value, capital, the machine, and more, treating them as dramatis personae—works metaphorically to further develop his critique of the contradictions of capitalism. These staged dialogues point to the simultaneous absurdity and necessity of conceptual abstractions, which never correspond to actual lived reality but which are nonetheless essential as theoretical mechanisms through which a totality can be comprehended. A talking commodity calls attention to the foolishness of theoretical models that mistakenly locate subjectivity in things rather than in humans. At the same time, it implicitly raises questions about the vexed nature of the *subject* within a capitalist mode of production that is in some regards constitutive of subjectivity; as Marx puts this in *The German Ideology,* "consciousness, therefore, is from the very beginning a social product."[39] That is, Marx uses these anthropomorphisms to point out the ways in which agency, if not subjectivity itself, is doubly located in the individual human and in the network of so-

cial relations produced under capitalism. His theorization of fetishism as a communicative process, then, elucidates the contradictory
nature of capitalism, which attributes subjectivity to objects even
as it works to turn laborers into alienated automatons, and which
works in some regards as an agentive social system, complete with
laws and principles, that actively conditions the consciousness of
those subjects who labor and own under this particular mode of
production.

Tellingly, the Bank, too, makes bold claims about the dialogic
nature of financial exchange, though with little evidence of Marx's
performative critique of communicative subjectivity. Consider the
fetishizing impulse of the following quite typical 1946 address by
Meyer, which converts products of international trade into the social hieroglyphics of cultural dialogue. Meyer argues to a group
of political scientists that an emerging postwar global division of
labor generates not only increased economic efficiency, but also a
meaningful social interchange between cultures: "Increased world
trade must go hand in hand with increased production resulting
from increased efficiency. There can be no better means of raising the living standards everywhere than the ready interchange
among peoples of what each is able to produce most economically. And it is equally true that there can be no better basis for
friendly relationships and mutual understanding among peoples
than commerce of this sort."[40] World trade functions as the communicative medium for cultural exchange between peoples who
would otherwise remain segregated. The division of labor within
the Taylorized factory becomes the model for both efficient global
production and international cultural exchange. Meyer trumpets
"mutual understanding," and McCloy crows that international investment "should lead to wider understanding, exchange of ideas
and mutual respect."[41] As we have seen, Marx's theorization of
value anticipates this strange communicative capacity attributed to
the products of trade, through which the further abstractions of
"peoples" or "nations" are placed into staged dialogue, masking
the real social relations between individual producers. Of course,
Marx harbors no illusions that commodity exchange produces
"friendly relations" or "mutual understandings." He articulates
the coercive nature of this dialogue rather more bluntly in the
Manifesto, contending that "the cheap prices of its commodities
are the heavy artillery" with which capital "compels all nations,

on pain of extinction, to adopt the bourgeois mode of production," seeking always to "create a world after its own image."[42]

To analyze midcentury claims about the reproduction of a *world* in its own *image* invites the introduction of cultural theory via the Frankfurt School, particularly Max Horkheimer and Theodor Adorno's 1947 critique of reification and the culture industry. Their argument is that that mass culture—financed by monopolist industrial capital—extends the instrumentalizing logic of Taylorizism into all aspects of daily life, including so-called leisure time, by bombarding consuming audiences with formulaic and clichéd repetition. For Adorno and Horkheimer, any perceived difference between Ford cars and Warner Brothers films collapses in the age of mass reproduction. Whereas the modernist work of art contains the negative potential to transcend and critique reality, mass culture only covertly reproduces the ideology of capitalism: "To speak of culture was always contrary to culture. Culture as a common denominator contains in embryo that schematization and process of cataloging and classification which bring culture into the sphere of administration."[43] That the Bank would turn to the promises and allures of mass culture to sell the idea of Detroit should come as no surprise. Rather, we should take seriously the fact that the early Bank archive is peppered with comments like McCloy's, which heroically portrays the World Bank as "pioneering with a radio and a motion picture at hand."[44]

Although McCloy and other Bank spokespersons may suggest that the case for modernization is advanced most effectively through the communication technologies of the culture industry, the radio and film industries in which he imagines himself to be pioneering serve in effect as metaphorical figures for the actual sorts of development projects that the Bank funds—energy, transportation, industrial infrastructure, and the like. If the styled life of a Hollywood actress or the life-style connoted by a chrome-finned Cadillac works to extend the reifying logic of capitalism through mass culture, a parallel, though not identical, process is at work in Nehru's famous dictum that mega-dams are the "temples of modern India." Likewise, in national contexts as different as Nkrumah's Ghana, Nasser's Egypt, and many others throughout the developing world, the mammoth concrete structures of development became freighted with the burden of national culture. In these and other cases, the ideological work of mass culture appears to be inverted. That is, Adorno and Horkheimer point to the obfuscating power of mass culture that effectively masks its status as commodity: a Cadillac seems to "speak" more loudly than the pavement on which it is driven; a Hollywood romance appears to communicate values and ideas infinitely more complex than the mute screen on which it is projected. In contrast to the rigid, machine-stamped standardization that marks large-scale industrial production, mass culture appears flexible, personal, and expressive, responding to the ever-changing needs and desires of a consuming public.

The example of development-sponsored dams (or, in Nasser's case, *not*-sponsored, and therefore nationally funded as a pointed critique aimed at the United States and the World Bank) functions as a revealing parallel case, where the logic of mass culture is simultaneously extended and inverted. Infrastructural installations and the means of industrial production become the fetish objects of decolonizing nationalisms, signifying well in excess of their use value. A far cry from the feeling of micropersonalized responsiveness that is the hallmark of the culture industry, the mega-dam signifies because of its monumental engineering, a permanent symbol of modernizing industrial might. Far from being cloaked in the illusory sheen of glamor or the jungle rhythms of jazz, industrialization, classification, and administration—in other words, reification itself—become the celebrated characteristics of the new mass-cultural products of development. Here, the concrete speaks as loudly as the chrome. Where McCloy uses Hollywood as a metaphor for the export of American development, Nehru, Nkrumah, Nasser, and many others throughout the developing world use mega-dams as a metaphor to assert simultaneously their national independence and their global modernity—precisely because, paradoxically, the nationalist monuments of development call stark attention to their own reifying logic and to their status as products of capital-intensive monopolist industrialization, the very characteristics masked by mass culture in Adorno's and Horkheimer's critique.[45]

But if trafficking in mass culture shoulders the ideological work of social reproduction, it simultaneously performs the opposite function as well, making visible systemic inequities that threaten to undermine rather than shore up the self-image of the world that the Bank has constructed. McCloy, like Iliff, is greatly concerned

about the "impatience to get on with development" that stems
from "the intimate knowledge and pressure of what is going on
elsewhere in the world."[46] This "impatience," it seems to me, signals a function of mass culture akin to the utopian promise theorized by Fredric Jameson.[47] For Jameson, following the Frankfurt
School critics, the ideological work of mass culture is inevitably
paired with its obverse: the utopian potential, present in all mass
culture, that remains "negative and critical of the social order
from which, as a product and a commodity, it sprung."[48] The circulation of mass culture "works" to produce the popular desires
that Iliff and McCloy term "impatience." In the Bank's reading,
"impatience" signals the desire for the capacity to consume more.
The export of Fordist-Keynesianism promises to fulfill this desire,
though in a form that is incremental rather than insurrectionary:
given patience, the development of an industrial base will raise
standards of living and increase the availability of manufactured
goods. The ideological work of such a promise masks the instru-
mentalization and exploitation of labor that accompanies Fordist
industry, as well as the extraction of wealth from periphery to center
that accompanies the chase for new markets.

   At the same time, however, global circulation of mass culture—
motion pictures as well as mega-dams—carries within it critical utopian potentialities. *Impatience* might just as easily be read to signal
an awareness of systemic exploitation and deprivation; at minimum,
it expresses deep dissatisfaction with the status quo. Might not the
lifestyles witnessed or heard via film or radio, or those promised by
nationalist leaders at the unveiling of modernization enterprises,
spark a new awareness of global inequity? Embedded in the mass
cultural products of development, real and symbolic, lurks the radical utopian ideas of appropriating the means of production, nonexploitative labor conditions, and equitable redistribution as just
alternatives to the Bank's preferred model of universal economic
growth. (It should come as no surprise that, even while mega-dams
continue to have purchase as symbols of nationalist progress, modernity, and self-sufficiency, these installations have also produced
the opposite effect, galvanizing local and global opposition both to
Bank-sponsored development and to the mismanagement and corruption of postcolonial nation states. From this oppositional perspective, mega-dams function both as specific targets of activism
and as broader systemic metaphors, making possible alliances be-

tween radical social movements struggling against the World Bank and neoliberal privatization schemes, and in support of indigenous rights, displaced peoples, environmental protection, and the like.)

Black, like McCloy and Iliff, can only understand the desires constituted by and for mass culture as emulative: "After all," Black boasts, "we ourselves are largely responsible for creating something called economic man and causing millions in the world to want to emulate him."[49] Fanon, discussing the reasons why Algerians might desire to purchase a radio, articulates a very different perspective: "Sometimes people wonder that the native, rather than give his wife a dress, buys instead a transistor radio. There is no reason to be astonished. The natives are convinced that their fate is in the balance, here and now. They live in the atmosphere of doomsday. . . . The native and the underdeveloped man are today political animals in the most universal sense of the term."[50] Fanon's point here is that the radio itself becomes a tactical device rather than a luxury status item. It offers a means to stay informed of revolutionary activity, prompting audiences to actively and critically interpret messages in order to read between the airwaves, so to speak, by deciphering information about the anticolonial struggle through extracting tiny nuggets of European news programs.[51] In this sense, Fanon offers us the reception side of Jameson's production argument. The two are by no means mutually exclusive or antagonistic. Utopian potential in Fanon's passage is located in the appropriation and interpretation of the mass-cultural radio program, whereas Jameson identifies a repressed utopian impulse embedded within mass-cultural expression.

Connecting Black and Fanon, I am arguing that the utopian promise within the mass cultural investments of development make visible persistent and deliberate patterns of global inequity, and thus contain the potential to discredit the Bank's logic of systemic economic growth and to plant the radical idea of nonexploitative redistribution: the potential to transform *economic man* into *political animal,* or, put differently, to politicize economics. The Bank, as we have seen, worked assiduously to produce and reproduce an antiseptic notion of development economics, purportedly outside of politics, outside of ideology. When it traffics in mass culture—when it goes "pioneering with radio and motion picture in hand"—the Bank recognizes the vast ideological potential for transforming impatience into emulation. But it also appears to recognize and repress, even if it cannot fully understand, that the *impatience* it has identified carries with it the utopian promise of redistributive equity, which threatens to undermine the world made in the Bank's own image.

Cultural Radicals in the Age of Three Worlds

Denning's account of the cultural turn is compelling in large part because it locates the contemporary understanding of *culture* in the contradictions and contestations that arise from a specific historical moment: the age of three worlds. Culture and cultural study take shape in the context of the postwar global expansion of U.S.–led Fordist-Keynesian capitalism, the bipolar political and military struggle between the United States and the Soviet Union, and the breakup and reconfiguration of colonial empires—to name but three historical processes with obvious planetary scope. The previous chapters have suggested that the Bank contributed to shaping this historical moment, but that it too was a product of the age, responding to as much as instigating the constantly shifting economic, political, social, and intellectual pressures of the "short half century" that Denning examines. Here I elaborate on the idea that culture and cultural study are the historical product not only of three worlds, but more specifically of the dynamic upheavals and antagonisms of an emerging third world and the dynamism of national liberation movements.[52] That is, not only is Eagleton correct when he argues that culture became "a transformative political force, in what remains the most spectacularly successful radical movement of modern history,"[53] but it is likewise true that radicalism and movements became a transformative force in the conception of culture.

The well-chronicled examples of émigré Frankfurt School critics, or the history of working-class educational activism at the root of Birmingham School British Cultural Studies, reveal that there are any number of historical urgencies that give rise to the postwar theorizations of culture as a sphere of political contestation and consequence. It would be possible, no doubt, to trace the historical dialogue between the Bank and these intellectual/ political movements, documenting, for instance, the institution's specific responses to European fascism, or examining biographical connections of a figure like Keynes to both the Bank and the Bloomsbury circle. My argument here, following and perhaps extending Denning's claims, is that the emergent political necessities and exigencies accompanying third world decolonization—more specifically, national liberation movements—must be considered as a central catalyzing process in the theoretical reconsiderations of culture.

The collective body of work from anticolonial intellectuals— Amilcar Cabral, Aimé Césaire, Suzanne Césaire, Cheikh Anta Diop, Margaret Ekpo, Frantz Fanon, Ché Guevara, C. L. R. James, Albert Memmi, Ho Chi Mihn, Jane and Paulette Nardal, Kwame Nkrumah, Funnilayo Ransome-Kuti, Walter Rodney, Léopold Sedar Senghor, Mao Zedong, to name just a few—constitutes a foundational corpus of cultural and postcolonial studies. Their interventions into historicism, economics, psychoanalysis, Marxism, and more interrogate such analytical categories as race, identity, the unconscious, dependency, the nation, peoples or masses, revolution, liberation, democracy, base/superstructure, town/country, gender,[54] and of course, culture itself. This diverse body of thought provides an inescapable set of landmarks for what we now take to be the intellectual and political exigencies of cultural study. As Denning argues: "Our moment is not the moment where liberation and culture are the key words. But we have much to learn from a left for whom they were the key words, and, as we try to build a newer left, a global left whose symbolic antagonists have been the IMF and the WTO, the new enclosures which are privatizing the commons established by the social movements of 1848 and 1968, we would do well to keep alive the promise and problems of a half-century of radical cultural analysis."[55]

Denning's insistence that contemporary cultural studies reflect on the lessons learned from its past struggles is no doubt correct; this book represents, in part, my own efforts to make good on such a challenge of historical memory. That said, we should not forget that, although the WTO may be a more recent symbolic antagonist, the IMF and the World Bank were on the minds and in the crosshairs of a generation of anticolonial leftists for whom *liberation* and *culture* were the key words. Sometimes the Bank and the IMF are named explicitly, as in Nkrumah's 1965 *Neo-Colonialism: The Last Stage of Imperialism*. Following Lenin's critique of imperialism, Nkrumah locates the World Bank's role within the increasing tendency toward monopoly capitalism, arguing that the Bank works to extend and facilitate the vast control of Northern banking and financial interests in Africa, which have become increasingly indistinct from the industrial corporate giants of Europe and the United States. That is, Nkrumah sees the World Bank's internationalism as a way to distance capitalist monopoly from the legacy of colonial rule, working tirelessly to make Africa profitable to Northern capital regardless of whether national liberation movements win or lose.[56]

In other cases, although the Bank is not explicitly identified, the practice of multilateral aid is excoriated as the vehicle for the export of Fordist-Keynesian capitalism. Here my methodological framework shifts somewhat, as I endeavor to overlay the history of the World Bank with the history of culture study. My argument to this point has insisted that we not reduce the Bank to a metaphor; I have worked to historicize the institution, uncovering its shifting, tactical interventions. But, although I believe it counterproductive to treat the Bank solely as metaphor, I find it important to recognize that the institution does function as a symbolic antagonist for a vast array of social movements throughout the age of three worlds and beyond. The name *World Bank* comes to signify, in Nkrumah's words, "the neo-colonial trap [of] 'multilateral aid' through international institutions."[57] As I work in the remainder of this chapter to map the history of culture and culture study onto my analysis of the Bank's public record, then, I oscillate between reading for historical facticity and reading for symbolic or metaphoric signification. As indicated, my goal is not to locate direct or causal links between the Bank and midcentury cultural radicals—to find conspiratorial backroom meetings between the two. Instead, I am trying to map the more imprecise notion that a shared engagement with questions of globality, economics, and culture connect the two spheres in ways that at times become conscious and explicit, and at other times remain more murky and associative. Both the Bank and the cultural radicals, I suggest, are products of a historical moment—products of the global cultural turn—even as they themselves contribute to shape that phenomenon. As I trace this historical convergence, I look for ways to locate the Bank's presence in the texts of this age. At times, the Bank appears as a decisive historical subject, making specific financial interventions. At other times, it lurks as a misty presence within the postwar cultural imaginary, linked metaphorically to the processes of global interconnectivity, international governance, and the new manifestations of post- or neo-colonial forms of economic power, typically associated with U.S. industrial and financial dominance.

For example, Aimé Césaire's Marxist–Surrealist anticolonial polemic *Discourse on Colonialism* (1950) warns that the "American hour" of "Violence, excess, waste, mercantilism, bluff, conformism, stupidity, vulgarity, disorder," is at hand.[58] Césaire, with characteristic rage and perspicuity, lays bare the fiction that the United States might legitimately claim to be in solidarity with, or even the intellectual precursor of, anticolonial nationalism (claims we saw being made by the Bank in the previous chapter). Commenting on the same 1949 Truman inauguration speech that occupies such a central place in the work of Arturo Escobar and Gustavo Esteva (among other theorists of development), Césaire stages an ethical debate between the critical narrator of *Discourse* and a more gullible straw man who sees the emergence of U.S. hegemony as preferable to Europe's history of colonialism. The passage is so rich, in both language and content, that I find it difficult to excerpt in brief:

> And indeed, do you not see how ostentatiously these gentlemen have just unfurled the banner of anticolonialism?
>
> *"Aid to the disinherited countries,"* says Truman. "The time of the old colonialism has passed." That's also Truman.
>
> Which means that American high finance considers that the time has come to raid every colony in the world. So, dear friends, here you have to be careful!
>
> I know some of you, disgusted with Europe, with all that hideous mess which you did not witness by choice, are turning—oh! in no great numbers—toward America and getting used to looking upon that country as a possible liberator.
>
> "What a godsend!" you think.
>
> "The bulldozers! The massive investments of capital! The roads! The ports!"
>
> "But American racism!"
>
> "So what? European racism in the colonies has inured us to it!"
>
> And there we are, ready to run the great Yankee risk.
>
> So, once again, be careful!
>
> American domination—the only domination from which one never recovers. I mean from which one never recovers unscarred.
>
> And since you are talking about factories and industries, do you

not see the tremendous factory hysterically spitting out its cinders in the heart of our forests or deep in the bush, the factory for the production of lackeys; do you not see the prodigious mechanization, the mechanization of man; the gigantic rape of everything intimate, undamaged, undefiled that, despoiled as we are, our human spirit has still managed to preserve; the machine, yes, have you never seen it, the machine for crushing, for grinding, for degrading peoples?[59]

Although not limiting themselves to any one form of neocolonial "aid," Césaire's references to Truman's underdevelopment speech, to the bulldozers, to the "massive investments of capital," and of course to "The roads! The ports!" explicitly critique the broader project of development, and implicitly target the World Bank's significant role within it. Césaire leaves little doubt as to his evaluation that Fordist-Keynesianism—which produces sycophantic lackeys along with toxic cinders—functions as a capitalist "machine for crushing, for grinding, for degrading peoples," a neocolonial extension of Gramsci's "new type of worker and man."

Likewise, Fanon, in his classic 1963 treatise on national liberation struggle, *The Wretched of the Earth,* argues with lucidity about the hegemonic shift (couched very much in Gramscian terms) toward the ascendancy of high finance over coercive force. "The military will of course go on playing with tin soldiers which date from the time of the conquest, but higher finance will soon bring the truth home to them."[60] Extending Lenin's argument that capitalism's constant need to expand in order to continue reaping profit will lead to situations where capitalism becomes "overripe,"[61] Fanon provocatively contends that national liberation movements bargain with high finance from a position of strength not weakness. Convinced, like Marx, that capital's need for new markets will chase "the bourgeoisie over the whole surface of the globe," Fanon nevertheless believes "the appalling state of the population as a whole immediately after independence" will effectively dampen that mad scramble, given private investment capital's "fear of taking any risk" and its need of "political stability and a calm social climate." The barricades of national liberation struggle become, for Fanon, barricades to the flow of international capital, leaving it "blocked" and "frozen." "Capital no longer circulates, or else its circulation is considerably diminished," he predicts, arguing that with the continued success of national liberation movements, "international capitalism is in desperate straits."[62]

The contradiction that Fanon identifies between capital's unquenchable need for expansion and its powerful aversion to risk could hardly articulate a more accurate job description for the World Bank. With its stated mission to "supplement private investment" by lending for projects that would otherwise be too risky—in other words, precisely to unblock and unfreeze the flow of international capital—the World Bank steps in to bridge the contradiction upon which Fanon stakes his argument. And it does so, in large part, by courting the nationalist bourgeoisie and ruling elites that Fanon so accurately portrays as stunted and corrupt, incapable of fulfilling the "historic role of the bourgeoisie"[63] to innovate and develop the modern means of production. What may be Fanon's largest theoretical misstep in *The Wretched of the Earth*—his conviction that national liberation struggles could freeze or fossilize capital in Europe, bringing about systemic crisis and revolution—founders in no small part against the corruption, conceitedness, temerity, and ineffectuality of a national bourgeoisie and postindependence ruling class, the theorization of which constitutes what is perhaps Fanon's most prophetic analysis.

A brief aside about this nationalist ruling class: the Bank made concerted efforts to court a number of the African postindependence leaders, even some with socialist leanings, most notably Léopold Senghor of Senegal (who, along with Césaire, founded the Negritude movement), Julius Nyerere of Tanzania, and Kenneth Kaunda of Zambia. Jomo Kenyatta of capitalist Kenya was hailed for his "astute leadership" that had helped to keep "latent tribalism in check." McNamara had a particularly close relationship with charismatic Nyerere, and throughout most of the 1970s the Bank overlooked economic indicators that would have raised red flags in other instances, enthusiastically supporting Ujamma, Tanzania's rural development program. Nyerere was enlisted by the Bank to lobby European nations for IDA contributions, including a 1975 effort to persuade Olaf Palme of Sweden. This was a strategy that the Bank used "not infrequently," according to Kapur, Lewis, and Webb, including a notable instance when Indira Gandhi made a personal plea to Margaret Thatcher for a generous IDA contribution in 1982.[64] Although these relationships, especially those between the Bank and African leadership, in many cases deteriorated

significantly during the debt crisis of the 1980s, they were cultivated with care and genuine respect, during the early postindependence years, from both sides.

If Fanon fails to foresee the role that the Bank will play in facilitating the rise of a self-interested and compliant nationalist bourgeoisie, collaboratively marshalling the rhetoric of nationalism and
the apparatus of the nation state to enable the global expansion
of capitalism, he succeeds admirably in articulating the political
imperatives for social movements interested in contesting such arrangements. When read against the Bank, these imperatives take
two forms: severing development from growth, and severing national culture from the nation state. Fanon unapologetically demands reparations and redistribution of wealth rather than symbolic independence or system-wide economic growth (what I have
been calling "the bigger pie"). He writes, "The question which is
looming on the horizon, is the need for a redistribution of wealth.
Humanity must reply to this question or be shaken to pieces by
it."[65] But redistribution, here, is entirely distinct from development
or "aid," for which he holds only contempt:

> We are not blinded by the moral reparation of national indepen-
> dence; nor are we fed by it. The wealth of the imperial countries
> is our wealth too. . . . Europe is literally the creation of the Third
> World. . . . So when we hear the head of a European state declare
> with his hands on his heart that he must come to the aid of the poor
> underdeveloped peoples, we do not tremble with gratitude. Quite
> the contrary; we say to ourselves: "It's a just reparation that will be
> paid to us." Nor will we acquiesce in the help for underdeveloped
> countries being a program of "sisters of charity." This help should
> be the ratification of a double realization: the realization by the
> colonized peoples that *it is their due,* and the realization by the
> capitalist powers that in fact *they must pay.*[66]

National independence is sufficient only if the nation state is considered the end of national liberation struggle. For Fanon, the state
more often functions as an obfuscating apparatus using the nationalist trappings of local tradition or custom to protect the interests of
capital. He understands national culture, by contrast, to be constituted by the living, dynamic struggle of a people: "the whole body
of efforts made by a people in the sphere of thought to describe,
justify, and praise the action through which that people has created

itself and keeps itself in existence." In native dress, food, and rituals, Fanon locates only exoticized residual customs or traditions—the literal and figurative "outer garments" of a people. By contrast, national "culture has never the translucidity of custom; it abhors all simplification."[67] Never static or passively inherited, national culture constantly remakes itself out of the emergent contemporary struggles of a people for liberation and equity. [68]

Although Césaire and Fanon may not name the Bank as their chief antagonist, then, their theorizations of liberation and culture are crafted in direct response to the pressures and antinomies of the World Bank era, and in tacit opposition to the kinds of strategic maneuvering at which the Bank proves so adept. In response to the neocolonial interventionism of the Bank, and to the broader spread of Fordist-Keynesianism—both threatening to undermine the revolutionary movements of national liberation—Césaire and Fanon (among any number of anticolonial thinkers) offer nuanced, cogent attempts to theorize the complexities of social collectivities that draw on national culture and the dynamism of national liberation movements, but that do not rely upon or aspire to the (often repressive) bureaucratic institutions of the nation state. Although attempting to account for the particular nature of capitalism in those parts of the world struggling with the historical legacies of colonialism—particularities that include everything from the history of slavery to the introduction of World Bank development "aid"—Césaire and Fanon insist that movements, not states, provide the means, and that democracy and equity, not independence, remain the ends of struggle.

Bankers at Bandung

The political commitments to movements for equity championed by anticolonial intellectuals stand, for the most part, in uneasy opposition to the network of postcolonial nation states that emerge from decolonization, and in stark contrast to the interests of the World Bank. The previous chapter examined the Bank's "uncomfortable intimacy" with decolonizing nationalisms, arguing that the Bank attempted to curb radical demands by claiming to be the intellectual forefather of anticolonial national liberation, linking the idea of independence to the "revolutionary *business* of development" through the apparatuses of the nation state and the system of internationalism. There is perhaps no better historical example through which to witness the struggle between movements for equity and the interstate system of development than the April 1955 Asian-African Conference held in Bandung, Indonesia, (and thus typically referred to as the Bandung Conference), an event frequently cited as a landmark of third world nationalism and (mistakenly) of the Non-Aligned Movement. This event, which American novelist Richard Wright hailed as "a meeting of almost all of the human race living in the main geopolitical center of gravity of the earth,"[69] and which a Portuguese daily paper disparaged as a "vast whirl of panic" among an "enormous wavering mass," bound together only by "hate for the white master of former times, or of today,"[70] offers perhaps the best illustration of my claim that the Bank underwrites culture in the age of three worlds.

As a symbolic performance of third world solidarity, Bandung proved a resonant historical marker. Twenty-nine leaders, almost all heads of state, who came as representatives of Asian and African nations that had recently or would shortly achieve national independence, gathered at Bandung to discuss the prospects for regional economic and cultural cooperation, and to consider both the shared historical legacies and potential future contributions of once colonized peoples. Representing the five sponsoring nations, the so-called Colombo Powers, were Nehru of India, Sukarno of Indonesia, Mohamed Ali of Pakistan, Sir John Kotelawala of Ceylon (Sri Lanka), and U Nu of Burma. Other prominent attendees included Zhou-En-Lai of China, Gamal Abdel-Nasser of Egypt, Kwame Nkrumah of (not yet independent) Gold Coast, and heads of state from across Asia and Africa, with the purposeful exclusions only of South Africa, Israel, and Korea. Most scholars credit the French demographer Alfred Sauvy with coining the term "third world" or *"tiers monde"* as early as 1951, but it is only after Bandung that the term became part of a worldwide vernacular. As much as any other single event, Bandung helped forge a worldwide conception of the third world as a coherent, potentially unified political bloc, bound by a shared hatred of the former colonial masters as much as by triangulation with capitalism and socialism (the first and second "worlds").

Bandung is often mistakenly equated with the Non-Aligned Movement; historians as different as Robin D. G. Kelley in his introduction to Césaire's *Discourse*,[71] and Kapur, Lewis, and Webb in their fiftieth-anniversary history of the World Bank[72] (to cite just two examples) use *non-alignment* as a near synonym for *Bandung* and *third world*. Even Neil Larsen, in his otherwise accurate and insightful assessment of Bandung's contradictions, erroneously places Yugoslavia's Marshal Tito (along with Nehru, the other chief architect of non-alignment) at the Bandung proceedings.[73] The misconceptions about non-alignment at Bandung, and the illusions of a homogenous third world bloc, can be quickly dispatched. The significant absence of any Latin American or Caribbean nations (the former having in most cases fought their independence struggles in the nineteenth century, and the latter, despite a revolutionary history of slave revolts such as the one famously chronicled by C. L. R. James,[74] for the most part gaining independence only in the decades following Bandung, roughly contemporaneous with African decolonization), marks an obvious disparity between Bandung and the conceptual geography typically associated with either the third world or the Non-Aligned Movement. Even for those nations present at Bandung, non-alignment was not a universally embraced principle. Although Nehru, U Nu, and others consistently voiced the principles of non-alignment—including Nehru's equivocal dictum "We do not agree with the communist teachings, we do not agree with the anticommunist teachings, because they are both based on wrong principles"[75]—the conference itself was riven with alignments and fractures.

To dispel the notion of a unified bloc, one needs look no further than the rift between India and Pakistan, two of the sponsoring countries. Further, the presence of Zhou-En-Lai, whose invitation came at the urging of Nehru after his state visit to China the previous year, caused great consternation among many participating nations that feared China's imperial aggression, its connection with Moscow, and the threatening specter of fifth-column infiltration posed by its large diasporic population in countries like Indonesia. China's presence was most threatening to the United States, whose allies from the recently formed South East Asian Defense Treaty Organization (SEATO)—including Pakistan, Turkey, the Philippines, Thailand, and Japan—were urged by Washington (after some initial hesitation) to attend the conference to refute Communist arguments and to put forward concrete proposals for economic development. Numerous news reports from the period, such as these from the Philippine papers the *Daily Mirror* and the *Manila Times,* pick up on the fear, among those aligned with the United States, that the conference would "furnish a convenient point of departure for the propaganda of the puppet Peiping Communist regime,"[76] necessitating a response that could "stand up to the Communists in a much wider arena than the Conference hall at Bandung—and make the communists back down."[77] Far from homogenous and nonaligned, then, the Bandung Conference attempts to produce, and perhaps to some minor degree succeeds in producing, a form of collectivity from a sedimented and fissured political landscape striated by a host of (frequently competing) alliances between and among the attending nations and the major power blocs of the United States and the Union of Soviet Socialist Republics.

These rifts and alignments reticulate the Bandung gathering, often undercutting, or at minimum complicating, the conference's foundational objectives to "promote goodwill and cooperation among the nations of Asia and Africa," and to "explore and advance their mutual as well as common interests."[78] Like that of most any large, symbolic gathering, the spectacular gesture of the event accomplishes some of its work; Bandung signifies third world unity in part because the leaders of the decolonizing world met in one spot over the course of several days, suggesting the possibility of a coherent, if not single-minded, collective force that might act on world politics. Beyond the symbolic performance of unity, however, the work of negotiating lasting relationships and organizing collective strategies that might "advance" and not just "explore" the region's "mutual as well as common interests" would have required a longer-term process of organizing and movement building. Collectivity does not emerge, fully formed, from a conference gathering (a lesson the World Social Forum [WSF] must learn as well). The argument can certainly be made that the leaders at Bandung had little interest in such long-term organizing, that the conference was a bit of political theater and little more. As Aijaz Ahmad has expertly demonstrated in his reading of Nehru's participation, the rhetorical maneuvering at Bandung must be read in the context of national and regional politics as well as third worldist aspiration.[79] The analytical challenge of critically assessing Bandung is not to ask whether the conference produced a unified third worldist bloc—it did not, nor could it have, given the internal divisions among its participants and their varied relationships to first and second world blocs—but rather to enquire into the grounds upon which the participants attempted to forge commonalities and to what ends. That is, how did the Bandung participants attempt to resolve, or, more accurately, to defer, the underlying contradictions and internal divisions that threatened to fracture the meeting, foregrounding instead the collective interests of potential benefits (individual, national, regional, and global) that might stem from such a gathering? My argument is that Bandung effectively defers many of its internal contradictions by relying upon the newly visible category of *culture* as a suddenly consequential politicized sphere of action, and the paradoxical visibility and invisibility (or perhaps, to use a Fanonian term, *translucidity*) of the newly consequential World Bank. Culture and the Bank do not work in isolation or opposition at Bandung. Rather, they are paired in an uneasy tension, as the attendees wrestle with the radical energies of decolonization, global polarization and militarization, their own class and political affiliations, and much more.

No World Bank representatives were invited to attend Bandung, of course. To the consternation of many in Europe, North America, and Australia who cried "racialism" at being snubbed, the conference delimited its membership to Asian and African nations in conscious juxtaposition to colonial conferences of the past such as the 1885 Berlin conference (which divided the continent of Africa among European powers) or, for that matter, Bretton Woods (which divided the world among financial powers).[80] Nevertheless, the Bank's influence at the conference was considerable. Consider, for example, the conference's Final Communiqué, from which we can glean some understanding of the Bank's role in suturing together both the alignments and the nonalignments of Bandung. Asserting that the "Asian-African Conference recognized the urgency of promoting economic development in the Asian-African region," the first item in the Communiqué, collectively authored by all twenty-nine attending nations, reads as follows: "The proposals with regard to economic cooperation within the participating countries do not preclude either the desirability or the need for cooperation with countries outside the region, including the investment of foreign capital. It was further recognized that the assistance being received by certain participating countries from outside the region, through international or under bilateral arrangements, had made a valuable contribution to the implementation of their development programmes."[81] In plain terms, this passage, inserted at the urging of Pakistan, endorses SEATO and the prospects of foreign development assistance through bilateral funding. Tacitly, however, it also sanctions the funding arrangements that underpin the ideal of non-alignment. Recall that India is the Bank's largest borrower in 1955, and that its ballooning debt, as much as anything else, convinces the reluctant Eugene Black to create the IDA. It is also worth noting that the Bank arranged a highly unorthodox lending package for Tito's Yugoslavia after its 1948 break from the Soviet Union. Fearing reactions from both Soviet Union and the U.S. Congress, George Kennan believed the Bank to be the ideal vehicle to deliver "discreet and unostentatious support" for Tito, and Black maintained that, although the loan "would be very difficult to explain to the market," it was worth the risk because, in his words, "it's also very important that Titoism succeeds."[82] For his part, Tito was apparently more concerned with the Bank's endorsement than with the loan itself, assuming that he would be able to secure Cold War–motivated bilateral funding from the United States. All this is to say that, for both Nehru and Tito, the "principled" position of national non-alignment was made possible by the availability of multilateral funding, never mind that those loans were disbursed in *U.S. dollars.*

The Final Communiqué makes explicit, two items later, the Bank's influence at Bandung, recommending "the early establishment of the Special United Nations Fund for Economic Development" and the "allocation by the International Bank for Reconstruction and Development of a greater part of its resources to Asian-African countries."[83] The creation of IDA in 1960 as an attempt by the Bank and the United States to outflank SUNFED, then, should be read in part as the result of pressure from Bandung. The obverse is also true, however; to whatever extent the heads of state attending Bandung were able to voice a unified front of once-colonized nation states, the coherence of such solidarity relied upon the availability of World Bank funding and the institution's appearance (or transparence) as a discreet, nonpolitical, multilateral body, allegedly outside the historical legacy of colonialism and the contemporary Cold War global alignments.

My argument here is that the Bank's lurking presence at Bandung is both symptomatic of a broader cultural turn taking place at the inception of a third world, and a precipitating agent that makes such a turn possible. The Bank, as we saw in chapter 3, was loath to venture into social lending; that it began funding in areas such as education during the 1960s speaks to the pressures being transferred up the line from restless populations to nationalist leaders and in turn to the international bodies of governance. At Bandung, a nationalist ruling elite, acutely aware that its own well-being is dependent upon material improvements in living conditions for its expectant, newly independent populations, solicits an expanded global role for the World Bank in no uncertain terms, calling explicitly for its evolution from a bank into a development agency. From a different vantage, however, the Bank's cultivated image of institutional transparency and objectivity (its own version of non-alignment) plasters over fractious questions of defense pacts and spheres of influence that might otherwise have ground the conference to a halt. Effectively displacing political and economic considerations onto the arena of culture where certain shared bonds between Bandung attendees can be discovered and exploited, the Bank's presence contributes to the cultural turn that marks the conference.

That *culture* is a keyword of the conference is evident as well in the Final Communiqué, which declares that "among the most powerful means of promoting understanding among nations is the development of cultural cooperation."[84] The document argues for an understanding of culture that is predicated on the enriching interchange between civilizations, suggesting that the historical interruption of Asian-African contact by colonialism "not only prevents cultural cooperation but also suppresses the national cultures of the people." Although the Communiqué presumes the significance and weightiness of the phrase "*national cultures* of the *people*," it offers precious little in the way of specific elaboration about the implications of any of these three key terms, each of which has been invested with new significance by the radical movements of national liberation. In this regard, the document is symptomatic of the global cultural turn, and seeks in its own elliptical way to intervene in critical debates about the role of culture. Implicitly a response to the radical theorists of culture and liberation, the document struggles to rein in culture, constructing it as a sphere of consensus and commonality rather than protest and critique.

In effect merging the Arnoldian and Tylorian traditions, the Communiqué asserts, for instance, that the continents of Asia and Africa "have been the cradle of great religions and civilizations." Culture, here, encapsulates both the finest expressions of human experience, and the complex whole. It serves as the vehicle through which the conference attendees can celebrate localism and traditional (not "primitive") custom, precisely those cultural values and expressions denigrated and suppressed by colonialism. With an emphasis on presumed universal foundations of spirituality and values that trace a direct genealogy back to the cradle of civilization, culture in this sense takes on an Arnoldian–Tylorian valence, appearing to exist outside of time and outside of capitalism.

But the document's conception of a static, inherited culture is conflicted, troubled by global flows in which national identity becomes increasingly defined by the circuit of commodified cultural production. Thus, when the Communiqué speaks of "cultural cooperation" and "cultural exchange," the document adopts language strikingly similar to Meyer and McCloy's assertions, cited earlier, that international trade and investment will result in "wider understanding, exchange of ideas and mutual respect."[85] Here again, the phrase "national cultures of the people" takes on the characteristics of the fetishized mass-cultural commodity, freighted with the duties of ambassadorship. In this model, the nation state serves as protector and regulator of cultural/commodity exchange. A far cry from Fanon's notion of "national culture," the term here serves to reinforce a sense of patriotic nationhood presumed identical with the sovereign borders of the state; "national culture" in this sense carries overtones of value-added marketing, the local color that differentiates Indonesian wood carving from that of Thailand or Ghana. Embedded within the language of exchange and dialogue, the document reaffirms divisions between nation states as natural, creating barriers to the formation of collectivities beyond the imagined community of nationhood.[86] Read in this context, the cultural exchange championed in the Communiqué places culture wholly within the logic of economic exchange, affirming the sovereign borders of the nation state and displacing the social relations between producers back into the fetishized realm of commodity circulation.

We can get a still fuller sense, however, of the ways Bandung participates in the struggles of the global cultural turn from Richard Wright, the black American expatriate writer and former Communist Party member, who travels to Bandung for the conference. Wright's quasi-journalistic, quasi-sociological coverage and analysis in his fascinating book *The Color Curtain* illustrates the stakes and competing forces at Bandung, often more clearly than do the conference documents themselves.[87] Upon learning of the conference, he asks himself what these nations could possibly have in common to bring them together: "The despised, the insulted, the hurt, the dispossessed—in short, the underdogs of the human race were meeting. Here were class and racial consciousness on a global scale. Who had organized such a meeting? And what had these nations in common? Nothing it seemed to me, but what their past relationship to the Western world had made them feel. This meeting of the rejected was in itself a kind of judgment upon that Western World."[88] Wright searches here, and throughout the book, for a commonality that can be articulated in the affirmative rather than the negative. The negative affiliation between the Bandung participants is evident: a bond forged from a common history of colonial exploitation, their shared status as *noncolonies*.

The affirmative commonality that Wright identifies takes the form of a collective judgment based upon a global race *and* class consciousness. Class consciousness on its own, for Wright as for any number of anticolonial intellectuals, appears inadequate for the task of analyzing the contradictions of colonialism and the promise of national liberation struggle. (Consider, for example, Fanon's claim that Marxist analysis needs to be "slightly stretched" when analyzing colonial problems because there "economic substructure is also a superstructure. . . . The cause is the consequence; you are rich because you are white, you are white because you are rich."[89] C. L. R. James offers a complementary analysis when he argues that the "clash of race, caste, and class" that structure West Indian cricket allow him to finally see the "pyramid whose base constantly widened, until it embraced those aspects of social relations, politics and art laid bare when the veil of the temple has been rent in twain as ours has been."[90]) Attempting to better account for the complexities of race, Wright begins to identify something that might be understood (to switch into the register of British Cultural Studies) as a *structure of feeling,* "not the absence, the unconscious, which bourgeois culture has mythologized," but rather, in Raymond Williams's words, "a kind of feeling and thinking which is indeed social and material, but each in an embryonic phase before it can become fully articulate and defined exchange."[91] Race consciousness in Wright's sense is not *merely* superstructural, nor is it *merely* a matter of the unconscious; instead race, like class, is understood as a material product of capitalist imperialism.

Bandung, for Wright, represents the embryonic attempt to articulate the ways that race and class—social and material, thought and felt—can provide the basis for an affirmative collective judgment. He writes: "There was something extra-political, extra-social, almost extra-human about it; it smacked of tidal waves, of natural forces. . . . *And the call for the meeting had not been sounded in terms of ideology.* The agenda and subject matter had been written for centuries in the blood and bones of the participants. The conditions under which these men had lived had become their tradition, their culture, their *raison d'être.*"[92] Wright shifts his analytical focus away from a strict Marxist ideology critique and toward an interrogation of the blurry line between nature and culture. The language of this passage, reminiscent of Foucault or Hardt and Negri as well as Marx, draws attention to the ways colonialism, and now anticolonialism, "had been written . . . in the blood and bones of the participants." One could argue that the critique remains materialist, but Wright's assessment of the conference seeks at times to articulate a biopolitical, rather than a historical, materialism.

Perhaps the more significant fault line that Wright unearths in this passage—a line that signals Bandung's place within a global cultural turn, and enables us to connect Wright to Fanon and Williams, and ultimately to the World Bank—is the distinction, or lack thereof, between tradition and culture. The syntax of the final quoted sentence of the passage makes Wright's position difficult to pinpoint with certainty. Lived conditions under colonialism, presumably including both oppression and resistance, appear to produce, in Wright's formulation, both tradition and culture, providing the ontological foundation, the raison d'être, for the gathering at Bandung. However, the two verbs *had lived* and *had become* locate both tradition and culture in the past, contributing to the impression left by the sentence structure that Wright is using the two terms almost synonymously. That is, culture, though elevated to a position of prominence as *the* coherent field of action on which the agenda of Bandung will be played out, appears at the same time relegated to a past-tense construction of tradition, akin to those "great religions and civilizations" cited by the Communiqué.

This reading of Wright's sentence certainly places it in opposi-

tion to Williams's insistence upon theorizing the social formations
at work in the contemporary moment; as he puts it, the "regular
conversion of experience into finished products" represents "the
strongest barrier to the recognition of cultural activity."[93] Likewise,
Fanon contends that national culture is forged in the dynamic, living complexity of the present, fully at odds with the "mummified
fragments" of custom; tradition for Fanon amounts to merely the
"outer garments" of culture, an exoticized reflection "of a hidden
life, teeming and perpetually in motion."[94] Whether Wright's passage in *The Color Curtain* actually equates culture and tradition
remains to my mind an open question; I am inclined to see the
pairing more as a field of inquiry that structures much of Wright's
analysis of Bandung than as a settled argument. Throughout the
text, Wright presents perspectives from people he interviews in
Europe and Indonesia, many of whom seem to return to the question of how to square tradition and custom with a conception of
contemporary, dynamic culture. One interviewee, according to
Wright, would like "to see Indonesia thoroughly industrialized,
but he wishes that the woodcarving, music, and dancing skills
of the people could be saved," though he is "afraid that won't be
possible."[95] Another of Wright's Indonesian discussants argues,
"We don't have a national culture yet; we have many cultures.
We are trying to find a culture."[96] On the whole, Wright's notion
of culture, like that of these two interview subjects, is probably
more static—tied to tradition, the arts, and localism—than either
Williams's or Fanon's. Nevertheless, there remains an uneasy sta-
sis. The twin modernizing pressures of industrialization and the
nation state trouble any straightforward conception of culture
that is either tied to past tradition or conceived of as fractured and
identity-based "ways of life," a series of localisms.

   This poses a problem for Wright, certainly, but also for the
heads of state who participate in the agenda, and for whom Wright
has such high regard. (There is a certain amount of hagiography
for the exiled, ex–political prisoner, national leaders in *The Color
Curtain,* "men to whom sacrifice and suffering had been daily
companions."[97]) Nehru, for instance, declares that nations gain
respect "because they are not only great in military might but in
development, in culture, in civilization."[98] Sukarno, likewise, suggests that, although the Bandung nations do not, as yet, constitute a military or economic bloc, "the peoples of Asia and Africa,

1,400,000,000 strong, far more than half of the human population of the world," speak as a political force because they can mobilize the *"Moral Violence of Nations* in favor of peace."[99]

Somewhere between the 1.4 billion people and the nation states and nationalist leaders that purport to speak for these masses, between living culture and mummified tradition, we can locate the cultural fault lines at Bandung. These fault lines manifest themselves in the pervasive atmosphere of anxiety and fear that reigns at the conference. The first world, the United States most of all, is certainly concerned about the revolutionary leanings of this 1.4 billion people—roughly 60 percent of the world's population—not to mention, as we saw in the previous chapter, the threats of violence and racialism associated with emerging nationalisms. The United States is concerned about the prospect of economic cartels that might emerge from regional trading blocs. It is particularly concerned about China's presence at Bandung and the prospect of Communism spreading in Asia and Africa, a situation that comes to a head during the conference with the United States threatening to deploy so-called tactical nuclear weapons in defense of Chiang Kai-shek and the islands of Matsu and Quemoy.

The insecurities of the nationalist leaders who called the conference are no less evident. No doubt they are genuinely afraid of the unprecedented concentration of military power, particularly nuclear power, such that a war between any two or more nations would hold potentially disastrous ramifications across the entire globe; Eisenhower's and Dulles's threat to launch nuclear strikes against China, issued during the conference, would have done nothing to quell this deep anxiety. Many of the attending nations are also concerned about the imperial aggression of the United States, of the Soviet Union, and (in some cases) of their fellow participant, China. Further, there exists an overriding fear among these nationalist leaders that they may lose their grip on their recently acquired power; ironically, then, the anticolonial heroes of Bandung, often European-educated nationalist elites, are in many cases afraid of the same mass movements that frighten the first-world observers. That is, they fear losing power to leftist revolutionary movements of peasants and workers, and likewise fear that anger and resentment arising from deprivation will manifest itself in religious fundamentalism, racism, xenophobia, or particularly violent expressions of nationalism. Tellingly, the fears of the Bandung leaders

have much more in common with those of the first world and the
World Bank than they do with the fears of the 1.4 billion people
whom they allegedly represent.

Wright is perceptive enough to understand both the urgency of
the situation and the complexities of satisfying the demands of the
restless and impoverished masses of the South. Although he may
not see, with the clarity of Fanon, the full class contradictions posed
by the representatives at Bandung, Wright nevertheless is aware
that the westernized Asians at Bandung face the enormous task of
translating national independence victories into material improvements in the living conditions of their peoples. Once again the di-
lemma of growth versus redistribution comes to the fore. Wright,
an ardent believer in the social benefits of modernization (benefits that he sees as both economic and secular/humanist), argues
that the problems facing the emerging third world cannot be solved
without a significant redistribution of wealth. When he declares
that "BANDUNG WAS THE LAST CALL OF WESTERNIZED ASIANS TO
THE MORAL CONSCIOUSNESS OF THE WEST!" he means to suggest
that, to resolve the explosive situation that has transformed the so-
called underdeveloped world into "the main geopolitical center of
gravity of the earth," substantial and rapid sacrifices, not token
lip service, must be forthcoming from the world's richer nations:
"To have an ordered, rational world in which we all can share, I
suppose that the average white Westerner will have to accept this
[economic parity between East and West] ultimately; either he accepts it or he will have to seek for ways and means of resubjugating
these newly freed hundreds of millions of brown and yellow and
black people. If he does accept it, he will also have to accept, for
an unspecified length of time, a much, much lower standard of living."[100] Redistribution of wealth and a "de-Occidentlalization" of
the globe announce themselves as the planet's most urgent imperatives. The West's failure to make *immediate* and *substantial* sacrifices will result in chaos, perhaps in the form of a leftist revolution,
more likely, in Wright's estimation, from *"a racial and religious
system of identification manifesting itself in an emotional nationalism which was now leaping state boundaries and melting and
merging, one into the other."*[101]

For Wright, the question becomes how to structure a transfer
of wealth to promote or sustain a worldwide secular, rational,
modernity. To this end, the concluding pages of his book stage a

debate between proposals suggested by various of his interviewees. On the one hand, Wright prints his exchange with a self-described "Jeffersonian Democrat" from the United States, who insists "we will help, but we won't interfere." This man argues that, for Indonesia to make progress, it needs technical assistance and training from the West: "above all, it needs personnel trained in modern techniques."[102] When asked by an incredulous Wright about the time frame for such assistance, the man replies "fifty or a hundred years." On the other hand, Wright interviews a liberal American social scientist working in the nascent academic field of economic development who, echoing Wright, argues that the "hour is late, very, *very* late."[103] This interviewee recommends a capital investment on such scale as to make the Marshall Plan look inconsequential: "if the scale of such assistance is big enough to provide a 'shock treatment' . . . there is good reason to suppose that the social and cultural barriers to further development will melt away."[104]

For his part, Wright agrees in principle with the recommendations of the development researcher, but rejects the proposal as unrealistic, arguing, "Human engineering" on the scale proposed by the researcher, "would bankrupt the United States in a year."[105] Wright's own suggestion is somewhat different. Rather than argue for transferring capital from West to East through direct loans, he argues for the industrialization of Asia and Africa, enabling these regions to process their raw materials and export (or use) manufactured goods. To Wright's mind, such industrialization would alter the dynamics in the worldwide mode of production, necessitating "a radical adjustment of the West's own systems of society and economics," a sacrifice he believes less severe than the alternative, "to face militant hordes buoyed and sustained by racial and religious passions."[106]

Triangulated between the Jeffersonian democrat, the WPA-style investment of the social scientist, and the industrialized secular rationalism of Wright, stands the World Bank, waiting just off stage, eager to play the role of midcentury culture warrior. Again, I maintain that the antinomies of Bandung, which so often play out in the contested sphere of culture, are resolved—inadequately, and unevenly, to be sure—through the institutional presence of the World Bank. The World Bank underwrites culture at Bandung. For the emerging cadre of World Bankers, the three positions outlined by Wright as possible solutions are in fact one; or rather, all three can be effectively collapsed into the logic of development so as to appear settled and accounted for. As we have seen, the Bank proves adept at responding with its own version of Jeffersonian democracy (recall Black's evocation of Jefferson's legacy in his address to the University of Virginia), offering precisely the kinds of technical assistance and modernized training that Wright's interviewee calls for, and suggesting the same century-long time frame to complete the process. Although not disclaiming the right to moral interference, the Bank does insist that its advice and its lending come unvarnished by political or ideological consideration. Moreover, by claiming that anticolonial national liberation movements are the intellectual inheritors of an American tradition of anticolonial independence, the Bank takes a rhetorical position that distances it from an imperialist history of *interference* while still holding out the promise of altruistic *intervention* through aid. That Sukarno approvingly cites Paul Revere's midnight ride, during "the first successful anticolonial war in history,"[107] in Sukarno's opening address to the Bandung meeting, provides some credence to the notion that appeals such as Black's were to a degree persuasive, at least to those "westernized Asians" at the conference.

Likewise, the Bank has proven adept at forestalling the massive capital transfers suggested by the social scientists' urgent plea for a third world Marshall Plan. The Bank provides nowhere near the scale of lending this researcher suggests is necessary. At the same time, however, the Bank has effectively marshaled a very similar rhetoric of crisis to justify its continued existence and prominence. With the creation of the IDA and the institutional focus on "poverty alleviation" and social lending, the Bank attempts to outflank calls from Bandung and elsewhere for SUNFED, while minimizing the damage to itself and its richest members. For this reason, the prominence of the IDA within the Bank's public representation of an institutional image stands in stark contrast to its meager lending budgets; the IDA and social lending appear to address the same urgencies identified by Wright's social scientist, while avoiding—by a long shot—the fear of bankruptcy introduced by Wright.

Finally, Wright's own plan of uplift through industrialization merely rearticulates one of the central pillars of the Bank's institutional practice. That he never explicitly mentions the Bank in *The Color Curtain* is somewhat surprising, given the institution's prominent place in the Final Communiqué. Regardless, Wright's proposal, like the Bank's, amounts to the globalization of Fordism, with an expectation that industrialization will bring employment, economic stability, and modern, secular values to the developing world. Where the two paradigms diverge is around the notion of redistribution. Wright believes that reapportioning the global division of labor and relocating the means of production will necessarily entail a redistribution of wealth and power. The Bank, on the other hand, has seen to it that the export of Fordism sets as its objective a bigger pie rather than a more equitably divided one. It has accomplished this through, among other things, the Keynesian bargain among capital, nation states, and labor; many of the leaders at Bandung were themselves the beneficiaries of this bargain, consolidating national power and in some cases lining their pockets in the process. If any redistribution has been achieved through the modernization and industrialization championed by Wright, it has only insured that the "haves"—residing in both the North and South—now sweeten their meals with an even larger slice of pie, while the "have-nots" are left with fewer crumbs than before.

We should not lose the thread of culture in all this. My argument has been that the Bandung attendees look to culture as a space of commonality, a way to plaster over deep-seated political and economic conflicts and find a ground upon which to build a sense of collectivity. For Wright, this takes the form of race consciousness ascending to the level of class consciousness—a color curtain that divides the globe into three just as much as the iron curtain splits it in two.

This challenge to the economism and the Eurocentrism of Marxist critique announces one of the ongoing currents of debate within cultural studies. We find too an active inquiry into the relation of culture to past and present: the contested break between culture as tradition and localism, and culture as a dynamic force of the contemporary moment. Moreover, this latter sense of culture as contemporary, always moving and transforming, takes multiple forms at the conference; we may identify, for instance, a split between articulations of a *development culture,* focused on the ways culture adapts to the pressures of modernity and industrialization, and a *culture of movements,* which wrestles with questions of how to produce and sustain collectivities. National culture in Fanon's sense of forging *a people* through liberation struggle butts heads with *nation-state culture,* where the state is identified as the singular repository of tradition, custom, and identity.

As one of Wright's interviewee's comments, the divide between national culture and the culture of nation states calls democracy itself into question. "How can a man's worth be measured when he votes?" he asks. "If Democracy means the opportunity of each man to develop to his highest capacity, then a mere counting of heads is no Democracy"; instead, he provocatively remarks, "Democracy is a means of protest, not a method of construction."[108] There is little doubt that the leaders at Bandung, in their effort to move from the insurrectionary moment of independence to the permanent establishment of political institutions, prefer to think of democracy-as-construction rather than democracy-as-protest (if, that is, they are willing to entertain any notion of democracy at all). The same might be said of their likely preference for culture-as-construction—locked securely in the past—rather than culture-as-protest. Nevertheless, these fault lines, like the rifts of alignment, political representation, and the many contradictions of the conference, remain unsettled at Bandung, where the figures of 1.4 billion and 60 percent—that is, the figures that attempt to represent, to *account for,* masses and multitudes—are never far away, not yet neatly contained by the census, the ballot box, the military draft, or any of the other state mechanisms for counting heads.

These fractures indicate the lines of debate that structure the global cultural turn. To be sure, the Bank cannot be blamed or credited for producing these fault lines. I have tried to suggest, however, that the institution contributed to shaping the historical conditions that are being addressed at Bandung, perhaps most notably the export of Fordist-Keynesianism. Further, the Bank played a crucial role in helping to manage the contradictions of Bandung, contributing to establishment of postcolonial nation states and working to dampen radical nationalisms of both the Left and Right. It cannot resolve these contradictions, in no small part because deep internal political rifts striate the conference and the national liberation movements themselves. Nevertheless, there are many cases where the Bank underwrote solutions that provided a simulacrum of resolution, contributing to the thickening of capital's saturation of the globe, and to whatever degree of stability has accompanied the postcolonial nation state and the postwar system of internationalism of which it is a part. The fault lines over culture at Bandung are not mere squabbles or differences of emphasis; they are genuine antinomies. The Bank's ability, in collaboration with private capital and the nationalist elites at Bandung, to provide the appearance of resolution has effectively deferred but not dissolved many of the contradictions. They are with us today, often with magnified intensity. To examine the role of the Bank at the origins of the culture turn, then, is to identify lines of struggle that have continued relevance for anyone interested in constructing, to return to Denning's phrase, an "emancipatory transnational cultural studies."

5. Success Stories: NGOs and
the Banking Bildungsroman

In the Bandung era, culture emerged into plain view for the radicals of anticolonial liberation struggles, the national elites of independence movements, and the World Bankers who underwrote the global cultural turn. For midcentury theorists and practitioners, culture was a sphere suffused with economic and political struggle, not removed from it. Firsthand witnesses to decolonizing movements across the Global South, and to the emerging system of international governance and finance, these intellectuals became ever more clear-eyed about the ways that the transforming nature of imperial power inevitably shaped and was shaped by cultural movements. However, the World Bank's specific role in these transformations remained (as we saw in the previous chapter) somewhat murkier for the midcentury cultural radicals. Although the institution's presence could be felt in the Bandung Communiqué, and although some anticolonial theorists named it a political antagonist, more often than not the Bank is found lumped into a loose constellation with multilateral aid, development, Americanism, neocolonialism, industrial modernization, and the like. Although this lack of analytical clarity about the specificities of the institution does not negate the significant intellectual convergences mapped in the previous chapter, it is true that the World Bank drifts hazily in and out of critical focus for the cultural radicals of the 1950s and 1960s.

If we jump ahead to the present era (as we do in this chapter), this can no longer be said. Radical social movement actors in the first decade of the twenty-first century have the Bank trained clearly in their sights. At times their analysis lacks historical precision (in, for instance, the tendency to equate the Bank with the era of globalization). Nevertheless, an extraordinary spectrum of contemporary social movements define themselves in stark opposition to the World Bank. Several decades of progressively intensifying resistance to the Bretton Woods institutions have sharpened activists' focus on the World Bank as a force of global immiseration.

Equally stark is the reason behind this critical shift: in a word, debt. The Bank's prominent role in the debt crisis that ravaged the borrowing nations of the Global South throughout the late 1970s and 1980s threw into high relief the institution's historical role as a neocolonial mechanism for the transfer of wealth from South to North. The causes of the debt crisis are many and multilayered.[1] The Nixon administration's decision to decouple the dollar from the gold standard, in response to balance of payment problems stemming from overextended foreign investments and the expenses of the Vietnam War, amounted to an $80 billion default on financial obligations, offloading U.S. debt onto the rest of the world by severely depreciating the value of the dollar. Further, though the Bank was concerned about the rising debt levels of many of its borrowers, India chief among them, it continued to lend liberally (as we have seen). When Indira Gandhi proposed to reduce India's borrowing to zero, in an effort to achieve national "self reliance" (another version of non-alignment), McNamara responded that such a policy was "dangerous and counterproductive."[2] Although aware of the crippling consequences of indebtedness, the Bank was not about to put itself out of business by encouraging self-reliance. By the mid-1970s, however, only the internal shuffling of funds between the IBRD and the IDA kept the Bank from negative transfers; that is, the Bank began to profit directly from its loans, collecting more in interest payments than it loaned out—but, for a "development agency" whose mission was presumably poverty alleviation, profitability was a public relations disaster, laying bare the illusion of development "aid." The oil crisis of 1973–74 brought the situation to a boil. Expenditures skyrocketed for those nations dependent on imported oil. The corollary sweeping profits for oil exporters, mainly the OPEC nations, provided the "petrodollars" that soon flooded an already saturated debt environment.

Borrowers turned for advice to the Bank, the world's leading authority on development financing, and it fanned the flames by counseling additional borrowing to pay the balance. When interest rates spiked at the end of the decade, the debt crisis erupted in full, leaving the bankrupted economies of Southern states unable to make loan repayments to Northern banks. The crisis was particularly severe in Latin America (where the 1980s are referred to as the "lost decade"), but it reverberated throughout the entire third world with devastating effects.

While the Bank's role in producing the debt crisis afforded it a certain global visibility, its role in managing and containing the crisis likely did more to cement its newfound institutional notoriety. In conjunction with the IMF, the Bank hastily put together a series of new loan packages—laden with "structural adjustment" conditions—to forestall default. In effect, these loans amounted to a massive bail-out of financially exposed Northern banks. Using divide-and-conquer tactics, the Bank and IMF successfully negotiated lending arrangements with individual national governments, enabling states to continue making interest payments, but placing them under still more severe debt burdens for the future. Looking back on the events, even Bank officials were surprised that the debtor nations did not default en masse. David Knox, the Bank's vice-president for Latin America, argued, "if they played their cards correctly, Latin American debtors would in fact have very considerable power to default partially or wholly." Ernest Stern, one of the most senior Bank officials, agreed, suggesting "I accept the proposition that the debtors have been too supine. . . . If debtors had been willing to play a role, or had been encouraged to, the legal framework would not have turned out to be such a [straitjacket]."[3] Such advice was not forthcoming to the debtor nations at the time of the crisis, however, and the Bank successfully protected the overextended financial interests of Northern banks against widespread default by isolating individual nation states and displacing the financial burden of debt onto the poorest and least powerful members of the South through the policies of structural adjustment.

The debt crisis, then, marks the moment at which the Bank is forced into a posture of chronic public defensiveness. An interconnected (if not internally coordinated or organized) wave of popular unrest in the form of austerity protests, also called "food riots" or "IMF riots," swept across the Global South, articulating an unambiguous critique of the "free market" reforms of liberalization, privatization, and structural adjustment. In their valuable history of this insurrectionary period, John Walton and David Seddon count 147 violent protests occurring in thirty-nine countries across Latin America, the Caribbean Basin, Asia, Africa, and Eastern Europe between 1976 and 1992.[4] Environmentalist movements in opposition to World Bank projects, including most notably the Polonoroeste development in Brazil and the Narmada River Valley dams in India, gain visibility and political clout during the late 1980s and early 1990s (emblematized by Bruce Rich's influential book *Mortgaging the Earth,* published in 1994). These movements have altered both the nature of the critique and the tactics of opposition (organizing with NGO campaigns, particularly those directed at pressuring national parliamentary bodies such as the U.S. Congress to withhold IDA contributions), adding to the ongoing public scrutiny and mounting pressure under which the Bank is forced to operate. For many activists (and media outlets) in the United States, the Bank returns to sharp focus as one of the agencies most responsible for global austerity only after the landmark 1999 WTO protests in Seattle and, shortly thereafter, the April 2000 Bank protests in Washington, D.C.; however, it should not be forgotten that tens of thousands of demonstrators mobilized to protest previous World Bank/IMF meetings in Berlin (1988) and Madrid (1994). And in the post-Seattle era, ongoing protests marked by increasingly robust networks of North–South and South–South alliances continue to hound the World Bank.[5]

The Bank's heightened visibility under the now focused scrutiny of radical opposition provides the political and rhetorical context for this chapter's inquiry into the institution's cultural work in the contemporary historical moment. I contend that, in the face of pointed critique, the World Bank turns to ever more mediated modes of public address. Now on the defensive, the institution works to deflect and diffuse critique in new ways. Perhaps more than ever, the Bank self-consciously traffics in culture, placing increasing emphasis on "the local," "the micro," and "the participatory."[6] This chapter analyzes one aspect of this newly redoubled attention to culture: the Bank's specific address to literary culture as a mechanism by which to authorize development. I offer a close reading of a short story (of sorts), authored by Becky Wachera and Matthew Meyer, the cofounders of the African NGO EcoSandals, and posted to the World Bank Website as a particular brand of *success story*. Although this chapter continues to analyze the rhetorical maneuvering of Bank presidents—in this case, James Wolfensohn—its primary focus turns to this NGO-authored text as a means of exploring the Bank's new modes of authorial mediation, and some implications of what I term its *appeal to the literary*.

World Bank Literature

Before taking up the EcoSandals story, I turn briefly to Amitava Kumar's edited collection *World Bank Literature* to raise questions about the relationship between literary and cultural studies and the contemporary World Bank. Kumar's introduction to the collection argues provocatively about the implications of replacing the longstanding and frequently taught world literature course with the more politically responsive category of World Bank literature. He argues that an "analytic shift from the liberal-diversity model of 'World Literature' to the radical paradigm of 'World Bank Literature' signals a resolve not only to recognize and contest the dominance of Bretton Woods institutions but also to rigorously oppose those regimes of knowledge that would keep literature and culture sealed from the issues of economics and activism." The phrase "World Bank Literature" functions for Kumar as a scholarly and pedagogical heuristic, "intended to prompt questions about each of the words in that constellation; it is a term that is designed to invite inquiry into globalization, the economy, and the role of literary and cultural studies."[7]

World literature reconceived as World Bank literature: a clever turn of phrase, to be sure, but is that the extent of it? After all, at the curricular level Kumar might be accused of flogging a dead course. Within the U.S. academy in any case, although world literature courses continue to be taught in some undergraduate curricula (typically more conservative and slower to respond to disciplinary changes), the fields of postcolonial studies and, more recently, variations on globalization or transnational cultural studies have almost fully displaced the more Eurocentric tradition of world literature at the graduate level and in published scholarship. It must be said, of course, that Kumar also intends "World Bank Literature" to expose the political horizons of postcolonial studies. Referring, presumably, to the liberal-diversity model that structures many courses taught under this rubric, as well, Kumar asks quite pointedly, "Can 'World Bank Literature' be a new name for postcolonial studies?"[8]

A more substantive criticism of the term is raised by Bruce Robbins in his afterword to the collection, where he raises doubts about whether the adjective *World Bank* adequately captures the contemporary global flows and forces that Kumar hopes to evoke in the phrase:

> In focusing on banking, the title suggests that finance, the domain in which globalization has proceeded fastest and furthest, can stand for the world economic system itself—that what has and has not been globalized in the domains of production and trade, for example, can be smoothly assimilated into it. But this does not go without saying, and the disparities are worth some attention. Nor can it be assumed that, a synecdoche within a synecdoche, the World Bank can properly stand even for the domain of global finance. Unlike other bodies, it has shown itself capable of at least some degree of internal critique. The World Bank may have won a place in this book's title over the World Trade Organization, which has been the object of more interesting contestation from without, in large part because it has one less word in its name.[9]

Robbins rightly voices concerns about the conceptual weakness of cultural studies arguments that too quickly make claims about the World Bank and globalization that rely on this double synecdoche: global financial exchange stands in for the world economic system as a whole (ignoring production), and the World Bank stands for this exaggerated conception of economic globalization. To my mind, however, the problem lies in the manner in which critics have treated the Bank rather than in the nature of the institution itself. As I have demonstrated throughout the present book, my interest in the Bank—as opposed to, for instance, the WTO (which emerges out of the 1994 Uruguay Round of multilateral trade discussions about the GATT)—is precisely that it allows us to examine an institutional history that spans a sixty-year postwar era, and thereby oversees and participates in a series of conceptual alignments and periodizations including colonialism, decolonization, and postcolonialism, the three-worlds system, the development era, and the age of globalization. Precisely because it cannot be conflated simply with globalization, and as a result of its historical relationship to the theoretical categories of culture and cultural study, the Bank presents a substantially different figure for institutional critique than does the WTO.

A different kind of objection to the radicality of World Bank Literature might come from scholars of globalization who cast the World Bank as a relic of midcentury internationalism, incapable of responding to the new theoretical challenges of supranational globalization.[10] Recognizing that the Bank still wields substantial influence, they nonetheless would see it as an outmoded institution, scrambling to define its relevance—an organization, constituted in an era when the nation state enjoyed unquestioned sovereignty, but which is now struggling to adapt itself to a new set of global realities that privilege corporate rather than national actors. In claims of this nature, we find an uneasy convergence between critiques from the political Right and from the Left—Bush's pre–Iraq War critique of the United Nations, and Hardt and Negri's claims about supranational sovereignty of Empire—both of which foresee the impending collapse of a moribund system of internationalism, though for different reasons and with decidedly different imagined ends.[11]

But reports of the Bank's demise are often overstated. Parallel to, or rather in extension of, arguments about the continued efficacy of the (albeit transformed) nation state—both in its historical role as the protector and facilitator of capital, and as the site of necessary activism to ensure the protection of welfare services— evidence would suggest that the World Bank as an institution is far from obsolete. Although the contemporary Bank is undoubtedly under significant public scrutiny at the moment, it continues to exert tremendous influence through its legitimization of neoliberal trade policies, its lending practices, and its ability to shape the research agenda of development.

In fact, I would argue that many of the epochal arguments about the radical newness of our contemporary moment of supranational globalization find unwitting parallels in the Bank's attempts to represent itself as an agency in radical transformation. This is a constant refrain in recent Bank promotional materials. Consider, for example, the Bank's glossy brochure "10 Things You Never Knew About the World Bank."[12] Upon opening this brochure, the reader confronts what may be understood as the *face of culture* placed in dialog with a transforming Bank. On the inside flap of the brochure's cover we find a striking *National Geographic*–style photographic close-up of a painted, perhaps scarred or tattooed, indigenous face. The subject directs a confident gaze intently at the camera/reader. Its gender is ambiguous, as is its ethnicity or national origin (at least to those audience members not familiar with the signifying logic of the paint or the cloth that covers the head), and the text offers us no indicators about how to *place* this visage. The Bank, apparently, need not offer any specifics; this is the face of global indigeneity, rendered in a variant of the familiar "native savage" trope. The face signifies *culture unchanged,* a celebration of local custom and tradition as diversity and precious heritage (precisely the image that Fanon so despised).

Conceptually juxtaposed to this static, enduring face of the native Other (though textually superimposed upon the right-hand side of the photo frame and occupying the entirety of the right-hand brochure page) is the bold pronouncement that "The World Bank's Priorities Have CHANGED Dramatically" (the word "changed" is in a font size several times larger than the other text). The passage claims that the Bank now prioritizes social lending, with education funding replacing energy as the sector receiving the largest percentage of Bank money. It goes on to argue that the institution "is doing development differently and is addressing newer issues, like gender, community-driven development, and indigenous peoples, as well as working to provide vital infrastructure for the poor." In effect, "doing development differently" amounts to an extension of the 1960s social turn, repackaged as *dramatic change.*

As a whole, the photo and text clearly hope to celebrate cultural difference, suggesting that the Bank's new emphasis on social lending will provide "vital infrastructure" for local communities. Indeed, the photograph signifies precisely the conjuncture of gender, community, and indigeneity with which the Bank wants to associate its "new" work. Critical readers, however, would be hard-pressed to find a more apt visual metaphor for the notion that the Bank's institutional transformation amounts to little more than a cosmetic makeover. The image's dehistoricized, decontextualized representational trope of enduring and unchanging native Otherness cuts against the celebration of plurality, difference, and "the local" implied by the mutability and performativity of the photo's painted face. Likewise (at least for those familiar with Bank history), the loud social-turn echoes of McNamara and the IDA drown out the brochure's claims of radical newness. Nevertheless, here as elsewhere, the Bank's claims of institutional transformation—persistent appeals to newness and change— become essential, even defining, elements of its public persona.

A differently inflected illustration of this trope of transformation is evident in Wolfensohn's response at a 2002 press conference, where the Bank president grouses that critics ought to "change their tune and tell us we haven't done enough on the next level of things that we are doing, rather than going back to things that were addressed five years ago and to which I think we have been particularly responsive."[13] Implicitly, Wolfensohn directs his audience to documents such as the "10 Things" brochure, asking that they read up on all the ways in which the Bank has worked to educate girls, to stop HIV/AIDS, to alleviate third-world debt, to expand biodiversity, and (particularly important in the context of this chapter) to strengthen its participatory dialogues with NGOs and civil society groups and to promote institutional openness, accountability, and transparency. Wolfensohn asks his audience to acknowledge the Bank's public abandonment of the term *structural adjustment* and the ten principles of the Washington consensus in favor of the "post–Washington consensus." In sum, he spotlights the Bank's willingness to accept critique and reform its policies and procedures accordingly.

This might all be read as signs of retreat and decline, even crisis—signs of an institution desperately trying to keep up with the times. Bank watchdog groups such as the Bretton Woods Project (www.brettonwoodsproject.org), Fifty Years Is Enough (www.50years.org), and the Bank Information Center (www.bicusa.org) will argue, however, that these new reforms represent but one more in a long line of rhetorical makeovers by the always-protean Bank, and that the core aspects of "Washington consensus" neoliberalism—liberalization, privatization, and fiscal austerity—remain at the heart of the Bank's new "poverty reduction" strategies, and continue to have devastating effects on the peoples of the underdeveloped world. I agree in large part. The Bank's central economic principles of liberalization, privatization, and austerity remain firmly in place, and the institution remains an enormously potent global-historical actor. Nevertheless, I take seriously the Bank's rhetoric of transformation. If the Bank has not yet been pressured into radical reform or relegated to obsolescence, its apparent need to systematically respond to opponents suggests that the institution recognizes its vulnerability to critique from below. A careful reading of the Bank documents from this era can tell us much about how the Bank understands the nature of that pressure and how it plans to react. In much the same way that Detroit was freighted with an excess of signification at mid-century, NGOs appear variously in these contemporary materials as audience, author, message, and participant. Not only does the rhetoric of transformation work to contain and diffuse particular critiques (in this case, from NGOs and civil society groups), such rhetoric also endeavors to alter the structural relationship between the Bank and its critics, thereby transforming the nature of the critique possible. Persuasion, after all, is a form of coercion.

In short, the World Bank's continued institutional authority along with the significance of its rhetorical maneuverings both contribute to a productive critical urgency that underpins Kumar's term *World Bank literature*. Indeed at the level of the symbolic, the struggle over signs and signifying practices, the Bank has never been more relevant—both as the world's preeminent development agency and as a galvanizing antagonist for radical social movement critique. We will now examine the ways an analytical distinction between rhetoric and literature may be of use in decoding the signifying practices of the Bank's public documents.

Success Stories

Kumar understands his collection's title to be "a provocation" rather than a category that assumes "a distinct referent."[14] I would like to explore a more specific application of the term *World Bank literature,* one that reads this term *both as a provocation and as a referential category*. To give the term *World Bank literature* a distinct referent is warranted, I believe, because, although the practice is not often noticed, the Bank has increasingly turned to literary narrative as a key element of its self-representational strategies.

This was no accident. In the mid-1990s the Bank hired media/marketing consultant Herb Schmertz to run its public relations campaign. Known for his aggressive media tactics in response to critics, Schmertz devised a substantial media campaign to counter the charges made in Rich's *Mortgaging the Earth*. This strategy is evident in the 1994 *World Bank: Current Questions and Answers* (the updated version of the booklet discussed in chapter 1), where entire sections are devoted to Rich's book with specific instructions about fending off critical questions from the media. Another key part of the public relations strategy was to "tell success stories from the field," which led to the Bank's publication of a press kit for its fiftieth anniversary that contained one hundred brief entries of successful Bank projects. (Although, as Catherine Caufield reports, these projects were not named or identified in ways that would allow researchers to independently evaluate the "success.") This practice continues today in printed brochures such as "The World Bank in Action: Stories of Development," which contains forty-eight short stories about, for instance, "How 'Bollywood' Music Videos are Boosting Literacy in India," "Educating Girls in Bangladesh," "Extending Credit to the Rural Poor of Vietnam," and "Gaza Water and Sanitation Services." In a slightly different vein, the Bank has published a two-volume set called *Voices of the Poor,* which collects an extensive set of interviews that chronicle "the struggles and aspirations of poor people for a life of dignity."[15]

Variations on the Bank success story have become so pervasive that it is possible to use the term *World Bank literature* to refer to a very specific genre of narrative promotional document. Consider, for example, InfoDev, the Bank's information technology division (www.infodev.org). Since 1999 (coincidentally, the year of the WTO protests in Seattle), InfoDev has sponsored a literary contest of its own called "ICT Stories," soliciting, judging, and publishing the most poignant success stories about local ICT (Information Communication Technologies) initiatives in the developing world.[16] The 2004 winners include stories about wiring rural villages in India, hybrid radio/Internet–projects in Nepal, and finally a dot-com sandal business in Nairobi, which can serve as a generic example for analytical purposes.

The ICT story, "Sole Comfort Dot-Com: Bridging the Global Income Gap through Hard Work, Quality Sandals, and ICTs," introduces us to Roselyne, a worker at the EcoSandals factory and a resident of the desperately poor Nairobi slum of Korogocho where the workshop is located:[17] "Two years ago, she would wake up each morning and set out in search of some way to earn money. . . . She never had formal employment and had little education. She really had nowhere to go and little to do but tried to achieve her singular goal each day, each week, each year: to find enough money to keep her family alive and, where possible, keep her five children in school." Not surprisingly the story narrates a transformation whereby hard work at EcoSandals changes Roselyne's life from a precarious struggle at the margins of subsistence to a life of fulfillment and growth. In fact, "Sole Comfort" narrates Roselyne's new life not as factory work, but rather as a creative contribution to the Internet community. Roselyne is figured as the paradigmatic digital worker, and the Bank gleefully exhibits the example of development-sponsored "immaterial labor."[18] The story recounts Roselyne's rags-to-riches tale as a metamorphosis, or perhaps *conversion*, into a global citizen (particularly given the word play in the story's title, one feels compelled to reference the long line of conversion narratives elicited by colonial missionaries, the original NGOs): "As orders increased and revenues jumped and an increasing number of people visited the Project's Korogocho workshop, individuals like Roselyne began to see their own lives in a different light. Roselyne, previously a mother of five children struggling to provide the basic necessities, became Roselyne the Webizen, an Internet user who designs and produces quality footwear products and markets them to other Internet users worldwide."

The Bank stories, as this example would indicate, often appear hackneyed. By and large, they have a strong bent toward the formulaic and the allegorical. Frequently they contain Horatio Alger–like parables about hard work, sweat, tears, innovation, a desire to succeed, much pulling up of bootstraps, and so on. Typically, too, the stories revolve around the generically mandated plot device of a loan and the subsequent "making good" on that loan. Narrative clichés notwithstanding, I find telling the centrality of a trope such as the emergence of the global citizen or Webizen. In a context where Bank lending is still funneled through the institutions of the nation state (witness the explicit national designation of each of the winning ICT stories: Nepal, India, Kenya, etc.) but the neoliberal economic principles of the Bank push toward deregulation and the opening of national borders to international imports, the Bank has substantial figurative and literal investment in the figure of the global citizen.

In the emergence or becoming of this figure, the paradigm of development through lending is reaffirmed time and again in the

Bank stories—development as bildungsroman. In many ways, "Sole Comfort" can be read as a traditional coming-of-age story of formation and education. Interestingly, this particular form of *bildung* may share more in common with some of the proletarian and socialist realism novels than with the classic bourgeois bildungsroman novels in that it eschews the internal psychological transformation of an individual subject in favor of something that appears like a concern for the fate of the worker and her place within the factory and the community. But an examination of the story as bildungsroman—particularly if understood as an extension, conscious or not, of a socialist literary form—enables us to identify more precisely what is being masked in the figure of Roselyne's education or formation into a Webizen. On the one hand, this is simply the valorization of global capitalism played out in the socialist setting of the factory floor. That is, EcoSandal's extraction of surplus value from wage workers like Roselyne, and the Bank's extraction of surplus value from EcoSandals or Kenya in the form of interest payments on loaned money, are here narrated as a story in which Roselyne's participation in the global circulation of commodities produces personal satisfaction and achievement: "As orders increased and revenues jumped . . . individuals like Roselyne began to see their own lives in a different light."

On the other hand, there is much at stake in the simple fact that the story, though apparently about Roselyne's transformation, implicitly casts the Bank in the role of hero–protagonist. It is after all the Bank, not a workers' revolution, that effects Roselyne's transformation. That is to say, we can read "Sole Comfort" as an autobiographical tale (again resonant with the bildungsroman tradition) by and about the World Bank. In this sense, it narrates a teacher/student story in the *Pygmalion* tradition, where education and progress ultimately come to be understood as dialogic and mutually enriching rather than pedantic or disciplinary. Here, both Roselyne and the Bank develop into global Webizens, the former through World Bank instruction and financing, the latter through cosmopolitan contact with the rich diversity of local cultures and peoples. With the question of digital access to communications technologies as its subtext, this story amounts in part to a digital-age updating of McCloy's argument that the Bank of the 1940s went "pioneering with a radio and a motion picture at hand."[19]

The irony that the Bank would choose to represent its work

through the character of a poor African working woman should not go unremarked. Cynthia Enloe's pointed (and poignant) question "Where are the women?" presses us to consider this educational tale in the context of the Bank's effect on women and girls. Enloe encourages scholars to look not only at the point of exploitation, but also at the broader social "combination of allies and ideas" that do the vigilant daily work of "keeping women's labor cheap."[20] One unfortunate limit of the current research project is that I am unable to develop the analytical roundness or depth that the best transnational feminist scholarship provides—for instance, about the specific working conditions at EcoSandals or the broader social constructions of gendered identification that help articulate Roselyne's subject position within the Korogocho slum of Nairobi.[21] Nevertheless, it is worth noting that representational practices do contribute to this vigilant, gendered policing of everyday life. And from its inception the Bank has represented its own work through the figures of women. Consider briefly the concluding image of Eugene Black's address to a group of investment bankers in 1947:

> Just at sunset on the last day of my tour of the Island [of Walcheren in Holland], I noticed imbedded in the great dunes along the shore, a number of grotesque masses of concrete—pill boxes and other fortifications that the Germans had build to protect themselves from an invasion by the Allies. In the doorway of one of these fortifications a Dutch woman (in the native Dutch dress) stood smiling and waved to us as we went by. Nearby the family wash was hanging on the line and off in the distance construction of hundreds of new houses was going on.
>
> That sight gave me a great feeling of inner satisfaction as I knew that I had contributed in a small way to obtaining the funds that were necessary to make that scene possible.[22]

In Black's argument about the value of international investment for European reconstruction, the native woman (Dutch here, Kenyan when extrapolated to the case of Roselyne) in her native dress becomes the public face of Bank lending. She figures normalcy, domesticity, and everyday life. Her very presence is a sign of health. To Enloe's question, "Where are the women?" the Bank responds, "See, they are here—everything will be fine."

But if the Bank's lending has worked to make everything fine for investment capital, the same cannot be said about its effect on women. In reading Roselyne's story and in analyzing the Bank's representational strategies in its depiction of native women, we should keep in mind the devastating impact that Bank policies have had on women and girls across the global south. Chandra Talpade Mohanty makes this point eloquently:

> In fundamental ways, it is girls and women around the world, es
> pecially in the Third World/South, that bear the brunt of globaliza-
> tion. Poor women and girls are the hardest hit by the degradation of
> environmental conditions, wars, famines, privatization of services
> and deregulation of governments, the dismantling of welfare states,
> the restructuring of paid and unpaid work, increasing surveillance
> and incarceration in prisons, and so on. And this is why a feminism
> without and beyond borders is necessary to address the injustices
> of global capitalism.[23]

The figure of Roselyne offers evidence that the Bank has heard this feminist critique. Part of its rhetoric of transformation has spot-lighted the Bank's extensive efforts to educate girls, as well as its institutional shift from a focus from "Women in Development" to "*Gender* and Development" in an attempt to better account for so-cial construction and performativity in gendered subjectivities and subjections.[24] But, although it is hard to argue against the principle of educating girls, it is important to ask how they are being edu-cated and what they are being educated for. The many examples of vast, Bank-funded "free trade zones" throughout the Global South ought to be enough to give us pause. The education of girls, and the efforts to free women from the allegedly nonproductive or *merely* reproductive realm of domestic "women's work," finds its class expression in the feminization and "third-worldization" of labor within the enormous garment and assembly factories that produce the bulk of the world's manufactured goods. I cannot speak with firsthand knowledge about the labor conditions in the Eco-Sandals factory. But the Bank's interest in narrating a story of education and formation that features an African woman as protagonist, and that is set in an NGO-sponsored micro-investment setting, ought to be read as a deliberate attempt to represent itself as an advocate for women's empowerment and an attempt to dispel its institution-al association with sweatshop labor.

Another important direction for an analysis of this sort is to examine the complex questions of authorship (and their necessary relationship to the equally complex questions of citizenship and personhood) that are raised by this reading of World Bank literature. To position "Sole Comfort" as a bildungsroman, and therefore in some kind of formal continuum with Goethe's *Wilhelm Meisters Lehrjahre,* Joyce's *Portrait of the Artist,* or Gladkov's *Cement* is to raise important questions about the status of the corporation or institution as author, citizen, and subject. Who authors this tale and what is being authorized? Although I have been calling this a World Bank story, in fact Becky Wachera and Matthew Meyer, the cofounders of EcoSandals, wrote the text itself. All of the ICT stories, for that matter, are written and submitted by people affiliated with Bank-funded NGOs or projects, rather than by the Bank itself (i.e., Bank *employees* whose intellectual property is contractually transferred to the institution). But, as the stories are written only for the Bank, are collected and posted only on the Bank's Website, and in effect function as a means of defining the function, scope, direction, and objectives of the Bank as an institution, the line between patron and author begins to blur (not to mention what happens with the slippages between patron and creditor). In effect we see the instantiation of the corporate author—corporate both in the sense of multipartied collaboration and in the sense of authorship by a financial corporation and in the direct interests of corporate capitalism. At stake here are a set of legal and philosophical issues about the degree to which authorship, citizenship, and subjectivity can be embodied by a corporation.[25] Although this admittedly brief treatment only alludes to the complexities of these questions of authorship, it is certainly worthwhile to reference stories such as "Sole Comfort" within the framework of legal rulings that grant corporations the rights of citizens in certain instances, and trade agreements, such as the Trade Related Intellectual Property Rights (TRIPS), that go to great lengths to extend protections ensuring the profitability of corporate-owned intellectual property exports, from modified genes to Hollywood blockbusters.[26]

Here we begin to see why the World Bank would like nothing more than to represent itself as a global Webizen with all the related rights that come with personhood and citizenship, but with obligations that can be refracted or deferred back onto individuals such as Roselyne, Becky Wachera, or Matthew Meyer. Of course, this opens up an important set of questions about the rhetorical analysis that I have presented throughout this study. I often refer to presidential remarks by Black, McCloy, McNamara, and so forth (even statements from Bank officials such as Ilif, Knapp, or Stern) as *representative of a World Bank position*—that is, as speaking for or on behalf of the institution. This functions to construct an imagined, coherent, *authorial* World Bank speaker, rather than a portrait of a necessarily schizophrenic organization being pulled and pushed by the individual subjects whose labor produces the World Bank as an organization (even as the institutional structures surely condition those individual subjects as well). Careful rhetorical analysis demands, then, that we inquire into whether, for example, the Black Founder's Day address to the University of Virginia that featured so prominently in the discussion (chapter 3) of nationalism constitutes an official World Bank position or simply Black's personal intellectual disposition. That said, Black's case involves an acting World Bank president, with enormous executive authority to direct the operations of his institution, speaking to a university audience in his official capacity as the head of the Bank. The distance in this case between individual and institution, though rhetorically significant, is miniscule when compared to the authorial diffusions and deflections enacted by the Bank-funded (and -scripted), NGO-written, ICT Stories. The contemporary moment still sees Bank presidents offering speeches, of course; but part of my argument in this chapter is to suggest that the ever-greater degrees of authorial mediation evident in the turn to Banking stories indicate a specific World Bank response to perceived pressure from external critique.

Tellingly, deferral itself is a frequent, perhaps defining, characteristic of the Banking tale. The success story is the requisite form of World Bank literature, but complete or total success stands necessarily outside the narrative form. Success as the end or closure of the romance is a generic and an institutional impossibility. The Banking bildung, though teleological at some level, demands the privileging and perpetuation of movement over and above closure. It has an address to a particular future, to be sure, but it projects that future based on the partial successes of the present; in other words, it isolates vectors of movement from the past to the present and narrates that movement as *progress*. Unqualified success would necessitate the narrative representation of an achieved *telos* of global development as a state rather than as a process, and thus the end of the development narrative. Instead, the Bank stories must figure success as partial, individual, and always precarious—minor, even miraculous, successes in the context of overwhelming conditions of failure. For instance, the sandal business, however proud it may be of its role in creating Roselyne the Webizen, must recognize that her newfound global citizenship does little to change the endemic poverty of Korogocho.

> If we started this Project in a perfect world, we would not need our Project. We have no real strategy to confront these problems in a long-term manner, except to continue being creative, committed, and having fun to try to solve them. We also hope, we dream, that somewhere among our sandal-makers, maybe just one among them, sits the person who will one day revolutionize the Kenyan exportation industry. Maybe just one sandal-maker will work up through our Project and become the telecommunications expert who transforms the Kenyan infrastructure. Perhaps just one of our current sandal-making trainees is going to somehow bring peace to the streets and alleyways of Korogocho. We see problems all around us, problems that caused the Project's founding seven years ago. But we also believe that the solutions may be among us.

Leaving aside the question of how peace might possibly stem from export or "tel-com" reforms, this admission of having "no real strategy" to address systemic poverty represents another structural requirement of the Banking tales. That is, the stories actively articulate the conditions for their reproduction. They must declare the possibility of success while still demonstrating the enormity of the task that remains ahead. And in doing so, they implicitly make the case for the necessity of perpetual World Bank involvement, all the while placing the full burden of finding solutions onto indebted workers in the South.

Roselyne is precisely the kind of worker whose *material* labor and class position in relation to production and the extraction of surplus value make it so difficult to imagine the new modes of resistance that Hardt and Negri describe in *Empire,* in which "each struggle, though firmly rooted in local conditions, leaps immediately to the global level and attacks the imperial constitution in is generality."[27] In a sense, this networked leap is what "Soul Comfort" narrates. Roselyne's communicative access to a networked community of global Webizens allows her to understand her own subjec-

tive transformation in terms that are immaterial and affective—
she comes to see her life in a "different light." Her wages from
EcoSandals likely provide her with some material benefits that aid
in her "singular goal" of keeping her family alive and her children
in school, but the broader logic of the story's denouement insists
that we accept personal comfort as broadened horizons, and forego thoughts of any systemic transformations entailing a radical redistribution of wealth. (In fact, we are told that EcoSandal's "revenues jumped," but learn nothing about whether Roselyne's salary
reflected that surplus.) *Empire*'s Deluezean appeal to the "communication of singularities"[28] would seem to describe Roselyne's conversion all too well. That is, the collectivity with which she identifies, the global Webizens, fosters only an affective change while
necessitating the abandonment of collectivities—class, place, gender, etc.—that might be capable of performing the slower, more
laborious work of organizing for material systemic change.[29]

Residual Formations

Let me step back briefly to clarify the way I am framing this analysis of World Bank literature. Certainly the Bank stories, the Bank
Website, even the Bank itself may be understood as *texts* or as *discourse*, and therefore available for critical interpretation of the sort
employed throughout the book. However, this does not, in and of
itself, address the question of genre, the question of the *literary-
ness* of World Bank literature. My concern in this chapter, therefore, has to do with what if anything may be gained analytically by
looking at a particular subset of the Bank materials as *literary* in a
stricter sense. At the risk of recanting what has become something
of a cultural studies truism, let me emphatically state that, in trying to give World Bank literature this distinct referent, my intention
is not to somehow isolate *the literary* as above or outside of "the
cultural," "the economic," or "the social." Quite the opposite. As I
implied earlier in pointing to the similarities between the Bank stories and socialist realism, literary form does not determine political
commitments. Rather, cultural practices emerge from particular
historical circumstances and are mobilized for particular political
purposes and with particular effects. To examine the specificity
of the literary in World Bank literature—to analyze the particular
rhetorical effects of texts that self-consciously signify as literary—
is to begin analyzing how the Bank stories function hegemonically:

that is, to begin reading the literary in World Bank literature as an active element, constituted by and constitutive of the contested claims issued by both dominant and subordinate social movements in their ongoing and multilayered struggles over the social sphere.

In asking why the Bank has chosen to adopt a self-consciously literary persona in so many of its promotional materials, then, I have found it useful to return to Raymond Williams's well-known distinction among dominant, residual, and emergent cultural formations.[30] Williams's account of culture as a complex, dynamic, active process argues against an "'epochal' analysis in which a cultural process is seized as a cultural system," in which dominant or hegemonic cultural forms are taken to represent the totality of a static historical/cultural moment. Although any cultural analysis must certainly account for the dominant, *no dominant social order ever in reality includes or exhausts all human practice, human energy, and human intention.*" Williams suggests the categories of *residual* and *emergent* as ways of accounting for certain alternative or oppositional cultural practices that have been excluded from the dominant, but that inevitably contribute to the actual hegemonic struggles and negotiations that define any cultural moment.

Most work in cultural studies that employs Williams's distinction has (understandably) concentrated on identifying and theorizing instances of emergence—those "new meanings and values, new practices, new relationships and kinds of relationships . . . which are substantively alternative or oppositional to [the dominant]." This may, however, be part of the reason why Williams's terminology is sometimes understood or applied in ways that are reductively schematic. As Michael Denning correctly observes about such scholarship, "[to] label a culture or subculture—rave, ethnic studies, or surfing—as alternative, oppositional, residual, or emergent was more subtle than praising or denouncing it as progressive or reactionary, but the logic was not dissimilar."[31] Williams, however, was keenly aware of the tendency of cultural critics to lionize instances of resistant practices, and is therefore at pains to clarify just how conceptually difficult it is to distinguish in any given moment between new or novel forms of the dominant culture and truly emergent practices, let alone between those emergent practices that are merely alternative (connoting difference without critique) and those that are oppositional (articulating a radical vision of a future in conscious opposition to the prevailing cultural dominant). He cautions, "Again and again what we have to observe is in effect a *pre-emergence,* active and pressing but not yet fully articulated, rather than the evident emergence which could be more confidently named."

Although much cultural studies scholarship, in its search for the new and the counterhegemonic, has focused on identifying instances of emergence—and the best of such identification accounts for the careful distinctions between alternative and oppositional, and is mindful of the impulse toward critical exuberance that Williams attempts to rein in through his insistence on the term *pre-emergence*—less attention has been paid to the implications of residual cultural forms and their complex relationship to the dominant social order. It is here, in the movement between dominant and residual, that I would locate the energies of World Bank literature.

Obviously, despite their apparent novelty as a genre, the ICT Stories are in no way emergent in Williams's sense. Foremost, these Bank stories must be read as dominant cultural practice; in its intimate relationship to neoliberal orthodoxy and global capitalism, World Bank literature offers almost unmediated access to the reigning ideas of this epoch's ruling class. Certainly the stories work to naturalize a very particular notion of development and to write the World Bank as the eternal protagonist of that narrative. Moreover, the stories offer little if anything in the way of formal innovation, relying instead on narrative realism, long the dominant literary mode of Euro-American modernity. In my reading of Williams's schema, however, the possibility remains open that a cultural practice may function simultaneously in more than one category. At the very least, Williams makes it clear that both emergent and residual forms are at any given moment always defined in response to, and must continually account for, the dominant social order; this intimate relationship frequently leads to their incorporation into the dominant. Whether we understand the Bank stories to function simultaneously as dominant and residual, or see them as residual forms that have been successfully incorporated into the dominant, the residual nature of World Bank literature needs to be accounted for.

In Williams's schema, *residual* implies the persistence of older traditions, values, and practices in contemporary life—religion, rural life, and the monarchy are Williams's primary examples. *Residual* is not the same as *archaic*, or a practice "wholly recognized as an element of the past." Rather the residual, for Williams, "has been effectively formed in the past, but it is still active in the cultural process, not only and often not at all as an element of the past, but as an effective element of the present." In one sense, then, the residual might be understood to represent the ways in which the conservative political power of nostalgia can be mobilized. Importantly, however, Williams applies the same subdistinction to residual forms that he does to emergent forms, arguing that the residual can also have either an alternative or oppositional relation to the dominant cultural paradigms.

My contention that these stories may function as residual in addition to dominant relies precisely upon a consideration of the specificity of literary form. One argument of this sort would see realism as waning in its generic dominance relative to postmodernism.[32] This line of reasoning would suggest that the realist bildungsroman structure of "Sole Comfort" harkens back to older narrative modes, and swims against the now dominant postmodern forms of multimedia hypertext, pastiche, surface without depth, and so on that have gained formal ascendancy on the World Wide Web, and in contemporary society more broadly. The crux of my assertion that World Bank literature is a residual form, however, is somewhat different. I am suggesting that *the literary* itself, even narrative realism, announces itself as ostensibly outside of, and prior to, what most would consider the dominant discursive mode of the Bank: the technocratic language of cost efficiency, statistics, and demographic analysis. Literature, that anachronistic form typically associated with troubadours and tweedy professors, apparently antithetical to the scientific, economic, modernizing presuppositions of the World Bank, taps into the residual desire for an ill-defined humanist appreciation for an Arnoldian conception of arts and culture,[33] with its corollary implications of individualist education, moral refinement, even a spiritual fulfillment of sorts (remember the allusion to Roselyne's conversion in "Sole Comfort"). That the residual may appeal to the personal, the private, the natural, or the metaphysical is not surprising; Williams says as much, indicating that these often appear to be the areas ignored by the dominant, "since what the dominant has effectively seized is indeed the *ruling definition of the social*. It is this seizure that has especially to be resisted" (emphasis mine).

What is most significant here is the way the Bank is able to place this ill-defined humanism into the service of a more sharply defined contribution to, or construction of, *the social* in the form of civil society. This is possible in part because civil society, NGOs, and not-for-profit groups also appeal to a notion of community that may be understood as residual—rhetorically invoking community as organic, natural, ante- and even anticapitalist. However, as Miranda Joseph has rigorously and convincingly demonstrated in her book *Against the Romance of Community*, this utopian promise of *community* is fully imbricated within—in fact, by Joseph's account functions as a Derridean "supplement" to—both capitalism and the modern liberal state by enabling the legitimization of exploitative social hierarchies.

In this context, then, we can read the stories as a more subtle articulation of the argument that Wolfensohn tries to make, at the press conference quoted earlier, when asked about the concerns of "the folks who are staging the rallies up the street this weekend." He responds:

> My short answer to them would be that we have come a hell of a long way; that the poverty reduction strategy programs include civil society more than they have ever dreamed of, officially, as part of the national process; that transparency has been enormously increased; that accountability has been enormously increased; country ownership has been enormously increased; that we are the people who have been leading the charge on trade and on debt relief. And I believe that there will always be a role for civil society to tell us that we haven't done enough, but I wish some of them would change their tune and tell us we haven't done enough on the next level of things that we are doing, rather than going back to things that were addressed five years ago and to which I think we have been particularly responsive.[34]

Note Wolfensohn's desire to collapse "those folks up the street staging rallies this weekend" into the containable category of civil society, conflating the Bank protestors with Bank-funded NGOs such as EcoSandals. Again, civil society here is imagined as an *outside* to the Bank, but an outside so diverse as to diffuse any

structural critique aimed at radical transformation rather than reform. Its role is to tell the Bank that they "haven't done enough"
rather than to question its fundamental premises or assumptions,
let alone to shut down its meetings, thwart its projects, or abolish
it altogether as an institution. Think back to the earlier discussion
about the particular form of corporate authorship evidenced in the
ICT Stories, whereby Bank-funded NGOs write not in the outsider role typically ascribed to civil society, but rather as organizations incorporated into, even at times metonymically figured as,
the Bank itself. A story such as "Sole Comfort" offers a published
account bolstering Wolfensohn's claims that the Bank is including
civil society "more than they ever dreamed of," that "actually, we
have helped them." The "we" and "them," which reiterate the con-
ventional understanding of inside/outside relationship for the Bank
and civil society, belie the ways the two support and sustain one
another. For the Bank, the category of civil society, with its address
to open, rational debate and dialogue, and its reliance upon romantic, residual notions of community, functions as a site of negotiation rather than one of critique or contestation. "Sole Comfort"
and the other Bank stories articulate a notion of the social that
casts the Bank not only as a committed partner, but importantly
as a contributing member of civil society. In seizing "the ruling
definition of the social" (to return to Williams's phrase) through
this construction of civil society, the stories work through a liberal logic of inclusion to contain the potentially radical energies of
protesters, energies that might produce a pre-emergent articulation
of the social through appeals toward democratic or anticapitalist
collectivities rather than toward a romanticized notion of community. And, perhaps because they are able to articulate this position
in a form not shaped by the agonistic setting of a press conference
where actual audiences might challenge a World Bank president,
they do so in a mode that appears more refined and less defensive
than Wolfensohn's "we have come a hell of a long way" remarks.

I read *the literary* in World Bank literature, then, as a conscious appeal to residual values and practices that appear alternative to—at times, even in opposition to—the dominant definitions
of development and global capitalism. That is, the residual here
functions largely, perhaps entirely, as rhetorical gesture; always already incorporated into the ruling logic of the dominant, the Bank
attempts to authorize its own work through an appeal to the al-

ternative residual values signified within the literary: values that
circumscribe the individual through an appeal to humanism, and
the social through an appeal to civil society; values that appear to
be outside of and prior to the dominant logic of global corporate
capitalism, but in fact serve to prop it up.

What is noteworthy about this argument is the way the residual
here marks a position of perpetual reaction, and reaction from very
different kinds of forces. The Bank's choice to adopt the residual
authority of literature as a principal form of self-representation illustrates not a position of creative security, but rather the degree to
which it finds itself, as an institution, in an embattled posture. On
the one hand we may read this return to the residual appeal of the
literary as a reaction to those forces of global corporate capitalism
that seem to have eroded some of the Bank's ability to orchestrate
the global financial system through its lending policies. Not an
institution that ever eschewed the motive of profit, the Bank has
nonetheless publicly maintained that philanthropy (another impulse that might be considered residual in the contemporary logic
of global corporate capitalism) is central to its mission. Might not
the new prominence of the literary, with its latent evocation of humanistic values, represent a rhetorical positioning of the Bank in
opposition to the purely profit-driven, dehumanizing ruthlessness
of global corporate capitalism?

More accurately, with the Bank attempting to position itself
in relation to transnational capital, the force against which the
Bank must react is "those folks up the street staging the rally":
the increasingly powerful critique directed against it by the network of alterglobalization social movements, of which the massive
demonstrations and *encuentros* in such places as Berlin, Madrid,
Chiapas, Seattle, Quebec City, Geneva, Prague, Porto Alegre,
Cancun, and Mumbai are only the most visible signs. Although
these gatherings are subject to critiques that point to the political
limits of "open spaces for dialogue" where a group of elite NGOs
(perhaps including EcoSandals), intellectuals, and disaffected but
economically comfortable youth meet for what at times seem like
global multicultural festivals,[35] the alterglobalization social movements have, I would maintain, at their core radical democratic and
anticapitalist energies that cannot be reduced to civil society in
the ways that Wolfensohn and the Bank would prefer. Although
the alterglobalization movement is certainly susceptible to the

romance of community that Joseph so astutely critiques, the collectivities produced and mobilized by this movement are not necessarily, and certainly not always, reducible to either civil society or community.

In the context of this chapter, however, it is worth briefly noting the importance and diversity of arts and creative expression within this alterglobalization "movement of movements"[36]: street puppets and street theater, music festivals that do more than provide a soundtrack for the World Social Forum or the Reclaiming Our Streets gatherings, visual arts projects (from the photography of Sebastião Salgado to the murals and graffiti on the walls of Porto Alegre and Mumbai), the innumerable video projects including those that emerge from the ever-expanding Indymedia network, and, especially pertinent to a discussion of World Bank *literature,* the centrality of an eclectic array of literary figures including Arundhati Roy, Mahaswetu Devi, Dennis Brutus, Nawal El Saadawi, Jose Saramago, Eduardo Galeano, and Subcomandante Marcos who marshal the literary in a very different manner than what we have seen the Bank do. "Sole Comfort" reads differently when mapped in relation to a cultural landscape where João Pedro Stedile of the Brazilian Movimiento Sem Terra (MST, or Landless Workers Movement) credits the photography of Salgado for giving "the Sem Terra Movement a global visibility in the field of the arts," and where, in response to a question about the funding sources of Narmada Bachao Andolan (NBA, or the Save Narmada Movement—which succeeded in forcing the World Bank to withdraw funding from the Sardar Sarovar dam project on India's Narmada River), Chittaroopa Palit quickly singles out Roy as someone who has "consistently supported us through her writings."[37] (I take up Roy's literary contributions in the following chapter, and the alterglobalization movement, especially in the form of the World Social Forum, in chapter 7.)

Instructive Critique

Within the framework of this argument that the Banking stories function as residual cultural forms in reaction to the pressures of both global capital and alterglobalization social movements, we can begin to address the question of audience and the more particular aspects of how and why World Bank literature performs the work of development. In some small way, of course, the tales might function as "best practices" or "how to" manuals for an audience composed of those nation states (or, more likely, NGOs) looking to borrow funds. But surely this explanation is insufficient. That the stories are only published in English is but one rather obvious means of discounting hopeful loan recipients in the South as a primary audience for the Bank's literary experiments.[38] And although the NGOs that may be applying for Bank funds are an important group, they would not seem to merit the extraordinary amount of public relations work (of which the success stories represent a not insignificant portion) that goes into producing what may be thought of as the World Bank *brand*.[39] It would appear, then, that the stories address an audience beyond potential borrowers. However, despite my earlier argument that World Bank literature should be read as a reaction to both global capitalism and alterglobalization movements, it would be presumptuous to suggest that the Bank's primary audiences are either corporate CEOs or the indigenous rights advocates, landless peasants, labor organizers, anarchist groups, environmentalists, human rights activists, and other actors that collectively make up the alterglobalization movement.

Who, then, does constitute the audience for these Bank-branded tales? A second unsatisfying, if somewhat more provocative, answer to the question of audience is that the stories exist on the Web in this form simply to interrupt what would otherwise be an unbearable silence. World Bank literature, especially as it exists on the Web, is the byproduct of a digital media environment in which one of the primary expectations is simply presence. Although the bulk of the Bank's enormous Website says very little of substance, imagine how loudly the silence would speak if there were no Website at all. In part, this is the very logic of branding, where the construction of a saleable public image becomes more important than, or at least can develop independently from, the actual products being sold. In addition, this question of silence should perhaps be understood in relation to the rhetoric of openness and transparency so often celebrated by both the Bank and its critics. The Bank, again in response to sustained critique, has at least gestured toward the goal of making its practices transparent for public scrutiny. It would seem, then, that for the Bank silence reads as opaque and inscrutable, whereas the literary reads as transparent, open, intelligible. This may at first appear antithetical to the way literary scholars like to understand the complexity of the texts they study, and therefore the essential role of interpretation in making sense of the deeply ambiguous literary object. But a closer look reveals that, although in one sense the Bank turns to the literary for apparent transparency, precisely the deeply ambiguous and layered production of this "realism" or rendering of "the everyday" makes the form such a potent hegemonic vehicle for the Bank. It is not only that the stories say nothing (which they do), or say something (which they do, as well), but also, as we have seen, that they say it in a way that produces authority while deferring and deflecting accountability precisely through the evocation of fictiveness.

A final speculation that I shall pursue here returns us to Kumar's point of departure: the World (Bank) literature course. It also returns us to an examination of bildungsroman as the preferred literary form of the Banking stories. I would like to suggest that the use of stories on the Bank's site is in no small part a pedagogical exercise, that Bank-brand development sells best when it is peddled through the other ideological apparatuses that work to reproduce a capitalist "ruling definition of the social"—most notably the school. It is no coincidence, certainly, that the Bank devotes huge sections of its Website to educational materials; the KidsDev Newsletter and the Learning and Knowledge sections of the Bank site contain enormous amounts of World Bank information explained through highly accessible prose and graphics. Geared most specifically toward students, the Web pages go so far as to include full course units for teachers to download, complete with quizzes, worksheets, and more. World Bank literature, then, functions as a core element within the Bank's extensive commitment to education, which in turn must be understood as an ideological cornerstone in the production of neoliberal globalization hegemony. In effect, the stories render education fully within the sphere of, perhaps even synonymous with, the ruling ideas of neoliberalism and development.[40]

Here again we can glimpse why the Bank sees such value in the literary form of bildungsroman. On the surface, the Banking bildungsroman tracks the education and formation of citizens from countries within the underdeveloped world, such as Roselyne's transformation into a Webizen. But as I am suggesting in these remarks about audience, the stories as a whole serve the broader function of *educating the rulers, not the ruled.* As a key component in the process of building the Bank brand, the stories' residual appeal to the literary is aimed to produce an audience defined by a consumer identity that imagines itself as responsive to "the local" in ways understood to be alternative or in opposition to global capital. "Sole Comfort," for example, is among other things, an advertisement for both EcoSandals and the Bank that targets the liberal, socially conscious consumer in the overdeveloped world, the consumer who might choose to buy a pair of pair of "locally made," "ecologically sound," African sandals from Roselyne's Korogocho workshop, rather than a similar pair of "faceless," sweatshop-produced shoes sold at Wal-Mart. Here we begin to unpack one aspect of the *liberal* in *neoliberalism,* and to see the obvious limits of resistance through commodity consumption (as well as the obvious appeal of such a construction for the Bank). I do not, however, mean to be entirely disparaging in this portrait; I count myself among those who avoid Wal-Mart shopping for just such reasons. But as Spivak (among others) has repeatedly implored us,[41] we must doggedly and self-critically interrogate the ethical complexities involved in the global circulation of capital, labor, and commodities, and we must recognize our own inevitable participation and complicities within these exchanges if we are to be politically effective in the long run. It is this very complicity, textualized in the narrative attempt to incorporate the residual alternative into the dominant, that marks the principal authority of World Bank literature. The Banking bildungsroman announces itself as consistent with, in fact constitutive of, the development of the ethically refined, socially conscious, liberal, global citizen—a citizen who is figured by a character from the Global South but who is more likely embodied by the consenting, consuming subject in the overdeveloped North. Character, author, and reader are all rendered as developing, but developing along entirely different vectors, each of which sustains and protects the central precept of development itself, and therefore the eternal role of the World Bank.

Here again, the complexities contained within the term World Bank literature, both as provocation and as referent, come to the fore. As do certain pedagogical imperatives and opportunities. To examine the privatization and corporatization of the contemporary transnational corporate research university is to see that World Bank literature has already been structurally incorporated into all levels of "public" education. Moreover, to read World Bank literature in its specificity is to see how the Banking bildungsroman is crafted with the pointed objective of seizing the very realm of education itself. In teaching World Bank literature, we are forced to invite the fox into the henhouse. Potentially we provide access to—perhaps even help to produce—an audience of liberal, socially conscious consumers that the Bank appears to be targeting. But to avoid teaching and writing about World Bank literature is to neglect the henhouse entirely, to presume that the foxes are either irrelevant or too numerous and tenacious to thwart. Kumar's insightful substitution of World Bank literature for world literature is useful precisely because it highlights pedagogy as a crucial site of hegemonic struggle. To teach World Bank literature, therefore, requires that we read carefully the contradictions and complexities inherent in its use of *the literary* and those undergirding categories of *global citizen* and *civil society*. Such teaching will also necessitate a redoubled effort to theorize aspects of the alterglobalization movements as pedagogical in nature, as well—potentially pre-emergent, potentially complicit, certainly having to make their way in a cultural dominant at least partially defined by the Bank. Both as a provocation and as a referent, Kumar's analytical category enables us to examine and critique the institutions of literature in ways that reveal new aspects of the cultural dominant (the nature of corporate globalization and of the Bank itself), the residual (in the form of the Bank's recurrent appeal to literary narrative in its documents), and the potentially pre-emergent and oppositional (in the practices of the alterglobalization movement against which the Bank must respond). Moreover, Kumar's phrase makes evident connections among these various institutions, forms, practices, and movements, as well as their intimate relationship to education and the disciplinary assumptions and practices of literary and cultural studies. Precisely because of this multilayered address to the contemporary moment and to the historical process involved in producing this moment, the category World Bank literature remains provocatively instructive.

6. Literary Movements: Impossible Collectivities in *The God of Small Things*

Permit me an excursus that returns us to the register of *the literary,* though from a somewhat different analytical frame than in the previous chapter. For the moment, I shall move the World Bank to the narrative periphery, in order to take up Arundhati Roy's 1997 Booker Prize–winning novel *The God of Small Things* as a means of thinking through the cultural politics of reading at the intersection of the World Bank, the World Social Forum, and the literary.[1]

Why turn to *GOST* and a more straightforward mode of literary analysis now, so near this book's end? At the surface level of biography, the enormous successes of *GOST,* as well as of Roy's subsequent books of nonfiction essays including *The Cost of Living* (1999), *Power Politics* (2001), *War Talk* (2003), and *An Ordinary Person's Guide to Empire* (2004), position her among the most prominent contemporary public intellectuals working within the movement for global justice and solidarity. Of particular relevance is Roy's close association with the World Social Forum (detailed in the following chapter). My objective at present is to read Roy's novel, *GOST,* with an eye toward literary and cultural politics in the contemporary historical moment. If the previous chapter suggested that the World Bank attempted to marshal the literary by tapping into a residual Arnoldian aura of *arts and culture,* with its corresponding values of civility, this chapter attempts to read the literary object—Roy's critically acclaimed, frequently taught, and widely sold novel—outside the distinctions of high and low, elite and popular.

I take my cues, here, from Michael Denning's claim that "mass culture has won. . . . All culture is mass culture under capitalism,"[2] as well as from Terry Eagleton's reminder, "Those radicals for whom high culture is ipso facto reactionary forget that much of it is well to the left of the World Bank. It is not on the whole the content of such culture that radicals should complain [about], but its function."[3] Although the present book has argued that, when pressed, the World Bank has often situated itself further to the Left than many straw-man arguments such as Eagelton's give it credit for, I nevertheless take his point. Merely reading Roy's novel as a novel, at once a favorite of the elite canon-setting academy and a successful mass-marketed commodity skillfully released during the fiftieth anniversary of India's independence, does little to reveal its political force. The more pressing question is one of function; what work does this text do, and what work can be accomplished through the act of interpretation? Rather than merely searching for subversiveness or critiquing complicity, this chapter is an attempt to analyze how *GOST* functions as a contemporary intervention into the intellectual and political currents that we have been tracing. That is, the chapter attempts to place Roy into a continuum with some of the midcentury cultural radicals including Césaire, Fanon, and Wright, situating the text in relation to New Left critiques of Marxism, to World Bank–sponsored development, and in particular to the problematic of constructing productive collectivities.

Spivak's shorthand distinction between philosophy and literature is suggestive in this context: "the first concatenates arguments," she writes, "and the second *figures the impossible*" (my emphasis).[4] Little wonder, then, that movements rallying behind the slogan "Another World Is Possible" would find the literary register so compelling. Although at first glance the WSF slogan appears to be at odds with Spivak's definition of literature, they are in fact obverse sides of the same utopian desire to probe at cracks or contradictions in the present social order so as to imagine alternative futures. Undoing the hegemony of TINA (There Is No Alternative) by imagining possible worlds that might emerge from the material social conditions of the present recurs as an insistent refrain unifying many otherwise divergent materials written or presented about the WSF as a cultural/political phenomenon. As Eagleton rightly reminds us in a recent book review, imagination itself does not necessarily correspond to progressive utopian desire (the imaginative Banking stories we examined in chapter 5 illustrate as much), but attempts to figure the impossible will at the very least avoid the delusional logic underlying any fantasies about a so-called end of history: "The future may or may not turn out to be a place of justice and freedom; but it will certainly disprove the conservatives by turning out to be profoundly different than the present. In this sense, it is the hard-nose pragmatists who behave as though the World Bank and caffe latte will be with us for the next two millennia who are the real dreamers, and those who are open to the as yet unfigurable future who are the true realists."[5] Eagleton's argument—particularly apt given the veritable moat of Starbucks coffee shops that encircle the Bank's headquarters at 1818 H Street in D.C.—reminds us that, although imagining other worlds is not in and of itself the marker of a progressive politics, no politics that aspires to ideals such as justice and freedom can avoid laboring to *figure the impossible*. To no small degree, this utopian construction of "realism" explains why the Social Forum has so eagerly embraced literary figures like Roy, and why Roy, in turn, has been so enthused about the prospects of an institution like the WSF.

Big Things

Roy has famously called Kerala home to "four of the world's greatest religions: Christianity, Hinduism, Marxism, and Islam," and one would be hard-pressed to locate anything sympathetic in Roy's representation of the Communist Party.[6] Marxism in the novel is roughly synonymous with a hypocrisy spoken with the conviction of communalist fervor. Chief among the sloganeers is the irredeemable character of Comrade K. N. M. Pillai, the dogmatic local organizer for Kerala's Communist Party of India (Marxist), or CPI(M), whose house is adorned with a plaque that boldly pronounces, "Work is Struggle, Struggle is Work" (254). Pillai is described as a "professional omeletteer," all too willing to break eggs in the name of "Inevitable Consequences of Necessary Politics" (15). When informed by the police inspector about the charges of rape and kidnapping leveled against Velutha, Pilllai refuses to intervene on behalf of the devoted Party worker despite knowledge of Velutha's innocence, all too eager to sacrifice a "Tribal" if it will help party organizing and, more pointedly, his own political ambitions. In Pillai's implicit sanction of police violence, Roy illustrates the complex stratification of power in the town.

Although Velutha is accused of rape, kidnapping, and murder by Mammachi and Baby Kochama, his "real crime" lies in violating the "Love Laws," Roy's shorthand for the conventions and apparatuses surrounding race, gender, caste, class, and the like that work to reproduce the social order by dictating "who should be loved. And how. And how much" (33). Committed to dismantling the unjust Love Laws, Velutha defends himself by citing the protection of the labor laws—a product of the CPI(M)'s political clout in Kerala—that give him rights as a worker that trump his status as a Paravan: "The days are gone . . . when you can kick us around like dogs" (246). It is the labor laws, not the Love Laws, that take priority in the eyes of the police force. Pillai's Janus-faced betrayal of Velutha undoes this secular political order, however. His sanction of police violence against a fellow comrade, presumably because Velutha's caste makes him both socially expendable and politically useful, indicates Pillai's unprincipled Marxism, his personal ambition, and/or his supplication to local custom and the metaphysical principles upon which the caste system is based. By proxy, then, the transcendent authority of the Love Laws, not the immanence of labor law, guides the police action, once sanctioned by Pilai.

On the one hand, then, Marxism in *GOST* is reduced to the emptiness of mantra-like slogans: "Another religion turned against itself" (272), Roy despairs. On the other, Marxism is reduced to Party politics and the corrupt exercise of power for personal gain. Here, Pillai is no different from the police inspector. Both are "Men without curiosity. Without a doubt. Both in their own way truly, terrifyingly adult. They looked out at the world and never wondered how it worked, because they knew. *They* worked it. They were mechanics who serviced different parts of the same machine" (248). The novel, therefore, offers a stinging version of a relatively familiar New Left critique of Party bureaucratization and corruption layered atop the determinism of orthodox Marxism. In the image of a Party chairman and a police inspector as twinned technocrats, *GOST* bemoans the fact that even the absolutes of Marxism corrupt absolutely when granted political power. Likewise, the novel elaborates the classically culturalist argument that the power relations of race, gender, caste, religion, and the like cannot be adequately explained or addressed as superstructural expressions of capitalist class relations: that caste is not class. The idealized, unblemished Velutha is the only character in the novel untouched by critique, and Roy seems convinced that the tragedy of his individual story will be swept aside and covered up by the grand narrative of Marxism, depicted as unable to account for the specific local needs, desires, contingencies of the individual. Even though hardly the first such critique, Roy's rebukes are particularly caustic, coming, as they do, from the state of Kerala, one of the few relative "success stories" of "actually existing socialism" in terms of relative rates of wealth redistribution, education, nutrition, life expectancy, and the like. If, as Denning curiously suggests, Roy is the "contemporary English-language inheritor of the Marxist traditions of India's Kerala,"[7] she remains deeply wary of that legacy in *GOST*.

Before returning to the question of *figuring the impossible* and the imagined construction of a collectivity that can somehow embrace and foster the creative, affirming individualism that Roy rebukes Marxism for ignoring, I would like to devote some specific attention to the novel's critique of development and the World Bank, a critique that, as I have mentioned, shares much in common with the novel's depiction of Marxism. For Roy, Marxism and the World Bank share the hubris of a totalizing vision that functions to obscure individual suffering behind a teleological narrative of progress. But whereas Marxism in the novel has a quaint, at times humorous, archaism about it, the World Bank (as we have seen repeatedly throughout this book) stands as a metaphor for the ruthless efficiency and conceptual murkiness of "new times."[8] The novel, however, resolutely refuses any Manichean third worldist critique that might consider Marxism and World Bank development simply as two variants of Western imperialist ideologies that have undermined and degraded an idealized notion of "local" Indian culture. Instead, World Bank–sponsored development is placed alongside Marxism in the novel's most disparaging category, "Big Things," joined both by imported grand narratives such as colonialism and Christianity, and endogenous variants of patriarchy, racism, and communalism. In some ways, Roy offers a Fanonian critique of foreign domination that operates with the full sanction and collaboration of local elites, overlaid with a psychological portrait (reminiscent of Albert Memi as well as Fanon) depicting an Indian colonial legacy that has, in Chacko's words, "made us adore our conquerors and despise ourselves" (52). But, in contrast to Fanon's work, in Roy's novel the sides of domination and resistance are never entirely clear.

Fanon's famous critique of Marxism in *The Wretched of the Earth* attempts to recast the base/superstructure metaphor by suggesting the foundational status of race in the colonies: "When you examine at close quarters the colonial context, it is evident that what parcels out the world is to begin with the fact of belonging to or not belonging to a given race, a given species. In the colonies the economic substructure is also a superstructure. The cause is the consequence; you are rich because you are white, you are white because you are rich. This is why Marxist analysis should always be slightly stretched every time we have to do with the colonial problem."[9] As we saw in chapter 4, this revision of Marxist thought, in one form or another, underpins much of the work that has come to be known as cultural studies. But race, as it is understood in the context of this passage, uses the biological language of "species" to talk about a distinction that is at core geographical and political. In the revision of Marxism that Fanon proposes here, race is a product of imperialist exploitation, and therefore maps starkly onto divisions of black and white, colonized and colonizer. If Marxism needs to be revised to account for race as a structural component of society in the colonies, the lines of exploitation remain clear for Fanon and the root of the problem lies in the imperialist violence of Europe.

For Roy, conversely, root causes are never so starkly delimited. Her reading of the neoimperialist intervionism of the World Bank remains sharply critical, but with an unwavering attention to the logical fallacy of *post hoc, ergo propter hoc* ("after this, therefore because of this"). The novel works insistently to undermine any attempts to read race and racism in India as straightforward products of colonial exploitation. Rather, Roy maintains that, if anything, patriarchy, caste, racism, and the various measures of social hierarchy that have stratified the subcontinent for millennia may actually provide the base onto which more recent foreign impositions of authority have been grafted. This reversal of a Fanonian, anti-imperialist rendering of base/superstructure is emblematized by the novel's discussion of how to read its own historical narrative or, more precisely, where to begin telling the story:

So to say that it all began when Sophie Mol came to Ayemenem is only one way of looking at it.

Equally, it could be argued that it actually began thousands of years ago. Long before the Marxists came. Before the British took Malabar, before the Dutch Ascendency, before Vasco de Gama arrived, before the Zamorin's conquest of Calicut. Before three purple-robed Syrian bishops murdered by the Portuguese were found floating in the sea, with coiled sea serpents riding on their chests and oysters knotted in their tangled beards. It could be argued that it began long before Christianity arrived in a boat and seeped into Kerala like tea from a teabag.

That it really began in the days when the Love Laws were made. The laws that lay down who should be loved, and how.

And how much. (32–33)

Roy's attempt to narrate the Bank's role in Kerala begins from a similar premise; though the Bank's arrival would certainly fit neatly into the list of devastating foreign interventions in Indian history, those moments of imperialist contact ought properly to be read as building upon, and working in concert with, a residual set of cultural practices based on the exclusions and exploitations of race, gender, caste, and the like.

Therefore, when Roy drops an offhanded reference to the Bank hardly ten pages into the novel, her explicit naming of that institution serves as a marker not only for contemporaneity, foreign exploitation, and the ravages of global capitalism (which it certainly does), but also for the ways in which the "new times" of Bank-sponsored development build seamlessly on—offer an extension and intensification of—the longstanding abuses of individuals at the hand of Big Things. "Some days," Roy writes, Estha "walked along the banks of the river that smelled of shit and pesticides bought with World Bank loans. Most of the fish had died. The ones that survived suffered from fin-rot and had broken out in boils" (14). Although the World Bank made agricultural loans to India as early as 1949, the presence of the Bank in this passage is undoubtedly meant to alert us that we are in the contemporary moment of 1990s globalization, marking the stark temporal break between the narrative time of Rahel's and Estha's childhood and the narrative present, twenty-three years later, when the twins have returned to their familial house in Ayemenem. Signaling contemporaneity, then, the Bank is linked to the severe degradation of the river's ecology, human and nonhuman alike, with parallels drawn between the abused and neglected environment and the twins' psychological condition, their emotional "fin-rot and boils." Although the Bank may function as a signifier of "new times," its presence registers more as a symptom of larger historical forces (Big Things) than as an isolatable, determinative cause. The river itself is a free flowing, living, dynamic force in the earlier narrative, but the fetid, stagnant state of the transformed river serves as an apt metaphor for the social setting that characterizes the Ayemenem of the twins' childhood, as much as for a newly repressive World Bank era; the social constraints of gender, caste, religion, race, and class stymie the movement, freedom, and growth of virtually every character in the novel, producing untold variants of "fin-rot" in those few who survive the small town. In other words, the transformations of Ayemenem, figured by the presence of the Bank, speak as much to the legacies of its past as to the arrival of new restrictive forces.

Not cast as a villainous agent of neocolonialism (or rather, not *only* as that), the World Bank is understood as one strand within a densely woven tapestry of internal and external forces contributing to the "production of locality"[10] in Roy's contemporary Ayemenem. Roy's insistence on specifying the World Bank by name does serve to underscore the ways that Bank lending is frequently structured precisely to deflect accountability and culpability away from the funding organization and onto inadequacies of local project design or implementation. But implicit in Roy's critique is a Fanonian condemnation of both Bank lending and local self-interested applications of its funds. It is the "influential paddy-farmer lobby" (never explicitly tied to the Bank) that dams the river to regulate salinity levels: "now they had two harvests a year instead of one. More rice, for the price of a river" (118). Although providing a presumed critique of the World Bank, Roy devotes her most scathing and cynical language to the local elites who selfishly profit from the direct exploitation of both the environment and the poor. The dominant features of the river's new geography become the rice farmers with their dams and pesticides downstream, the industrialists dumping untreated factory waste into the river upstream, and, just across from Ayemenem on the site of the History House where so much of the action is set, the five-star hotel chain *God's Own Country* selling commodified simulacra of Kerala culture, tradition, and heritage to rich tourists.

Literary Politics

Roy's novel not only illustrates but also performs the double bind of representing an antiglobalization critique. On the one hand, it desperately strives to make visible the environmental devastation and human suffering behind the polished façade of development; on the other hand, the metaphors announce their own inadequacies for carrying such a heavy burden. Again and again, the images that would appear to unmask such violence reveal themselves to be fully part of the development lexicon, and therefore impoverished or invisible as a site of critique.

We can read Roy's before-and-after comparison of the transforming river, for instance, as a literary response to Conrad's depiction of the venerable old river Thames at the beginning of *Heart of Darkness*, the classic developmentalist narrative of colonialism to which *GOST* persistently alludes. Conrad's stately, mature river represents civilization's apex, the *telos* of a Hegelian historical arc that traces the sun's progress from East to West: "The old river in its broad reach rested unruffled at the decline of day, after ages of good service done to the race that peopled its banks, spread out in the tranquil dignity of a waterway leading to the uttermost ends of the earth."[11] Roy's river, on the other hand, commands none of the respectful stature that Conrad attributes to age: "Once it had the power to evoke fear. To change lives. But now its teeth were drawn, its spirit spent. It was just a slow, sludging green ribbon lawn that ferried fetid garbage to the sea. Bright plastic bags blew across its viscous, weedy surface like subtropical flowers (119)." The "broad reach" of this dammed and polluted river, choked with weeds and garbage, shows none of the "tranquil dignity" of old age. Rather, it evinces the "fetid" and "sludging" horrors of aging, when body and mind fail piteously. In Roy's clear-eyed antidevelopment image, the river's wretched condition is not the result of natural maturation or inevitable decline: its precipitous devolution and decay can be traced directly to abuse and neglect at the hands of greedy developers such as the World Bank, the paddy farmers, the industrialists, and the resort ownership. If, as I argued above, Roy's metaphor of stagnation applies equally to past and present conditions in the novel, and her insistence upon the shared culpability of local actors and institutions works to destabilize any simplistic anticolonial or anti-imperial critique of outside interventionism, still there is no such ambiguity about the novel's indictment of capitalist development as the principal force behind the river's speedy decay.

If we are to read *GOST* as (among other things) a form of literary activism, we should probably look to locate the novel's political force in its *representation* of, in this instance, the abuses of capitalist development. That is, a literary politics relies to great extent upon representational practices that presume a latent potential in the visualization of the image; this is why so many terms of literary analysis rely on visual metaphor: portray, depict, figure, examine, bring to light, etc. To represent an object, to *depict* it, is to make that object visible, to expose its true or essential nature. A literary representational politics (representation still in the sense of "speaking of," not "speaking for" as might an elected representative) works on the premise that making certain truths visible will produce the appropriate political response from readers.[12] The ecological devastation wrought by capitalists on the ravaged river would appear a case with irrefutable, empirical evidence of misuse—evidence that, if unveiled, ought to produce outrage and action. Certainly, this is one of many instances where Roy's novel relies upon the power of representation to advance a critique of development (in its foreign–local partnerships), environmental degradation, and, more generally, those Big Things that dominate the novel's action. Exposing the oppressions of the caste system ought to help dismantle the caste system; exposing the misogynist underpinnings of marriage traditions ought to help bring about gender equity.

However, here, as elsewhere in the book, Roy seems to make visible not only the failures of Big Things, but also the limits of representation itself and of literary politics based in the logic of visibility. For example, Roy's simile in the passage above, which likens the nonbiodegradable plastic bag to a subtrobical flower, contains within it the seed of doubt. Suggesting that even the river's wrecked ecology might have a certain beauty if glimpsed in the right light or at the right angle (perhaps by an opportunist politician, by the foreign and incomprehending eyes of a World Bank mission, or even by a novelist looking for beauty amidst the ruin), Roy seems to acknowledge that the correspondence between visual exposure and public action offers, at best, an uncertain vehicle for political change. In part, of course, this speaks to the ambiguities involved with interpretation, the excess of meaning within any image that no author or producer can fully harness or contain. Comments that Roy has made in interviews would suggest that she embraces this ambiguity, and, moreover, sees it as one of the principal advantages that literature, novelistic writing specifically, holds over other representational forms, going so far as to suggest that the multiplicity of interpretive possibilities left open by literary writing enable the reader (as opposed to a filmic spectator) to engage in a democratic form of meaning-making.[13] In discussing why she has refused to turn the novel into a film, Roy has stated that she "set out to write a stubbornly visual but unfilmable book," and that it "would be a pity, don't you think, to let a single film-maker extinguish and appropriate all those [multiple readings], and force-fit them into a single, definitive one. This decentralised democracy is fine by me."[14] Likewise, Roy has repeatedly declared that she will work as an activist in support of Dalit rights, or with the NBA for water rights, but that she does not speak for these groups.[15] Given her scathing critique of representational politics ("speaking for"), in the form of the Marxist government's willing sacrifice of Velutha, this argument about the decentralizing democratic potential of literary representation is revealing.

But if the inherent openness and multiplicity of meaning in any image indicates a democratic possibility within literary representation, Roy nevertheless draws attention to a corresponding crisis of representation: the gap between interpretation and action. Although there is a celebration in the novel of the openness and playfulness of "stubbornly visual" literary language, there is a simultaneous malaise that accompanies the visual image in Roy's work. In a hypermediated world, the image, whether literary or cinematic, has lost its power to shock, to truth-tell (if it ever had such power). Reading Roy, one senses a deep nostalgia for the modernist faith in the transformative image, missing, however, the assured conviction of a Brecht or a Césaire in the latent political potential of the arresting power of language. Even though Roy argues that the literary figure may be more capable of evoking feeling than the cinematic image, neither seems fully capable of shouldering the burden of political action. The images of GOST may be able to truth-tell—to unveil or make visible an inequity or an injustice—but they also acknowledge the inadequacy of such an

act. The troubling gap between awareness and transformative action remains unresolved. The novel's visual "stubbornness," then,
stems in part from its persistent reliance on the image despite this
shaken conviction about its potency.[16]

For example, to return to Roy's depiction of life along the ir-
reversibly polluted river, the immiseration of human lives would
appear impossible to ignore given Roy's bleak description:

> On the other side of the river, the steep mud banks changed abrupt-
> ly into low mud walls of shanty hutments. Children hung their
> bottoms over the edge and defecated directly onto the squelchy,
> sucking mud of the exposed riverbed. The smaller ones left their
> dribbling mustard streaks to find their own way down. Eventually,
> by evening, the river would rouse itself to accept the day's offerings
> and sludge off to the sea, leaving wavy lines of thick white scum in
> its wake. Upstream, clean mothers washed clothes and pots in un-
> adulterated factory effluents. People bathed. Severed torsos soap-
> ing themselves, arranged like dark busts on a thin, rocking, ribbon
> lawn. (119)

The wealth of the rice farmers, factory owners, and resort opera-
tors stands in obvious juxtaposition to impoverished communities
scratching out a diseased subsistence on the banks of the polluted
river. Inequity remains the dominant feature of the social landscape
in Kerala, despite Communist Party of India schemes of wealth redistribution. Part of the "Small Things" politics of the novel would
thus appear to rely on the belief that making poverty and the lack
of power visible can serve to undermine the authority of those with
wealth and power.

Although political change requires that social inequities be exposed, an unblinking faith in the absolute efficacy of sunshine as
the best disinfectant no longer seems possible; simply shining light
on problems no longer can guarantee (if it ever did) the outrage
of an audience. If some degree of social visibility is necessary to
enact progressive change, visibility is certainly not sufficient. And
one wonders, with a novel like Roy's, whether, as with sunshine,
too much of a good thing may be harmful. Vivid though the river
scene may be in detail, the reader is left with a lingering sense of
stock photography. Has this scene of bathing and defecating in the
same river become *the image* of third world poverty, *invisible* in its
ubiquity? Consider the deep parallels to Richard Wright's descrip-

tion of Jakarta in *The Color Curtain*—his account of the Bandung Conference, which, appropriately for this comparison, might be understood as one of the originary moments in the imaginary production of the third world:

> I passed those famous canals which the Dutch, for some inexplicable reason, had insisted on digging here in this hot mudhole of a city. (Indeed, the site of Jakarta itself must have been chosen for its sheer utility as a port and with no thought of the health of the people who had to live in it.) I saw a young man squatting upon the bank of a canal, defecating in broad daylight into the canal's muddy, swirling water; I saw another, then another. . . . Children used the canal for their water closet; then I saw a young woman washing clothes only a few yards from them. . . . A young girl was bathing; she had a cloth around her middle and she was dipping water out of the canal, and holding the cloth out from her body, she poured the water over her covered breasts. . . . A tiny boy was washing his teeth, dipping his toothbrush into the canal. . . .[17]

If Wright's 1955 image of endemic futility—a degree of impoverishment that compels humans to perform hygienic acts in the most unsanitary conditions—was central to the initial constructions of the third world, then the scene's almost unaltered presence in Roy's novel functions as a reminder of the failures not only of development, but also of critiques from literary and cultural radicals from the age of three worlds. Whereas Wright might hold out hope that his journalistic image could convey the terrifying urgency of global poverty and convince the affluent nations of the world that they ignored the world's hungry masses at their own peril, Roy's almost identical scene carries no such expectation or conviction. If anything, Roy's recycled image illustrates that even the loudest, brashest exclamations of immiseration, hunger, and poverty can be ignored with surprising ease and few apparent consequences. The five-star resort hotel, after all, is built on the same foul river:

> The view from the hotel was beautiful, but here too the water was thick and toxic. *No Swimming* signs had been put up in stylish calligraphy. They had built a tall wall to screen off the slum and prevent it from encroaching on Kari Saipu's estate. There wasn't much they could do about the smell. . . .
>
> The trees were still green, the sky still blue, which counted for

something. So they went ahead and plugged their smelly paradise—
God's Own Country they called it in their brochures—because
they know, those clever Hotel People, that smelliness, like other
people's poverty, was merely a matter of getting used to. A question of discipline. Of Rigor and Air-conditioning. Nothing more.
(119–20)

The novel's literary politics run aground, that is, upon the
double bind of representation. Although it is necessary to expose
injustice, even the most visible abuses can be walled off, gotten used
to, and ignored with a bit of discipline, rigor, and air condition-
ing. The novel's images, then, do not announce their critique and
wait expectantly for outrage and action from the reader; instead
they stubbornly announce their critique but mournfully acquiesce
to a readership who will likely nod in agreement and then silently
return to everyday life, tacitly understanding that nothing can be
done about "History's Big Things."

If the visual exposé cannot be depended on to produce collective
action, neither can the state or traditional political party apparatuses. Or rather, in the novel, these organs are capable of transforming outrage into collective action—precisely what is missing
from the reader/spectator of the visual image—but not into *productive* collective action. The masses of *GOST* take on the familiar face of the manipulated herd, the mindless mob. The crowd is
far from powerless; Pillai's clever sloganeering can rouse sufficient
public anger to shut down the factory; in the novel's logic, however,
this anger feels misplaced, and Pillai's political work caries similar
theatrical trappings as "the Play" staged for Sophie Mol's arrival in
Ayemenem. Similarly, the Communist march that passes the family
on their way to Cochin depicts several of the individual demonstrators as bullying vigilantes, freed, perhaps even compelled, by the
perceived safety and anonymity of the mob to taunt and harass.

The mob is not without virtue, however. It materializes the collective rage of disempowerment, a rage that Ammu shares with the
marching workers. Upon seeing Velutha afterwards: "Suddenly
Ammu hoped it *had* been him that Rahel saw in the march. She
hoped it had been him that had raised his flag and knotted arm in
anger. She hoped that under his careful cloak of cheerfulness he
housed a living breathing anger against the smug, ordered world
that she so raged against" (167). Roy locates great potency in the

crowd's collective expression of dissatisfaction. It contains the seeds of disorder, the chaotic, anarchic antithesis to the structures of power. However, Ammu's own deep-seated anger (she is described as embodying both the "infinite tenderness of motherhood and the reckless rage of a suicide bomber" [44]) can find no collective solidarity with the marchers. The workers' singular focus on class struggle, prompted by the opportunistic dogmatism of Pillai and the CPI(M), prohibits any political alliance; in fact, Ammu is the object of their anger given her familial ownership of the pickle factory. Paradoxically, the novel figures Ammu's legitimate rage against Big Things through the image of the crowd and her identification with that collective, even as it forecloses the prospect that her own struggles against exploitation and oppression might find any meaningful expression within that social body. The construction of collective agency in GOST, though seething with potential, is hobbled by the fracturing of identification, fostered and perpetuated by the manipulations of power (including, perhaps especially, those like Pillai who appear to be on the side of the masses).

The distinctions made by Hardt and Negri in Multitude, which seek to illustrate the conceptual limitations of familiar categories used to describe collective agents, such as the people, the masses, the working class, describe precisely Roy's apparent apprehensions about public action. Hardt and Negri suggest that conceptions of the people are often predicated upon forced singularity. "The people has traditionally been a unitary conception," they argue. "The population, of course, is characterized by all kinds of differences, but the people reduces that diversity to a unity and makes the population a single identity: 'the people' is one." Likewise, they maintain that "the masses" (despite the noun's plural construction) has a similarly totalizing, soporific connotation: "The essence of the masses is indifference: all differences submerged and drowned in the masses." Finally, they contend that the category working class suffers from being an overly "exclusive concept," privileging a narrowly defined class of (often industrial) wage laborers over all those others, such as the poor, unpaid domestic laborers, or agrarian laborers, who work but do not receive a wage.[18]

Although it is perhaps conceivable to imagine public outrage and public action that would hold the police responsible for their violent, racist tactics, "the masses" in Roy's novel seem to lack the agency to do so in the absence of some organizing framework or charismatic leader. The masses as a political agent—not un-like the grand narratives of Marxism and Development—become characterized primarily by their reductive totality. The novel sug-gests that when the masses act, they act out of manipulation, fear, prejudice—attributes of a familiar construction of mob mentality. The "will of the people" tramples difference; it commits violence in the name of solidarity. Roy's novel locates subjectivity in the indi-vidual, never the collective, even if the individual is herself always already subjected to the reifying social authority of Big Things. Roy appears to be struggling with much the same problem as Hardt and Negri: how to imagine a form of collectivity that is an "open, inclusive concept" and that could avoid reductive totalities in favor of a "multiplicity of all these singular differences"?[19]

Figuring the Impossibility of Productive Collectivity

Hobbled by the impossible limits of a literary representational poli-tics, and the utter failures of both representational (electoral) poli-tics and traditional conceptions of *the masses, the working class, the people, the Party,* and the like, the novel looks for another way to imagine a productive collectivity that does not function at the expense of the individual. I argue that Roy's conception of produc-tive collectivity is best figured by the twinned couplings that close the novel.

On the one hand, with her depiction of Ammu and Velutha's sexual attraction, consummation, and brief two-week courtship, Roy pairs the promise of a future via heterosexual reproductivity with arguments about the productivity of both social transgression and labor. By the time we read about Ammu and Velutha's roman-tic consummation, the novel's foreshadowing has made it clear that Velutha's death is imminent and that Ammu's will come shortly after a few, lonely, tormented years. Like the two lovers, the novel puts its "faith in fragility," and "Stick[s] to Smallness" (321). Its final word, "Tomorrow" (231), which is the only promise that the two lovers can extract from one another after each clandestine ren-dezvous, lends a defiant optimism to a story that is otherwise un-compromisingly brutal in its depiction of how poorly Small Things fare in a world dominated by the ruthless self-interestedness of those who reproduce the structural hegemony of Big Things. The impossible future promised by the lovers' uttered "Tomorrow" borders on cliché, to be sure. But Roy has not written a saccharine morality tale about living for the little things, about stopping to smell the roses on the bumpy path of life. Ammu and Velutha's decision to risk the pleasures of Small Things leads to horrific consequences; however, they choose to see one another fully cognizant of the possible ramifications.

What makes this relationship worth considering in the context of figuring the impossibility of collective action is that it holds the promise of productivity, stemming from the curious coupling of "natural" physical attraction and social dissent. Roy writes, "Biology designed the dance. Terror timed it. Dictated the rhythm with which their bodies answered each other. As though they knew already that for each tremor of pleasure they would pay with an equal measure of pain" (317). After most of the novel has thoroughly undercut the "naturalness" of biology, it is significant that the attraction between Ammu and Velutha is couched partly in terms of a biological mating ritual, partly in terms of the fear that accompanies the transgression of taboo. Their physical desire is powerful, and Roy's evocative description of their mutual seduction celebrates this corporeal embrace as perhaps the only moment of unqualified loving joy in the novel. To say that "Biology designed the dance," then, is to suggest in part the instinctual, spontaneous, organic nature that produces the pulls and pleasures of bodily attraction between the lovers, a construction of the natural productive possibilities of romantic love between man and woman that is distinctly heteronormative.

However, the physical attraction between these two bodies is the product of, in addition to biology, dissent and disobedience. Terror times the dance that biology designs, and the physical desire and pleasure shared by Ammu and Velutha draws its strength in part from the disruption of social norms that is embodied in their union. Not unrelated, perhaps, to other forms of sexual thrill seeking, this particular relationship gains intimacy and intensity from the very real danger that each partner faces in transgressing cultural taboo. Although Chacko's dalliances with the women laborers at the factory are accepted, even encouraged, as the expression of "Men's Needs," Ammu's status as a divorced mother and Velutha's as a Paravan make them each subject to carefully guarded, tightly constrained sexual boundaries; almost the definition of ideology, Roy's "Love Laws" have so fully saturated social norms that they are policed not only by the inspector who taps Ammu's breasts coercively with his baton and calls her a *veshya*, but even by family members, including Mammachi, Baby Kochama, Chacko, and in particular Velutha's father Vellya Paapen, who exposes the lovers' illicit affair and goes so far as to offer to kill his own son as redress for the severity of Velutha's breach of societal mores.

The transgression of these rigidly policed boundaries can be read as the novel's only instance of productive dissent, productive despite the disastrous consequences for both lovers. Unlike the empty flag-waving and chanting of the march, this fulfilling, affirming sexual relationship serves as the one pedagogical moment of the novel. It provides the vehicle through which Ammu can effectively realize both sides of her personality—her maternal tenderness and her suicidal bomber's rage—and it hovers over the novel as the moral standard to which all forms of collective action must be held accountable. If collective action is to be considered productive, it must be founded in modes of collectivity that do not abandon the minority, the disenfranchised, the subaltern; it must identify modes of collectivity that can encompass not only economic and political well being, but also the affective needs of desire, pleasure, comfort, risk, courage, rage, and the like. The affair is not an explicit, courageous act of political expression, a statement by, or in the name of, those who are least empowered to speak through traditional political means. Rather, the affair figures both the affirmative potential of social transgression and disruption, and the materiality of affect, insisting that the corporeal and emotional fulfillments of specific, individual bodies—including rational choice and the sovereignty of the subject—not be sacrificed in the name of an abstracted social body such as *the masses, the people,* or *the working class.* The claim that the lovers' union figures an impossible form of productive collectivity requires a necessarily convoluted logic. We must somehow look past the normativity of the biological, reproductive prospects of heterosexual intercourse without overlooking the affective desires, suppressed by social conditions, fulfilled in the coupling. More, we must reckon with the ways in which this attraction is the product of, and in turn productive of, dissent and revolt against the normativity of social relations.

The focus on individual bodies draws attention, in turn, to the constitutive nature of labor. In describing Velutha's body, Ammu notes "the quality of his beauty," sounding surprising Marxist tones as she admires "how his labor had shaped him. Each plank he planed, each nail he drove, each thing he made had molded him. Had left its stamp on him. Had given him his strength, his supple grace" (316). Her body too is shaped by labor, though as much by the reproductive labor of childbirth and child-rearing as by the so-called productive labor of working in the Pickle Factory. In mentioning Ammu's not yet sagging breasts that "wouldn't support a toothbrush" (316), the seduction scene references an earlier moment in the novel when Ammu reclaims her body from her children and locks herself in the bathroom to weigh her youth and sexual vitality against both her body's past, made evident by her "seven silver stretchmarks from her two-egg twins born to her by candlelight amid news of a lost war," and the specter of a future of enforced celibacy in which she is prematurely aged by the "vinegary fumes that rose from the cement vats of Paradise Pickles. Fumes that wrinkled youth and pickled futures" (213–14).

I read Roy's fascination with her characters' labor-shaped bodies as making a point akin to Hardt's and Negri's conception of affective immaterial labor, which they define in *Multitude* as labor that "produces or manipulates affects such as a feeling of ease, well being, satisfaction, excitement, or passion."[20] In discussing the reproductive labor of the home, which has traditionally been called women's work, Hardt and Negri argue: "domestic labor does require such repetitive material tasks as cleaning and cooking, but it also involves producing affects, relationships, and forms of communication among children, in the family, and in the community. Affective labor is biopolitical production in that it directly produces relationships and forms of life."[21] Read through Hardt and Negri, the *productivity* of the relationship between Ammu and Velutha is not solely located in the biological—that is, in the possibility for reproduction through heterosexual intercourse—but also in the biopolitical, which is to say in the labor of producing and reproducing the relationships that can support living collectivities.

In fact, though these two lovers do not reproductively conceive Rahel and Estha, one could argue that their collective affective labor nonetheless produces the twins. For this reason, the second coupling, the incestuous sexual relationship between the two-egg twins, offers a more daring promise in its efforts to figure the impossibility of collectivity. Here the bio-logic of miscegenation is laid bare. The social hierarchies of caste and class, which prohibit mixture and cross-fertilization, constitute over time a form of biological *familiarity* akin to the incestuous relationship between twin brother and sister. If the notion of biological purity as applied to caste is socially acceptable (and, more extremely, defended at all costs by some), what precisely constitutes the "depravity" of the sibling relations? Here, Roy makes a different sort of effort to de-couple sex from biological reproductivity. Although Roy provides none of the arousing details of pleasure, desire, and sexual explo-ration that characterize her descriptions of Ammu's and Velutha's trysts, the sparser language describing the twin's union nevertheless suggests that the act of coitus takes place between the adult twins twenty-three years after Ammu and Velutha's affair. "There is very little that anyone could say to clarify what happened next," writes Roy, "Nothing that (in Mammachi's book) would separate Sex from Love. Or Needs from Feelings" (310). Of course, such phras-ing is an invitation to distance ourselves from Mammachi's Social Darwinism and attempt to do exactly what she would not—namely, to separate sex from love, and needs from feelings. Again Roy of-fers us a heterosexual coupling, necessitating that the possibility of conception remains (the fundamental issue that presumably levels all sexual intercourse in Mammachi's book). This coupling, how-ever, is driven not by sexual desire or by physical attraction (sex or needs), but rather by deep affection and shared trauma. One is reminded of Aimé Césaire's description in *Notebook of a Return to the Native Land,* when he suggests that what defines *negritude* is not biological Africanness or racial blackness, but a bond that stems from a historical "compass of suffering."[22] Similarly, Roy writes about the twins, "that what they shared that night was not happiness, but hideous grief" (311). This grief speaks not only to the trauma that binds Rahel and Estha, but more broadly to in-clude a compass of suffering that circumscribes histories beyond and before those of the twins.

Most notably, this passage pointedly mirrors the coupling of Ammu and Velutha. Although taking place decades apart, the two scenes are positioned back-to-back at the end of the novel. Rahel is said to whisper and kiss with "[t]heir mother's beautiful mouth" (310). Both scenes include a variant of the line, "It was a little cold. A little wet. A little quiet. The Air" (320).[23] And in its elliptical at-tempts to "clarify what happened," the narrative points to a recur-rent pattern but relies on the ambiguity of a pronoun to muddy the precise nature of that repetition: "once again," Roy writes, "*they* broke the Love Laws" (311, my emphasis). The invocation of the Love Laws with the phrase "once again" lends an atavistic tenor of prophecy and fulfillment to this passage, similar to what Benedict Anderson (following Walter Benjamin) has termed Messianic time, "a simultaneity of past and future in an instantaneous present."[24] In the context of such Messianic simultaneity, "they" would seem to refer to a plurality larger than just the twins. Although Rahel and Estha are the only explicit pronoun referents in the passage, the twins can hardly be said to have previously broken the Love Laws. At a minimum, the plural pronoun would appear to include Ammu and Velutha, who, most immediately, bear the guilt of Loving trespass echoed so powerfully in the incestuous coupling.

These narrative parallels, or better, recursivities, are revealing, particularly because the twins' sexual encounter, which takes place twenty-three years after Ammu's and Velutha's, precedes the chronologically earlier event in the novel's narration. Although many of the details are mirrored in the two love scenes, the reader meets them first with the incestuous encounter between the twins, and subsequently notices their repetition in the concluding love scene between Ammu and Velutha. The chronologically earlier love scene takes place on a patch of ground cleared by the twins' boat, "[a]s though Esthappen and Rahel had prepared the ground for them. Willed this to happen. The twin midwives of Ammu's dream" (318). The twins as children—in their parallel roles as life-burdening reminders of the past and life-affirming promises of a future—might therefore be understood to produce the conditions that make possible the love between Ammu and Velutha. Likewise, the admixture of mutually satisfying and self-affirming affection and desire, coupled with the boldness of social dissent, and the traumatic backlash that results from the lovers' just, if injudicious, decision to transgress social norms, may be understood as the productive prefiguring of this moment of shared "hideous grief," but also of intimate, loving reconnection, taking place between the adult twins as they "held each other close, long after it was over" (311).

The construction of collectivity in each love scene, then, relies upon a simultaneous uniqueness and a deep reciprocity, both between the individual partners Velutha and Ammu, and between the two cross-generational couples. This dialectic is figured in a slightly different sense with the twins, as the movement between the autonomy of any individual and the deep interconnectivity between us all. Describing the twins' encounter, Roy writes: "They were strangers who had met in a chance encounter. They had known each other before Life began" (310). As twins, of course, Rahel and Estha might be said to have known each other in their mother's womb. But the language here, echoing the passage cited earlier about the history of Love Laws stretching back to time immemorial—to long before the arrival of Christianity, colonialism, or Marxism—has an atavistic quality where, again, a sense of Messianic time informs the particular mode of knowledge. In the characters of Rahel and Estha, we find, paradoxically, absolute difference and indissoluble unity; they always already embody both singularity and multiplicity. "In those early amorphous years when memory had only just begun," writes Roy, "Esthappen and Rahel thought of themselves together as Me, and separately, individually, as We or Us" (4). The sexual relationship between the two siblings can be read as a moment of affective *enfleshment* that enables Estha and Rahel to produce and reproduce a mode of subjectivity both singular and multiple, the expression of a specific historical moment and an atavistic recursion. As "strangers who had met in a chance encounter," this multigenerational tangle of bodies constitutes a We; as lovers who "had known each other before Life began," the two constitute a Me.

I read these twinned couplings as an act of figuring the impossibility of a productive collective social body that assumes a form alternative to a nation, a people, a caste, a class, and so on. Here again, I turn to Hardt and Negri, whose work draws extensively from the models of organizing practiced and theorized by the World Social Forum and the broader movement for global justice. Building on their arguments about affective labor, Hardt and Negri use the concept of "social flesh" in an attempt to capture the "pure potential" and "unformed life force" of the multitude. Attempting to avoid the connotations of internal division and hierarchy within traditional metaphors of a social *body* (head over heart, for example), they choose the "elemental figure" of "a flesh that is not a body, a flesh that is common, living substance," and that "is maddeningly elusive since it cannot be entirely corralled into the hierarchical organs of a political body." Reversing Marx's metaphor for capital's parasitism on living labor, they argue that the "vampire is one figure that expresses the monstrous, excessive, and unruly character of the flesh of the multitude," given the vampire's "excessive sexuality" and the ways it "undermines the reproductive order of the family with its own, alternative mechanism for reproduction."[25] The reproductive "monstrosities" of miscegenation and incest can be understood to function in just such a manner for Roy. In the figure of collectivity embodied by the novel's twinned couplings, Roy glimpses the possibility of another world, even if that world is unimaginable in the hegemonic logic of the reigning social body; these monstrous relationships figure a flesh that is (to return to the words of Hardt and Negri) "aimed constantly at the fullness of life" and that allows us to "recognize these monstrous metamorphoses of flesh as not only a danger but also a possibility, the possibility to create an alternative society."[26]

The argument here has been a circuitous one, so let me return to an earlier point as a means of clarification. In using Spivak's notion of *figuring the impossible,* I have endeavored to address the function, not the content, of Roy's novel. As I asked at the beginning of this chapter, what *work* does this novel do? And what work may be accomplished in the act of interpretation? In this context, it would be a mistake to treat Roy's novel as a field manual, an updated edition of Che's *Guerilla Warfare* for the age of globalization. I analyze *GOST* not as a politically subversive treatise but as a compelling set of theoretical questions and figures that wrestle with many of the issues we have seen throughout this book. In reading the novel, I may at times nod in agreement with Roy's depiction of the World Bank's collusion with local capitalists; I may furrow my brow at her unrelenting caricature of Marxism as religious dogma, or her portrayal of the manipulated masses. Indeed, read as political acts, the twin couplings that close the novel should at best be considered mildly transgressive; at worst, they are selfish, irresponsible capitulations to heteronormative desire, far more likely to produce long-term trauma than personal fulfillment, never mind social transformation.

I have tried to suggest *not* that we can locate evidence of subversive resistance in the sexual play of Ammu, Velutha, Rahel, and Estha, but rather that these twin couplings *figure* a set of unanswerable problems. They figure the gap between the crises of today and a utopic future, suggesting that the means of political organization available in the current moment are inadequate to bring about the desired transformation. The critique is clear: racism, sexism, caste-ism, agism, capitalism are not only ineffectually addressed, but are often reproduced, by the available political forms, which are themselves marked by hierarchical, exclusionary, exploitative power arrangements. Taken as the outline of a political program, then, the novel is deeply despairing; there is hardly much consolation to be taken from a fleeting moment of tenderness and desire in the face of Velutha's brutal murder, Ammu's rapid and solitary decline, and the psychological anguish and debilitation of Rahel and Estha. Taken as a literary object, however, the novel may be said to name a horizon of possibility. That is, in figuring an impossible productive collectivity, it imagines a future beyond the limits of present vantage; it dares to ask the question, how do we get to Tomorrow from today.

The *realization* of an alternative society constituted by and from the social flesh of a multitude, a society that imagines forms of collectivity that are open, networked, nonhierarchical, vital, and productive is the organizing project of the World Social Forum. It is to that process, and to Roy's participation at Porto Alegre and Mumbai, that we turn next.

7. Minimum Agendas:
The World Social Forum
and the Place of Culture

Conference culture sutures the histories presented in this book. There are, of course, many ways to schematize a project of this sort, but one could do much worse than to isolate within *Invested Interests* an arc that stretches from Bretton Woods through Bandung, and finally to Brazil—or, more precisely, to the World Social Forum (WSF), an event with its roots in Porto Alegre, Brazil, an event that provides the focus for this final chapter. I have argued that the Global South, by virtue of its purposeful exclusion, hovered at the edges of Bretton Woods. Visible at first only in the imperial legacies of its founders, the so-called underdeveloped world would make its revolutionary presence felt in ever more urgent fashion during the World Bank's early decades, pressuring the institution to, among other things, address "the social." At Bandung, the Global North schemed and sulked from outside; nevertheless, the Bank found its way into the conference documents and into the writings of anticolonial cultural radicals, its presence helping to mask or defer historical contradictions. The World Social Forum, as we shall see, would pitch a tent broad enough to shade both cultural radicals (from North and South) and the World Bank from the Porto Alegre sun.

The WSF is an event and a process that represents one of the most intriguing, wide-scale, contemporary political challenges to the hegemony of the World Bank. Indeed, the WSF can be thought of as the specific historical product of the World Bank era, a crystallized expression of opposition to the forces of postwar capitalist globalization in which the World Bank played such a considerable and consequential role. Put differently, the WSF claims the World Bank as one of its constitutive antagonists.

On the one hand, the WSF reflects the post-1994 era of global opposition to neoliberalism.[1] That year marked the fiftieth anniversary of the World Bank, an occasion met with forceful opposition by the world-wide Fifty Years Is Enough campaign and the massive demonstrations at the annual Bank meetings in Madrid, both of which drew global attention to the disastrous consequences wrought by the Bank's neoliberal economic policies. The year 1994 also saw North American Free Trade Agreement (NAFTA) go into effect, an event rudely greeted by the emergence in Chiapas of the Ejército Zapatista Liberación Nacional (EZLN). The extensive and compelling case against *neoliberalismo* spelled out in the poetic communiqués of Subcomandante Marcos became touchstone theoretical critiques of globalization. These electronic missives enumerated the brutal costs of "free" trade, condemning the systematic destruction of indigenous peoples and cultures, the declining sovereignty of nations, and the privatization of the global commons. The intellectual acuity of the Zapatista critiques, along with the thickening interconnectedness of the activist networks through which they circulated, contributed to the defeat of the Multilateral Agreement on Investment (MAI) in 1998, the Seattle protests against the WTO in 1999, and the myriad of gatherings, actions, strikes, and so forth in the post-1994 era that have marked the anti- or alter-globalization movement.[2] Notable as well is the surge in radical unionizing in Brazil, South Africa, South Korea, and elsewhere, articulated in response to the global forces affecting local labor conditions.

But one may draw the circle wider still. The WSF is a product of *debt,* and of the historical trajectory outlined in the previous chapter extending back to the usurious lending practices of the 1960s. The contemporary critiques of neoliberalism (and of the World Bank's role in structuring the financial and juridical mechanisms of the global capitalist economy) should be understood properly as extensions of the global food riots that erupted widely and regularly from the late 1970s through the 1990s. The insurrectionary popular unrest that greeted almost every attempt at what was variously called "austerity reform," "economic restructuring," or "structural adjustment" signaled deep popular dissatisfaction with the concerted effort to shift the burden of indebtedness to the poorest sectors of the world's population. Central to this history as well are the corresponding shifts to post-Fordist labor practices and global supply chains, which see the industrial production of the world shifted in significant part to the Global South, including the vast so-called free trade zones or export zones so frequently funded by the World Bank.

The de-linking of the dollar from the gold standard in 1971, the oil crisis of 1973, the Mexican government's threat to default on its national debt in 1982, could all provide other possible points of origin for historicizing the movements against capitalist globalization. This set of historical transformations, in which the Bank often plays a defining role, provides yet another context within which to place the oppositional activities of the WSF.

Broader still, the WSF emerges out of the wider postwar World Bank era of cultural radicalism traced in this book; the WSF is a product of the cultural turn, with an intellectual lineage that stretches back to the anti-imperialist thought of Césaire, Fanon, James, Wright, and so many others. More than Berlin, Madrid, Seattle, Washington, Prague, Geneva, and many other landmark gatherings of the antiglobalization movement, the WSF is the direct inheritor of the South–South allegiances of Bandung. Northern activists and movements are not purposefully excluded as they were in 1955, but the ethos of the gatherings has been consciously third worldist. In this sense, the WSF has been a useful corrective to the perceived U.S.-centrism of Seattle, serving to highlight the radical social movements of Latin America, Asia, Africa, and the Middle East. Significant, too, is the fact that the WSF is a *forum,* not (solely) a protest; it has at its core a commitment to the intellectual work of collectively theorizing the contemporary moment, even as it seeks to change it. As such, it inherits the midcentury radicals' commitment to engage the interconnectedness between economy and culture. Drawing upon the legacy of cultural study, the WSF critically and self-reflexively interrogates the many ways that neoliberalism and global capitalism engender, racialize, proletarianize, and ethnicize—that is to say, how a specific mode of production actively *produces* peoples and collectivities, how it produces social relations, indeed how it produces social life itself. A hallmark of the cultural turn, this expanded theorization of the Marxist category *mode of production* underpins the multilayered analytical gaze of the WSF.[3]

If the WSF, as a product of the cultural turn, counts the Bank as a constitutive antagonist in these many ways, the institutions also find themselves coupled as strange bedfellows in Porto Alegre. The Forum, paradoxically, may represent the fullest expression of a democratic culture of protest and movement, and at the same time an ineffectual and accommodationist culture of global civil society—a World Bank culture. Or perhaps this is no paradox. Culture, as we have seen, flows untroubled and unimpeded in multiple directions. It is not enough to struggle for culture or to struggle through culture. The questions remain, as always, what kind of culture is worth the struggle, and what forms of culture advance that fight?

As this chapter will demonstrate, the fault line between radical democratic movements for equity and the liberal reformist politics of civil society runs just beneath the surface at the WSF. Its boldest advocates argue that the WSF will become, or at least will contribute to, seismic tremors and social upheaval capable of making a new world—or, in the Zapatista-inspired language of the Forum, a world in which many worlds are possible. But for this to be the case, the Forum itself will have to be radicalized. Or, as a minimum agenda, radical movements beneath the broader WSF umbrella will have to employ the structural spaces opened by the Forum to build, strengthen, and globalize their struggles for democracy and equity and in opposition to capitalist imperialism. If, instead, the Forum relies upon the World Bank and global civil society to help resolve its differences, it will likely go down as another Bandung: a spectacular if ineffectual political landmark, marred by unresolvable contradictions. The struggle over the Forum's future, a struggle of utmost urgency, must begin and end with the terms that have underpinned this project: *democratic movements* for *equity*.

A World in Which Many Worlds Are Possible

To describe the World Social Forum in any comprehensive sense is like clutching a handful of water. It defies capture. Attempts at representation run aground against the institutional structures and, it might be said, structures of feeling, that underpin the WSF.

Institutionally speaking, the Forum's Charter of Principles makes it clear that the WSF is not a representational body—it is not an agent. No one can speak on behalf of the WSF, nor can the WSF express any positions or call for any actions as a body. Its only official document is its Charter of Principles. "The meetings of the WSF do not deliberate on behalf of the WSF as a body," the charter declares; "No one, therefore, will be authorised, on behalf of any of the editions of the Forum, to express positions claiming to be those of all its participants. The participants in the Forum shall not be called on to take decisions as a body."[4] If no one can represent the Forum as a body, neither can representatives participate in the Forum's deliberations and actions. The charter prohibits only two classes of participants from inclusion in the Forum: "party representations" and "military organizations."[5] Representational politics (in the sense of "speaking for") is thus named as an antagonist to the objectives of the Forum, suggesting the WSF's deep distrust of hierarchical party structures, be they parties of the Right or the Left. It should be noted, however, that the charter backs away from this stance in a significant way, equivocating that "Government leaders and members of legislatures who accept the commitments of this Charter may be invited to participate in a personal capacity" (more on what might be called the "Lula clause" shortly).[6]

The WSF's Charter of Principles, its founders, and many of its participants have as an organizing premise the rejection of any unifying movement or platform that might in any way function to reduce diversity and multiplicity into a singular entity incapable of accounting for the vast complexity of individual desire and choice. Representational politics is thus constitutionally forbidden by the WSF, both in its prohibition of participants who speak on behalf of political parties, and in its insistence that no person or statement can claim to represent the Forum. In articulating the ideal that no person or group should be forced to choose between minority interests and the interests of the collective whole, the charter shares both with Roy and with Hardt and Negri the philosophical position that representation and democracy are fundamentally at odds. As Boaventura de Sousa Santos, one of the Social Forum's most thoughtful analysts argues, "The WSF rejects the concept of a historical subject and confers no priority on any specific social actor in this process of social change."[7] As we shall soon see, this subjectless position has raised crucial questions about whether the WSF ought to consider itself a movement (which advocates for positions, advances an agenda, organizes, participates in actions, and so forth), or whether it ought to think of itself as an open space for debate and reflection, where social movement actors meet but do not collectively act.

The Forum defies representation in another sense, that of its radical heterogeneity. In a well-known essay published as part of the *New Left Review*'s "Movement of Movements" series, Michael Hardt draws an analogy between the WSF and Bandung. Comparing the two landmark conferences, Hardt writes that, "whereas Bandung was conducted by a small group of national political leaders and representatives, Porto Alegre was populated by a swarming multitude and a network of movements," which in turn he describes as "unknowable, chaotic, dispersive."[8] At the level of representational description, this is certainly accurate. The Forum is a riot of activity. Over the span of a few days, several hundred thousand participants from around the world split time among marches, keynote addresses, thousands of self-organized panels, workshops and roundtables, music exhibitions, poetry readings, film screenings, art installations, demonstrations, youth camps, and more. And such a catalog of events captures nothing of the constant dialogue and interaction that provide the ongoing background noise of a happening of this scope. The topics discussed, formally and informally, are equally diverse. Although it is easy to be skeptical about the relevance of panels with topics such as "Football Supporters: Culture and Rights," "Flower Essences Therapy," "Music and Psychodrama Stimulation Lab," the vast bulk of the Forum's activities are devoted to what are clearly the most pressing concerns of our day: access to land, food, water, and other resources; the militarization of the planet, headlined by, but by no means limited to, the imperial aggressions of the United States; the struggles against racism, sexism, communalism (as the term is used in South Asia), agism, and the like; the migration and displacement of peoples; the exploitation of labor and the deepening saturation of the world capitalist system; and, of course, the global impact of international financial institutions (IFIs) and the glaring need for immediate, comprehensive debt relief, to name but a few. Participants come from a broad spectrum of activists, intellectuals, artists, and policy makers from across the globe; present are the tiniest NGOs as well as Nobel laureates, radical insurgents as well as reformist institutions. One could never describe a whole

World Social Forum gathering, then, because it would be impossible for even the most determined participant to see, let alone comprehend, more than a fraction of what was taking place over the course of the week.

I have been fortunate enough to participate in three international Forums and two local Forums, and in each instance I have come away overwhelmed and enthused by the mix of interaction, dissent, solidarity, hope, joy, logistical confusion, and theoretical antinomies that structure these events. The affective, experiential pulls of collectivity, coupled with moments of impasse and alienation, defy easy description. Hardt captures the hopefulness of this riotous process, arguing that the Forum's "overabundance created an exhilaration in everyone, at being lost in a sea of people from so many parts of the world who are working similarly against the present form of capitalist globalization."[9] That the radical heterogeneity of the Social Forum events defy representation, however, does not excuse us from the task of theorizing the Social Forum as both event and process. Overabundance and excess may provide a potent energizing aspect of the WSF, but they also constitute a pressing intellectual and political problem for analysis. Even though it is not possible to represent the entirety of any Social Forum gathering, a critical assessment of the Forum's radical potentials must nevertheless look to identify tendencies and emergences, as well as to contextualize the WSF with the half-century of New Left social movements.

A bit of background will be helpful here.[10] Founded in 1999, the WSF is variously conceived of as event, process, or space. It has developed into perhaps the most visible, dynamic, and coherent gathering of the antiglobalization or alterglobalization movement, sometimes also referred to as the "movement for global justice and solidarity." The Forum goes under the slogan "Another World Is Possible" and is described in its charter as: "an *open meeting place* for reflective thinking, democratic debates of ideas, formulation of proposals, free exchange of experiences and interlinking for effective action, by groups and movements of *civil society* that are *opposed to neoliberalism and to domination of the world by capital and any form of imperialism,* and are committed to building a planetary society directed towards fruitful relationships among humankind and between it and the Earth" (emphasis added).[11] Founded by several prominent civil society groups, primarily in

Brazil and France, the WSF is most readily associated with its annual international gathering that has been timed to correspond with the World Economic Forum (WEF), typically held in Davos, Switzerland. The WEF plays host to a few very powerful individuals (heads of state, important government officials, and influential corporate CEOs and officers) who meet each year to discuss how best to manage or steer the global economy. By deliberate contrast, the WSF consists of social movement activists, academics, artists, and an inclusive assortment of civil society groups, and bills itself as "a reinvention of democracy" and "globalization from below."

The inaugural WSF international gathering took place in January 2001 in Porto Alegre, Brazil, where four of its first five annual meetings took place. In 2004, the gathering was held in Mumbai, India, as part of a process of "globalizing" the Forum in hopes of increasing participation from Asia and Africa—the same two-thirds of the world's population that constituted the "center of gravity" for the Bandung meetings. Departing from the tradition of a single annual international gathering, the 2006 WSF was split into three "polycentric" regional Forums—in Caracas (Venezuela), Karachi (Pakistan), and Bamako (Mali)—to further diversify participation and to foster the notion of the WSF as a permanent process and not merely an annual gathering. Seeing value both in consolidation and in expansion, the WSF is moving toward an alternating biennial sequence, so that in 2007 a single international meeting was held, in Nairobi. Responding to concerns voiced by social movement actors that the time and money devoted to organizing annual WSF meetings takes away precious resources from ongoing local political struggles, the WSF International Council has formally agreed that the international gathering should be held every other year.[12]

Judged by the number of participants, the Forum has been wildly successful. The first meeting in 2001, which was more narrowly focused as an anti-Davos protest, drew roughly 10,000 participants, already a sizable number when compared to the hundreds of delegates at the WEF or the twenty-nine leaders gathered at Bandung. As it has evolved, the WSF has differentiated itself from the other anti-WTO, anti–World Bank/IMF, anti-G8 protests, becoming a more self-generative, reflective, analytical space; consequently, it has experienced dramatic growth. Estimates for the 2004 Mumbai WSF were as high as 150,000 participants, and the 2005 gathering in Porto Alegre may have drawn over 200,000. Further, numerous regional Social Forums take place throughout the year and across the globe, so that the WSF is properly understood not solely as an annual conference but rather as an ongoing set of actions at local, national, regional, and planetary scales.

The verdict on the WSF's effectiveness as a political agent of change, however, is less certain. This stems in part from the fact that the WSF "rejects the concept of a historical subject," to quote Sousa Santos again. The questions of ends and means, movement and space, therefore, have become central points of debate for the Forum. Chico Whitaker, one of the founding members of WSF and a leading activist with the Brazilian Committee for Justice and Peace, has published an influential argument in which he power-fully defends the idea of the WSF as an open space (his metaphor is a public square) rather than a movement. Whitaker's contention is that the WSF "speaks loudest" when it does not speak on behalf of anyone but instead provides an "open, free, horizontal" struc-ture that can create movements and amplify the struggle.[13] Here we can see the overlap with, and intellectual indebtedness to, clas-sic constructions of civil society and the public sphere as a space of free and rational debate, radical pluralism, and a commitment to nonviolence.

A liberal civil society theorist such as John Keane will insist that global civil society is not a sphere in which anything goes; rather, civil society is the "ethical *conditio sine qua non* of moral plural-ism. . . . [T]he ethic of global civil society celebrates social diver-sity, but it does so by asking after the universal preconditions of dynamic social diversity. . . . Which is to say, to put it most simply, that the durable co-existence of many moral ways of life requires each to accept unconditionally the need for the institutions of civil society."[14] Keane and Whitaker part ways politically in terms of their respective defense and critique of capitalism, but both share the construction of global civil society as a space that is open, but not open to everyone and everything. For Keane, global civil so-ciety must be militant, without being militaristic, precisely in its defense of pluralism against those who wish to enforce a singular vision of morality, be it party dogmatism, religious fundamental-ism, or imperialist state ambition. Whitaker insists that the WSF is an open space, embracing of diversity, but not a neutral space. Its objective is, according to Whitaker, "to allow as many individuals, organizations and movements as possible that oppose neoliberalism to get together freely, listen to each other, learn from the experiences and struggles of others, and discuss proposals of action, to become linked in new nets and organizations aiming at overcoming the present process of globalization dominated by large international corporations and their financial interests."[15] Both arguments, then, defend openness within limits. However, Keane, although critical of some of the excesses that accompany "turbocapitalism," nonetheless vigorously defends the inclusion of transnational corporations within his conception of global civil society. He sees "*the* market" as a defining feature of global civil society, and advocates that financial institutions be considered central participants in defining the stakes of a civil, social globe. Ford Motors and the Ford Foundation (and, of course, their long-time mutual friend the World Bank) serve as key stakeholders in the construction of a Keanian global civil society.

There is much to be critical of in Keane's work, but for the sake of brevity let me focus on one central concern. In the name of democratic pluralism, Keane includes as "participants" some of the the least democratic institutions on the planet. Consider that workers at a multinational corporation such as Ford are unable to share equitably in the company's profits, or to participate equitably in its decision making; likewise, the Bank can be faulted for its lack of democracy at the level of national stakeholders, not to mention the millions of people around the globe affected by Bank policies with no consultation or recourse whatsoever. To insist that these institutions be considered participants is to perpetuate the most disabling forms of "representation," giving disproportionate voice to institutions that have consistently and effectively worked to preclude the participation of the majority of the world's population.[16]

Whitaker, thankfully, shares none of Keane's illusions about equitable participation. He argues that the WSF is an open space in which those opposed to neoliberalism can meet to forge more diverse, powerful, creative movements that mobilize people both in resistance to particular instantiations of neoliberal economic principles and in the development of alternatives to the hegemony of global capitalism. It is to this openness-without-neutrality that Whitaker attributes "the great joy that reigns in this square," adding that it "is precisely this joy—the same joy we would all like to always see in the 'other possible world'—that takes hold of and in-

vigorates everybody, and that also destroys the divisions that segregate the struggles of different movements: the fact that we are *many*
in the *same* fight."[17] Whitaker and the organizers who authored
the charter are willing to name their antagonists—the World Bank
the chief among them, as part of "the process of globalization
commanded by large multinational corporations and by governments and international institutions at the service of those corporations' interests, with the complicity of national governments."[18]
If the Bank lurked in the Final Communiqué at Bandung, its presence is no less strongly felt in the WSF Charter of Principles; here,
however, it is the object of critique, not promise. Whitaker and the
charter repeatedly and unapologetically name "the domination of
the world by capital," "the mechanisms and instruments of domination by capital," "the process of capitalist globalization," and
the like.[19] In opposition to these "mechanisms and instruments of
domination," Whitaker proposes the mechanism of open space—
that is, horizontal, democratic pluralism, heterogeneity, diversity,
discursivity, debate, exchange, and the other keywords of the WSF.
His name for this open space, like Keane's, is *global civil society*.

If in theory the charter's line between participant and antagonist seems drawn clearly, in practice that distinction is blurred significantly. As we have seen throughout this book, the World Bank
is fully capable of embracing liberal constructions of openness
and inclusivity. This holds true for its regard of the WSF as well.
Consider the following document from the extensive section of the
Bank's Web site devoted to Civil Society Organizations (CSOs):

> CSOs' influence on shaping global public policy has also emerged
> over the past two decades. This dynamism is exemplified by suc-
> cessful advocacy campaigns around such issues as banning of land
> mines, debt cancellation, and environmental protection which have
> mobilized thousands of supporters around the globe. The most re-
> cent manifestation of the vibrancy of global civil society has been
> the World Social Forum held annually in Porto Alegre, which in
> January 2003 attracted some 100,000 participants to debate and
> propose more equitable and sustainable alternatives to current
> models of economic globalization.[20]

Hardly playing the part of chief antagonist, the Bank showers
praise on the dynamism of the WSF, casting the Forum as a partner in the fight for "equitable and sustainable alternatives." That

the Bank, always loquacious, could describe the Forum's purpose using the two verbs "debate" and "propose" points to the limits of constructing the Forum as an open space for dialogue.

Let me make the point clearer still. The difficulty of assuming, as Whitaker does, that "that we are *many* in the *same* fight," becomes immediately evident when reading the World Bank's January 2004 *Civic Engagement Newsletter* (its newsletter for and about civil society). The short article "World Bank at World Economic Forum in Davos, and World Social Forum in India" states:

> The World Economic Forum (WEF) is an independent international organization committed to improving the state of the world. The forum provides a collaborative framework for the world's leaders to address global issues, engaging particularly its corporate members in global citizenship. Incorporated as a foundation, the forum is impartial and not-for-profit; it is tied to no political, partisan, or national interests. WB is represented in Davos by two senior managers. The World Social Forum (WSF) is a gathering of global civil society which brings together tens of thousands of civil society activists from around the world to debate globalization and other broad policy issues. It was created as an alternative meeting to the World Economic Forum held annually in Davos, Switzerland. The 2004 Forum is being held in Mumbai, India on January 16–21. The Bank is present at the WSF through a team of 3 staff persons from Washington and the New Delhi Offices, who will be there as observers attending sessions, and maintaining informal discussion with the CSO participants. Additionally, Edith Brown Waiss [sic], Chairperson of the Inspection Panel, has been invited to speak at a seminar: *Can Internal Accountability Mechanisms of the IFIs Give Justice to Local Affected Communities?* . . . on January 19 and . . . hosted by the Bank Information Center.[21]

We need not belabor the issue. The Bank acts here as a paradigmatic member of Keane's global civil society. It willingly sends delegates to engage in dialogue with these corporate global citizens of the "not-for-profit" WEF (be assured that the WEF participants are very much *for* profit, even if the foundation does not make any) *and* to "debate globalization and other broad policy issues" with the civil society activists at the WSF. The founding antitheses of the WSF—its status as a counterpoint to Davos, and its opposition to neoliberalism—are effectively synthesized by the World Bank's simultaneous participation as a member of the global civil society in both the Economic and Social Forums.

The World Bank's presence at the Forum, then, suggests the limits and the dangers of the open space/public square metaphor. The further the WSF moves toward Keane's radical pluralism, the more difficult it is to be certain "that we are *many* in the *same* fight." Many of the same objections can be raised regarding the other celebrated metaphors for understanding the forum. Hardt, for instance, uses the figures of multitude and network, arguing that, "no one speaks for a network," and that the "multitude in movements is always overflowing, excessive, and unknowable."[22] Likewise, Arturo Escobar uses principles from complexity theory to argue that the Forum "could make up an inter-networked society of *intelligent communities,* centered on the democratic production of culture and subjectivity."[23] And Sousa Santos suggests that a "sociology of emergences" that "aims to identify and enlarge the signs of possible future experiences under the guise of tendencies and latencies, that are actively ignored by hegemonic rationality and knowledge," offers the most productive way to conceptualize the Forum.[24]

That the Forum has adopted the language of global civil society is, in my opinion, a mistake. *Global civil society* is a term "populated—overpopulated—with the intentions of others," as Bakhtin would say.[25] Severing civil society from its historical connection to capitalist imperialism amounts to a monumental undertaking. That Keane and the World Bank so willingly embrace the term suggests to me that to use it is not a rhetorical recuperation effort worth undertaking. Whether *network, multitude, intelligent societies,* and the like amount to a theoretically inflected repackaging of the same remains to be seen. At present, they function as figures, like Roy's novelistic writings, for the potentialities of collectivity. Struggling to determine the form that collectivity takes is the Forum's pressing task, a task that must be taken up by activist-theorists and theorist-activists alike. One of Richard Wright's Indonesian interviewees from *The Color Curtain* made the point "Democracy is a means of protest, not a method of construction."[26] That this emergent collectivity be constituted through protest as well as debate is essential; likewise, it must not forego considerations of equity and exploitation in its rush to form inclusive alliances. There is much to be enthused about with the WSF:

its willingness to name capitalism as the source of global inequity (though admittedly its focus on *neoliberalism* can at times obscure this critique), its efforts to theorize democracy, its embrace of participatory forms of organization, its commitment to alternative modes of noncapitalist production and exchange, its layered understanding of what may be thought of in geographer's terms as the "scales" of activism and organizing, its efforts to break down the simplistic division between intellectual and activist labor, and, importantly, its tremendously persuasive organizing strategies that have successfully mobilized hundreds of thousands, at times millions, of people across the globe (in part, it must be said, because of its inclusive address to civil society). These radical tendencies cannot be taken for granted, however. As we have seen, the World Bank, already speaking from certain WSF lecture podiums, eagerly awaits the opportunity of partnership.

A Collective Pain in the Ass

Richard Wright served as a guide of sorts to the Bandung Conference in chapter 4. Seeking someone to play that role as we work through the complexities of the WSF, I turn again to Arundhati Roy.

In the leveling of distinctions among its critiques of Marxism, Communist Party organizing, World Bank Development, racism, caste-ism, sexism, and so forth, *GOST* can be said to share an anti–Big Things zeitgeist of the World Social Forum. But, as I have intimated above, both the novel and the WSF share a utopian boldness, what I have been calling (following Spivak) an attempt to figure the impossible; they share an imaginative impudence that allows them to announce, and thereby begin to call into being, to make material, a future beyond the limits of our current political horizon. Roy's novel does what Spivak suggests that literature can do: it figures the impossible, constructing the theoretical ideal of a collectivity that can be imagined together as a "Me," and "separately, individually, as We or Us." The challenge for Roy's WSF speeches, on the other hand, is to galvanize the *immediately possible* without falling prey to a pragmatism that would fully obscure the novel's utopic address to an impossible future.

"Confronting Empire," Roy's 2003 address in Porto Alegre, sketches a roughly similar critique and offers a roughly similar conclusion to those that we found in *GOST*. In defining "Empire," she identifies not only "the U.S. Government (and its European satellites), the World Bank, the IMF, the WTO, and the multinational corporations," but also "nationalism, religious bigotry, fascism and, of course, terrorism," all of which "march arm in arm with the project of corporate globalization" and the global "dismantling of democracy."[27] Moreover, in one of the most frequently quoted passages from any document associated with the WSF, Roy concludes her address with what may be read as an echo and elaboration of the "Tomorrow," that punctuates *GOST*. Roy states, "Another world is not only possible; she is on her way. On a quiet day, I can hear her breathing" (54).

Departing from the author's cynicism in the novel, Roy's WSF address suggests that something called "public opinion" may exist and may matter. After her despairing portrait of "the masses" or "the people" in *GOST,* her statement that we "can continue to build public opinion until it becomes a deafening roar" (54) is striking. The WSF becomes in this formulation a pedagogical and activist space of hegemonic struggle. A far cry from the disparaging depiction of Comrade Pillai shouting slogans in front of Paradise Pickles is Roy's argument here that civil disobedience can be rhetorically persuasive and politically effective; that is, in her speech she posits the existence of a "public" whose collective "mind" perhaps can be swayed by the conviction and creativity of disruptive protests. With mischievous conviction, and to the exuberant delight of the crowd at the Gigançino Stadium that evening, Roy joyfully exhorted her audience: "We can reinvent civil disobedience in a million different ways. In other words, we can come up with a million ways of becoming a collective pain in the ass" (54). In contrast to *GOST,* where Roy delimits transgression to the narrow intimacy between the novel's main characters, her WSF speech entreats the audience "not only to confront empire, but also to lay siege to it: to deprive it of oxygen; to shame it; to mock it" (54).

Several things are worth noting about this exhortation to civil disobedience. First, because it is framed in terms of building pubic opinion, the explicit methods of "laying siege" that Roy mentions take a form that I have been rather awkwardly labeling "culturalist": we assault empire, she insists, "with our art, our music, our literature, our stubbornness, our joy, our brilliance, our sheer relentlessness, and our ability to tell our own stories" (54). Even more plainly than in Bandung, the battleground of the WSF is culture: "The corporate revolution will collapse," Roy argues, "if we refuse to buy what they are selling—their ideas, their version of history, their weapons, their notion of inevitability" (54). We might say, here, that Roy "marshals the literary" for counter-imperial purposes (ironically, to an audience full of representatives from NGOs not dissimilar to EcoSandals). This culturalist emphasis highlights, for instance, the rhetorical gesture of a Narmada Bachao Andolan (NBA) *dharna* (often translated as "sit in" or "demonstration"), or a Movimiento Sen Terra (MST) land occupation, in addition to the specific achievements of reclaiming and redistributing resources or seizing control of the means of production. Roy's primary focus appears to be on the *communicability of struggle*—that is, on the ways in which dissent and civil disobedience function to make a public case against the coordinated assaults of empire. Such a case would necessarily view the NBA *dharna* or the MST land occupation as not only a strike against dams and displacement in India, or against property rights of large landowners in Brazil, but also as components of a larger global counterimperial struggle that can communicate beyond local particularities.[28]

A second striking aspect of this Porto Alegre speech is the consistent, stable *we,* and by extension stable *they,* that Roy establishes: "We can hone our memory"; "We can turn the war in Iraq into a fishbowl"; "We can expose George Bush and Tony Blair"; "We can reinvent civil disobedience"; "We can come up with a million ways of becoming a collective pain in the ass"; "We be many and they be few. They need us more than we need them" (54). The stability of this "we" depends in part on the culturalist logic discussed above, in that it presumes communicability and cumulative effects, even in the absence of shared objectives or coordinated actions. That is, a local NBA *dharna* protesting the displacement of indigenous peoples and the privatization of communal water resources necessarily has a global ripple effect, transforming the perceived stakes, tactics, and analytics of other so-called local struggles, irrespective of any conscious globalizing objectives of the organizers in the Narmada Valley. Exposing the systemic interdependence of what might otherwise appear distinct phenomena, Roy suggests that "we" can begin to locate a politically ascendant mosaic of counterimperial struggle across the globe.

Beyond this broader presumed "we" of the counterimperial struggles across the globe, Roy's address seeks to unify the "we" of the WSF: the activists "gathered here today" in Porto Alegre.

As one of those participants, I find this aspect of her address—one that highlights the performativity of oration as well as the politics of spectacle, crowd, and the affective draws of public collectivity—of particular interest, and it intersects for me with broader questions about the function and form of WSF international gatherings. In a roundabout way, this particular "we" of gathered WSF participants speaks to one of the criticisms leveled by Naomi Klein (among others), that the 2003 gathering was "hijacked" by big stars. Klein bristles that:

> The key word at this year's World Social Forum, which ended yesterday in Porto Alegre, Brazil, was "big."
>
> Big attendance: more than a hundred thousand delegates in all! Big speeches: more than 15,000 crammed in to see Noam Chomsky! And most of all, big men.[29]

Klein is concerned that the overflowing crowds swooning over the recently elected Brazilian president Lula and then-embattled Venezuelan president Chavez would forget the fundamental New Left lesson upon which the WSF was founded—namely, that "[p]olitics had to be less about trusting well-meaning leaders, and more about empowering people to make their own decisions; democracy had to be less representative and more participatory."[30] She bemoans the fact that the 2003 Forum had fewer "circles, with small groups of people facing each other," and more big crowds being lectured to by those "big men." It is difficult to know precisely where Roy, obviously not a "big man," fits into this critique. Klein fails to mention that the fifteen thousand people who showed up to see Chomsky (I have heard crowd estimates as high as thirty thousand, and certainly the Gigantinho stadium, where the event took place, was filled beyond its seating capacity) were also there to see Roy, who in fact gave the final, headliner presentation of the evening.

Nevertheless, Klein's broader concerns about an emerging WSF cult of celebrity, and the corresponding audience passivity and disengagement produced by huge, didactic lecture presentations instead of more intimate discussions or workshops, are not invalidated simply by the appearance of a woman on the big podium.[31] In fact, Klein appears to be challenging precisely the presumptuousness of a stable "we" that underpins Roy's "Confronting Empire." Klein and the WSF have typically been more comfortable with the Zapatista formulations of "a world in which there is room for many worlds,"[32] and a movement of "one 'no' and many 'yeses.'"[33] Although Roy does proclaim that, "*we* can come up with *a million* ways of becoming a collective pain in the ass" (my emphases), this might be read as a negative articulation of collectivity: "many nos" rather than "many yeses." Roy's address underscores the idea of a single "no" by suggesting the systemic coherence of "Empire," but it does little to suggest the plurality of either the broader movement for global justice and solidarity, or the WSF participants. Rather, in a rousing performance that to Klein's ears may well have contained echoes of the dreaded bullhorn or pulpit, Roy's address and her considerable skills as an orator worked to produce a relatively untroubled sense of commonality among her audience, implicitly presuming that "we" shared analyses, goals, and tactics. This stable *we,* which adds coherence to Roy's oration and produces a (false?) sense of unity among her audience, could likely serve only to underscore Klein's opposition to the "big" format and its paradigmatic form, the mass political rally, with its undercurrents of fascistic coercion and manipulation that are no less worrisome merely when rallies are organized by parties on the Left.[34] I hasten to add that this sentiment is fully shared by Roy in *GOST,* as evidenced by her portrait of Comrade Pillai and the CPI(M); in her Porto Alegre address, however, (perhaps in part because of the presumed bona fides that she established with *GOST*), Roy seems more interested in producing a unified community than in trying to nuance or trouble such a notion.

I take Klein's point. She is right to be concerned that the WSF may turn into a Worker's Party (Partido dos Trabalhadores, or PT) organ. Moreover, it is undoubtedly the case that the prominence of Lula and Chavez at the 2003 event went against the Charter of Principle's prohibition of political parties. To say that these men's speeches were not *officially* part of the Forum, or to claim that they spoke as individuals and not as party representatives, is transparently hypocritical. This said, the much more uneven reactions to the two Leftist political leaders two years later at the 2005 Porto Alegre gathering—the anti-imperialist demagoguery of Chavez was more warmly received than Lula's Pollyannish evaluation of the PT's accomplishments, though neither "big man" commanded anything near the influence of Lula's 2003 appearance—suggests that the crowd's enchantment with electoral successes may have either waned significantly in the intervening years of (at best) mixed success for Lula's government, or been somewhat overestimated in the first place by Klein and others. My own impression after returning from the 2003 meeting and reading Klein's critique was that the WSF crowd may have been less enraptured by the big men than she believed. Certainly they were celebrating the unlikely ascent and victory of a Leftist presidential candidate, a development that held particular promise for the WSF crowd because of their (plausible) impression that the Lula triumph was to some extent a product of the visibility and successes of the WSF during the previous years. There was a decided optimism at the 2003 Forum stemming from a perception that the WSF was playing a significant role in shifting the assumptions and values of political debate nationally (hence Lula), continentally (hence Chavez, as well as the emergence of Evo Morales, who was scheduled to appear the same night as Chomsky and Roy but remained in Bolivia because of an intensification of the political crisis there), and globally (hence the enthusiasm about "globalizing" the WSF as it prepared, for the first time, to leave Porto Alegre for Mumbai). Uneven though this leftward drift may have been, it was nevertheless taken to be a sign of the WSF's growing efficacy.

But amid the exuberant revelry of the Forum, which punctuated every speech and gathering with long sing-song chants of *Luulaa . . . Lu-la, Lu-la, Lu-la*, there persisted much clear-eyed analysis not only about the limits of representational electoral politics as such, but particularly about the improbability that any single head of state, no matter how charismatic or committed, would be able to make significant inroads into a global economic and political system that punishes those who do not conform. I read the celebratory reception for Lula in 2003 as an expression of the politics of scale that, to my mind, underscores the WSF process. Electoral politics are assuredly not the answer in and of themselves, but they remain an important sphere of activist work that can bring immediate, measurable material benefits or detriments to the lives of real people. The open-space model of the WSF works on the premise that one can be opposed in principle to representational politics, and yet still recognize the short-term, tactical benefits that can accompany the victory of a progressive candidate. In this sense, the Forum is illustrative of (and responsive to) the dialectic of globalization that Fredric Jameson identifies between a celebration of difference and the standardization or Americanization of the globe. Rather than understanding these two positions as antithetical, Jameson argues that they exist in a dialectical relation of an antinomy that is best understood in terms of place: "that these differences do not have to do with Difference so much as where it is located or positioned." One's analysis and response to the processes of globalization "depends on the level at which a malign and standardizing or despotic identity is discerned."[35] That is, if the nation state is seen as a site of repression and exploitation, the play of local difference is affirmed and celebrated as resistant; if the transnational system of capitalism (variously inflected as transnational corporations, IFIs, juridical apparatus such as the WTO, etc.) is seen as the corrupting force, then the nation state can be called upon to defend the integrity of besieged local cultures. The WSF, at its best, works to facilitate this dialectical politics of scale, advancing what may be thought of as an aggregative or accumulative opposition to globalization that accounts for both positions within the antinomy that Jameson identifies, without privileging either. (one 'no,' many 'yeses').

In my view, the exuberant "big crowds," "big men," and "big events" of the 2003 WSF indicated not so much that the passive masses were being duped again by the empty promises of charismatic leftist party leaders, but rather a celebration of the possibilities for meaningful progressive reform that Lula's election offered, as well as the WSF's own growing influence as a "movement of movements" (to use Klein's phrase).[36] I would add that the celebratory enthusiasm at the mass events never eclipsed the pervasive commitment to, and ongoing analysis of, modes of participatory democracy, a redefinition and reclamation of the commons, open discursive space, and other affirmative innovations that Klein and others have lauded in the past. If anything, the Forum's triumphant atmosphere suggested less an inaugural gala for Lula than an inaugural celebration of the WSF—its arrival on the world political scene, marked by the growing force and popular appeal of its vision, "Another World is Possible," and its innovative political models of participatory democracy. Indeed, the former was widely understood to be a symptom of the latter.

I would like to defend Roy's address from a slightly different perspective as well, arguing that the "big event" format, which was featured much less prominently at the 2004 and 2005 gatherings (in Mumbai and Porto Alegre, respectively), in part as a response to critics such as Klein, plays a valuable role in the WSF process. For the most part, I have in this chapter steered away from discussions of Forum logistics, not because I think them unimportant—far from it—but because the debates around format, venue, organization of event spaces, scheduling, and the like seem more appropriate to the essayistic and journalistic writing most typically associated with the WSF (as evidenced by the now substantial archive of essays on the WSF Website and by the several anthologies of essays about the WSF). The *time* of such writing, coupled with its *dialogic* responsiveness—that is, the immediacy of short essays, editorials, and commentaries that react rapidly to specific issues in a manner that invites response, refinement, debate, and analysis from a broad community of WSF commentators—contributes to making such writing more suitable for debating the merits or limitations of logistical choices. Indeed, the body of such insightful commentary by critics such as Walden Bello, Peter Waterman, Jai Sen, Chico Whitaker, Tievo Teivainen, Patrick Bond, Michael Albert, Vandana Shiva, Immanuel Wallerstein, and many others, including Klein herself, have helped ensure that the Forum reflexively examines its own processes so that it may avoid the bureaucratic torpor of a large institution and so that it may become a more effective vehicle for social change. Because this logistical issue of "big events" speaks to the broader questions about collectivity, however, I think it worthwhile to address what is not solely a question of venue and format.

Although I recognize the legitimate concerns about a WSF star system, I would like to defend the importance of the big event and suggest that Roy, as much as any other Forum participant, understands the value of the grand stage. The untroubled "we" of "Confronting Empire" certainly cuts against the grain of the perpetually unstable constructions of collectivity that mark *GOST*. However, totalizing though it may be, Roy's address and her performance of "Confronting Empire"—with its unique weave of thoughtful analysis, indignation, joking playfulness, and ebullient optimism that infectiously energized the massive audience—also seem to acknowledge the productive aspects generated by the affective pulls of collective joy, celebration, participation, and the like. The seminars, workshops, and discussion circles that have constituted the vast majority of the scheduled events at the WSF are integral to the Forum's process; they provide venues where participants can catch a glimpse of the Forum's diversity by working with participants who come from other parts of the world, who speak different languages, who hold different priorities, and who bring different kinds of experience and strategy to a conversation. More pressing still, these events connect movement activists, educate participants, and enable new strategic alliances to be forged and older ones to be deepened. Every WSF participant should experience these more intimate venues, and my guess is that most do.

But crowds are also vital and indispensable to the WSF, particularly to the international gatherings. The sheer scope of the event is after all one of the things that sets the WSF apart from other activist gatherings. The WSF is in part about political spectacle. *Staged* at the same time as the WEF in Davos, the Forum is designed to be seen and heard across the globe, and as such the *images* of massive marches, enormous crowds, and a joyous, enraged, passionate exuberance of the participants provide a striking visual contrast to the news imagery featuring polite applause for CEOs and government functionaries in the famously "neutral" halls of Switzerland. But the teeming crowds are not merely spectacle. Gone (as I suggested in my discussion of Roy and Wright's scenes of third world hygiene) is the modernist faith in the denaturalizing power of the image to shock into action. Moreover, political spectacles are tricky things: one never knows precisely how they will signify, particularly in a global mediatized context.[37]

Beyond spectacle, the dynamism of WSF crowds is essential to the construction of collectivity as understood and felt by Forum participants. One need not romanticize a crowd as an organic community, or imagine that its myriad differences dissolve into unthinking unanimity, to recognize that the sense of commonality shared by participants in these big events—the affective relationships forged among individuals, and between a participant (speaker or spectator) and the larger crowd—are both real and consequential. The so-called big events shape participants' experiences of the Forum. In part this stems from the fleeting rush associated with "live-ness," where the sharp division between spectatorship and participant is rendered obsolete, if only temporarily, as audience members are swept up in feelings of being connected, being in the moment, being part of something bigger.

Is this a false sense of euphoric commonality? Likely. Are the tactical differences between reformers and radicals made any less significant because both cheer Roy? Is the lived experience of land-less peasants in Brazil or Dalits in India any more fathomable to a participating Northern academic like myself? Probably not. Are any landless peasants or Dalits even in the auditorium to listen to Roy? Some, perhaps—though certainly not with the numbers or di-versity that would challenge a recognizable commonality between a crowd that mostly shares some aspect of what were once called Western values and backgrounds. Subalternity in its various forms remains largely mute.

And yet, though all this is certainly true (and, I hasten to add, recognized by most in the audience), when Roy emphatically de-clares that "*We*, all of us gathered here, have, each in our own way, laid siege to 'Empire,'" a surge of collectivity is produced that cannot be reduced to mystification and manipulation by the rhe-torical sophistication of a charismatic leader, or to the comforting blindness of the essentially passive and unskeptical masses. To the contrary, the big events energize participants, recognizing and vali-dating the place that joy, hope, revelry, and excess hold in strug-gle. The powerful experience of being among a surging, chanting, dancing crowd that is, at least during the transient moment of the live event, entirely generous, welcoming, and joyful provides a physical and emotional reinvigoration and fortification for activists who face despairing challenges on a daily basis.

On the one hand, there is much value in the rush of the mo-ment. On the other hand, the affective bonds of commonality felt so powerfully in the passing moment of live performance and par-ticipation also carry over far beyond the event itself, and are gen-erative of ongoing commitments and energies that are actively re-flective, probing, and critical of the collective bonds forged in such moments. The big events play a crucial role in forging participants' experience of the Forum not only because of the momentary, spon-taneous joys of participation in what feels like a momentous hap-pening, but also because these events become fixed as the lasting touchstones that allow for ongoing deliberation and reflection long afterward. Because they figure moments of shared experience for many Forum participants, the big events frequently serve as the point of departure for subsequent discussions and analyses (like this one) in which specific instances of commonality and dissensus can more slowly emerge as participants consider, debate, refine, reinvent, and reinforce aspects of the WSF process.

Although the WSF crowds are not the ideal instantiation of an impossible collectivity theorized by Roy, Hardt and Negri, Klein, Marcos, and others, they do provide moments in which the carnivalesque excess of joyous bodies produces much more than a simple mirroring or amplification of a staged performance. Indeed, I would contend that the WSF crowds perform a thinking, feeling embrace of the impossibility of perfect collectivity, much more than an obfuscation or occlusion of real differences and divides. Roy's 2003 performance at the WSF enables us to understand this dynamic in ways that may be precluded by, for example, the electoral aspirations underpinning Lula's or Chavez's speeches from the grand stage.

Minimum Agenda

The Forum's intellectual reflectiveness about the value and the limits of such political rallies becomes all the more clear if we examine "Do Turkeys Enjoy Thanksgiving?" Roy's 2004 Forum address in Mumbai. The Mumbai address reaffirms the idea that shared affection and joyous commitment constitute necessary aspects of collective struggle, both as ends and as means, but nonetheless suggests that affective constructions of collectivity, such as those produced and experienced by WSF participants, offer a tactically insufficient response to the hegemonic dominance of what in Porto Alegre she called "Empire" and in Mumbai she calls "The New Imperialism," reminiscent of the language of midcentury cultural radicalism. The "we" of this latter address, which advocates for a "minimum agenda" to bridge internal differences among activists, is much more troubled and fractured than the "we" of "Confronting Empire," but it is a "we" charged with a much more consequential burden.

Although only twelve months had passed since her comments in Porto Alegre, the world seems to have changed utterly by the time Roy delivered the opening plenary address at WSF Mumbai. Her 2003 address closed, to raucous applause, with the lyrical, expectant assertion, "Another World is not only possible; she is on her way. On a quiet day, I can hear her breathing." Also to raucous applause, her 2004 address concluded with the more confrontational sentiment, "For these reasons, we must consider ourselves at war."[38] The intervening months had witnessed Lula's rapid fall from WSF grace as he, in Roy's words, busied himself "implementing IMF guidelines, reducing pension benefits, and purging radicals from the Workers' Party" (90). Klein's distrusting assessment about "big men" from the previous Forum was reiterated by Roy in Mumbai, who asserted, without venom but also without sympathy, "Time and again we have seen that when it comes to the neoliberal project, the heroes of our time are suddenly diminished. Extraordinary, charismatic men, giants in the opposition, when they seize power and become heads of state, they become powerless on the global stage"(90). With its shift of venue from Latin America to South Asia, the Forum itself faced a new set of regional challenges, most forcefully articulated by the Indian Left (including the CPI(M), which Roy savaged in *GOST*). A gathering called Mumbai Resistance (MR), spearheaded by so-called orthodox Marxists, staged a "counter-Forum" across the main road bordering the WSF site in the northern suburb of Goregon, pointedly critiquing the Forum's lack of a coherent anti-imperialist and anticapitalist platform as well as its cozy and largely unexamined alliances with funding organizations, NGOs, and global civil society. Most notably, of course, 2003 witnessed the United States invasion of Iraq, led by President Bush—who appeared entirely undeterred by global popular opinion, that imagined force invoked by Roy in 2003 and labeled "the World's second superpower" by the *New York Times* in an oft-quoted article about the February 15, 2003, antiwar protests around the globe, protests that were set in motion at the WSF regional meeting in Europe. Roy's confident predictions from Porto Alegre that empire, once exposed, would be too "ugly even to rally its own people," and that it would not "be long before the majority of Americans become our allies" (53), had gone confoundingly unrealized, a painful reminder of the easily learned and forgotten lesson about the limits of sunshine as disinfectant.

All this provides the background for a very different "we" constructed in Roy's Mumbai address, one that is both more combative and more constructive than the giddy, untroubled collectivity that Roy helped to forge in Porto Alegre. The 2004 address argues:

> This movement of ours needs a major, global victory. It's not good enough to be right. Sometimes, if only in order to test our resolve, it's important to win something. In order to win something, we—all

of us gathered here and a little way away at Mumbai Resistance—
need to agree on something. That something does not need to be
an over-arching pre-ordained ideology into which we force-fit our
delightfully factious, argumentative selves. It does not need to be
an unquestioning allegiance to one or another form of resistance
to the exclusion of everything else. It could be a minimum agenda.
(92–93)

The phrase "we—all of us gathered here" is almost identical to the
words she uttered the previous year. In this case, however, the oppositional presence of MR across the highway forces Roy's to account for a "them" (or are "they" a "we"?) only a "little way away"
as opposed to (or in addition to), a "them" residing in Washington,
corporate headquarters, war rooms, or places of fundamentalist
worship across the globe. The confident presumption and performance of an untroubled "we" in Porto Alegre finds itself unable to
bear the weight of a transformed historical setting in Mumbai. In
a reaction predictable to *GOST* readers, Roy recoils from the idea
of unanimity or any single "over-arching pre-ordained ideology,"
a sentiment downplayed if not forgotten in the rush of optimism
that had marked her address at the previous gathering. However,
although she embraces the liberal pluralism of "delightfully factious, argumentative selves," she argues that consensus, the "need
to agree on something," remains of paramount concern. Forging
a minimum agenda, then, becomes the pressing necessity for WSF
2004. Or, rather, it becomes a pressing necessity for "this movement of ours," a different construction of "we" that lays down an
implicit challenge to the WSF, which has steadfastly refused the
label of "movement" and the politics of minimum agendas.

I have chosen to read Roy's optimism in the Porto Alegre address not as naïveté (I believe that *GOST* more than establishes
her skepticism regarding the possibility of straightforward or un-
differentiated community), but rather as the performance of a
participatory, affective collectivity. Similarly, I understand Roy's
Mumbai address in terms of the construction of an emergent collectivity; however, both the stakes of such a collectivity and the means
by which it may be constituted are substantially refashioned in the
2004 speech. Gone is the blithe optimism (never quite believed) that
dares to imagine surging forward on the brink of a world-historical
wave of victories. In its place, Roy develops a more tempered as-

sessment of global crises, along with a firmer conviction that collectivity is forged through struggle and sacrifice rather than, or in addition to, carnival. Gopal Balakrishnan makes a similar, illuminating argument in his response to Benedict Anderson's thesis that the rise of print capitalism produces conditions that allow for the imagined community of nationalism. Unconvinced that print capitalism alone would be able to produce cultural affinities "sufficiently resonant to generate the colossal sacrifices that modern peoples are at times willing to make for their nation," Balakrishnan argues persuasively that the affective bonds of nationalism are forged in moments of collective risk and struggle: "Only in struggle does the nation cease to be an informal, contestable and taken-for-granted frame of reference, and become a community which seizes hold of the imagination." Although such imagined communities are therefore often the product of official, nation *state*–sanctioned militarism, Balakrishnan, following Anderson, rightly suggests that they need not be so, pointing out that the "mobilization of a people on a national basis has just as often played the decisive role in the more subaltern history of struggle against colonialism and foreign occupation."[39] In this regard, both Balakrishnan and Roy should be understood to echo Fanon through their foregrounding the ways in which (national) collectivity is forged through struggle.

Significantly it is *the nation* that re-emerges in Roy's address as the figure of collectivity most successful in its opposition to (New) Imperialism. On the one hand, this points to a problematic nostalgia within Roy's address. The references to courageous acts of civil disobedience such as Gandhi's Salt March seem to yearn toward a moment when the enemies were clearer, resistance more united, and tactics more effective: "It was a direct strike at the economic underpinning of the British Empire. It was *real*" (91). Reminiscent of Wright's deep admiration for Nehru at Bandung, Roy's speech also evokes the nation's first prime minister, lauding "India's proud tradition of being non-aligned" (86). The "big men" hagiography is a bit troubling, but even more so is Roy's romanticizing of Nehru and nonalignment. As I argued in chapter 4, the World Bank underwrites nonalignment: the extensive history of lending and borrowing agreements between Nehru's India and the Bank likely enabled both institutions to survive. As Dean Acheson said of Nehru, "he was so important to India and India's survival so important to all of us that if he did not exist—as Voltaire said of God—he would have to be invented."[40] To evoke this particular nationalist tradition in a critique of the New Imperialism rings hollow. A return to the moment of Bandung seems both unlikely and undesirable.

That said, we should recall Jameson's argument that a dialectic of globalization is best understood as a matter not of Difference, but rather of position, as it offers a useful rejoinder about the continued efficacy of a nationalist politics. Although the nation state may no longer seem sufficient as a political response to globalization, it remains a tactically valuable institution to the extent that it can defend borders against certain malign global flows. Patrick Bond has developed this case at length, arguing specifically for the nation state's capacity to "lock down capital" as a means to resist the developmentalist imperialism of the World Bank. Bond writes that radical democratic reforms will "necessarily be located at the scale of the nation state," which is why the state "remains the unit of analysis amongst even those who (like myself) consider themselves vigorous internationalists."[41] In Roy's speech, then, it becomes possible to read nonalignment as a figure for Indian nationalism tactically positioned in opposition to the privatizing tentacles of Haliburton and Bechtel.

But if we extend the dialectical logic that both Jameson and Bond offer us, we also can read nonalignment as a signifier for a certain internationalism that stands in opposition to the current Indian state's sponsorship of both communalist violence and nuclear weaponry. In this sense, Roy's address works to produce in the global movement for justice and solidarity the type of internationalism that Fanon seems to envision as the end of national struggle when he writes that "national consciousness, which is not nationalism, is the only thing that will give us an international dimension" (247). The *inter*nationalism that arises out of national consciousness, for Fanon, stands in stark opposition to the representative internationalism of the United Nations and World Bank to which he refers. Likewise, it stands in opposition, though much more equivocally, to the internationalism of Marxism, at once seeking to retain Marxism's analytical and revolutionary force while insisting on the need to address its Eurocentric blindnesses in relation to race, and the specific historical forces that condition the social relations of the colonial world. Roy's globalism in this Mumbai address, I am suggesting, bears a close resemblance to precisely such a Fanonian internationalism. Like Fanon, Roy dispenses an unambiguous critique of the World Bank and IMF as the henchmen of New Imperialism, and, despite her discomfort with MR's Marxist "over-arching pre-ordained ideology," she argues that a victory for the global justice and solidarity movement will require the coalitional or consensual tactics of agreeing with MR orthodoxy on a minimum agenda.[42]

Toward the end of defining such a minimum agenda, Roy looks to the war in Iraq as a specific site upon which broad consensus could be built. "The issue is not about *supporting* the resistance in Iraq against the occupation or discussing who exactly constitutes the resistance" (93); instead, Roy insists, "We have to *become* the global resistance to the occupation" (94). Specifically, she suggests that we start "with something really small" (93). Surely I am not the only *GOST* reader who sees some irony here. With a welcoming nod to any would-be Comrade Pillai who might be rousing the Mumbai Resistance crowd just across the way, Roy suggests, in effect, that *we* lay siege to the Paradise Pickle Factory:

> I suggest that at a joint closing ceremony of the World Social Forum and Mumbai Resistance, we choose, by some means, two of the major corporations that are profiting from the destruction of Iraq. We could then list every project they are involved in. We could locate their offices in every city and every country across the world. We could go after them. We could shut them down. It's a question of bringing our collective wisdom and experience of past struggles to bear on a single target. It's a question of the desire to win.[43]

This is hardly the "small politics" of *GOST*, where the window for meaningful resistance appears limited to the tiniest slivers of individual joy or, at best, mutual affection. "Small" here refers to widespread, coordinated opposition to the U.S. occupation of Iraq. The mass rally and the company boycott—treated with wariness at best, disdain at worst, by the novel—here become refashioned as tactical applications of the "wisdom and experience of past struggles." And shutting down the "single target" no longer rings of opportunist scapegoating, as in the case of Paradise Pickles, but rather turns the pressures of hypervisibility and market logic against offending corporations, demonstrating the "desire to win" that characterizes the global struggle Roy hopes to call into being.

To a large extent I embrace Roy's call for minimal agendas. The term, however, offers both a retreat and an advance. Minimum agenda for the WSF will likely founder against two problems. The notion pulls us on the one hand toward the politics of consensus and thus toward the politics of global civil society. Here, as we have seen, the Bank among others happily waits for the inevitable arrival of the WSF. On the other hand, it pulls us away from the utopian sphere of possibility; necessarily, *minimum* agenda means the abandonment of certain possible worlds in the decision to work toward others. But if the concept inevitably promises regression, it also implies much to be hopeful about.

Minimum agenda is meant, I believe, to spur the WSF in the direction of mobilization. It is an effort to radicalize the Forum to the extent that it moves toward the articulation of a shared affirmative agenda that would be generative of movement, rather than space—toward an agreed-upon set of "yeses" in addition to the single "no." It argues that the Forum's multitudinous weight can be, indeed should be, pressed into action. This logic has been embraced by others within the WSF, and in 2004 a group of nineteen prominent intellectuals released what was termed the Porto Alegre Manifesto, which contains twelve "proposals for another possible world." A minimum agenda of sorts, it nevertheless articulates the beginnings of a bold platform for activism.[44] Further, the concept of minimum agenda enables a response to the local/global dialectics that Bond and, particularly, Jameson frame so thoughtfully. That is, minimum agenda asks us to think about the ways that the WSF politics of scale may provide an important structure through which accumulative, multilayered forms of struggle can be concatenated into a form of politics more responsive to the complexities of globalization.

Finally, the notion of minimum agenda calls for the pedagogical and dialogic work of communicating struggle. Throughout this book, I have made clear that I applaud and value the theoretical provocation to figure the impossible. As Jameson has repeatedly reminded us, the utopian desire for another possible world remains integral to politics as such in its requisite address to a future horizon. But I part ways with Hardt and Negri when they suggest in *Empire* that "each struggle, though firmly rooted in local conditions, leaps immediately to the global level and attacks the imperial constitution in is generality."[45] This notion of networked intelligence and affiliation seems entirely too simple. When defining the constitutive components of politics, the obverse side of utopic desire is the labor of organizing. Global collectivities, like class formations, race formations, gender formations, and the like, are forged, not inherited. As Balakrishnan and Fanon remind us, such collectivities are typically produced not simply by interconnectedness or access to community, but rather through consequential sacrifice and struggle. Minimum agenda recognizes and accepts the difficult work of building political alliances.

In the end, minimum agenda is probably as much as the WSF will be capable of offering. An institutional structure designed to facilitate participation, not leadership or direction, the WSF charter itself will forestall efforts to make the Forum articulate a specific platform. This may be for the best; it places the onus for radicalism back onto the social movements that animate the WSF in the first place. They will set the agenda. The Forum's job will be to insist that this agenda not be an abandonment of its foundational democratic and anticapitalist principles—it must resist the pulls of so-called free associations and free markets, of global civil society. Indeed, at minimum the WSF agenda will need to include a response to what I earlier described as the Forum's constitutive antagonist: the World Bank. The first demand must be immediate and comprehensive debt relief. The second "first demand" in this regard should be the abolition of the Bank.

Placing Culture

Roy's insistence on real politics and minimum agenda can serve to refocus our attention on one of the founding antinomies of cultural studies—namely, the relation between economy and culture. During the course of this book, we have encountered this trope variously manifested as base and superstructure, industrial manufacturing and speculative finance, project lending and social lending, the material and the ideological, participation and representation, organizing and networking, and more. Eagelton rearticulates the fundamental schism by reminding us that "a monotonous biological round of need, scarcity and political oppression . . . has been the typical experience of by far the majority of human beings in history, and remains so today," leading him to conclude that "it is time, while acknowledging its significance, to put [culture] back in its place."[46]

In many regards, this book has been my endeavor to help *place culture*. As Eagleton suggests, this project demands that we reckon with the fact that the globe has been and continues to be marked by radical inequities, inequities that cannot be considered merely cultural. The real economics of subsistence and the *real* politics of subalternity cannot be reduced to culture. Nor, as Eagleton would be the first to say, are they entirely outside it. Similarly, the real work of addressing inequity and exploitation is in excess of culture. Networks and multitudes will not spring, ready formed, from the philosopher's pen. Rather, although historical models may provide some guidance, the long, hard work of building and linking *movements*—to my mind, the only plausible vehicle for radical change that can address the real inequities produced by exploitation and oppression—will certainly require the real labor of persistent, courageous organizing. This labor stands in stark distinction to an Arnoldian notion of culture as bourgeois aesthetics, or a postmodern notion of culture as discursive fluidity and play. But the work of producing collectivities, though not reducible to culture, cannot take place outside of the communicative, affective realm of culture, either. The real labor of imagining and actualizing collectivities of struggle is always cultural work.

We must develop a double vision that allows us to, at once, see culture and the economy as both distinct and inseparable. Culture, as we have seen, is not inherently political. It is politicized—for better and for worse. As I argued in chapter 3, the Bank's institutional embrace of social lending, along with its subsequent establishment as the planet's preeminent development institution, becomes possible only at the moment that it abandons any responsibility for global equity. The same may be true of a theoretical category like *multitude*: that is, the precondition of horizontal, networked forms of collectivity may likewise be the abandonment of a commitment to the principle of equity, or of movements defined by their struggle for equity and against exploitation. However, *multitude*, as I argued earlier, is a figure for a potentiality, not an empirical category of the present. Whether the WSF and contemporary social movements are emergent formations that may help produce that future remains to be seen.

I am inclined, for now, to work toward minimum agendas. The WSF provides an exceptional vehicle to do just this. To do so, however, it must move beyond the limits of global civil society. Or rather, the collection of social movement actors and activists that constitute the WSF must move it beyond these limits. Minimum agendas, as Roy suggests, look to identify shared projects upon which the collective weight of a global movement can aggregate pressure. Further, a strategy of minimum agendas suggests the WSF should continue to conceive of its role as supplementary rather than vanguardist; it will be most effective if it commits its resources to supplement the ongoing struggles of social movements encircling the planet, particularly the radical movements of the Global South. Among these struggles are the campaigns against the World Bank. Like the boycotts that Roy proposes of Halliburton, Bechtel, and the other war profiteers, struggles against the Bank *communicate* in part because of the spectacular visibility of the institutions. But as I have tried to show here, the campaigns to abolish the World Bank are not merely political theater, merely cultural; rather, they rely on the double vision that works to keep sight of both economy and culture.

The project of this book has been to analyze the role of the World Bank as a cultural institution and a world-historical actor in the age of three worlds and beyond. The Bank has not acted in a vacuum, however, and I have tried to situate it in relation to other cultural institutions (the conferences at Bandung and Porto Alegre, in particular), as well as to the radical anti-imperial social movements that have also shaped the World Bank era. In doing so, I have hoped to contribute to an emancipatory transnational cultural studies that works, in Denning's words, to "narrate an account of globalization that speaks not just of an abstract market with buyers and sellers, or even of an abstract commodification with producers and consumers, but of actors."[47] Exposing and interrogating those institutions predicated on capitalist exploitation and the perpetuation of inequity, while working to build and link those institutions that might create new mechanisms for democracy, remains one of the supplementary contributions that an emancipatory transnational cultural studies can pursue. Putting culture in its place is no mean feat. To do so requires that we look toward a potential future horizon while remaining firmly grounded in the realities of the present. Culture as such offers an inadequate vehicle for affecting radical change. But, of course, it makes no sense to speak of "culture as such." Culture is not a place; it is placed. And working to *place culture* in the service of *democratic movements for equity* remains a locus of struggle that dictates one of the minimum agendas of our day.

Notes

Introduction

1. Muhammad Yunus, "Preface: Redefining Development," in *50 Years Is Enough: The Case against the World Bank and the International Monetary Fund,* ed. Kevin Danaher (Boston: South End Press, 1994), x.

2. Bruce Rich, *Mortgaging the Earth: The World Bank, Environmental Impoverishment, and the Crisis of Development* (Boston: Beacon Press, 1994), 8.

3. Gayatri Chakravorty Spivak, *A Critique of Postcolonial Reason: Toward a History of the Vanishing Present* (Cambridge, Mass.: Harvard University Press, 1999), 372.

4. Michael Denning, *Culture in the Age of Three Worlds* (London: Verso, 2004). I develop this argument in much greater detail in chapter 4.

5. Ibid., 3, 1.

6. I, like many other scholars, find the term *globalization* theoretically wanting when used to describe either a set of coherent processes or a chronological period marked by a distinct break from other "phases" of capitalism. The literature is too vast to cite here, but an eclectic survey of seminal references would include: Samir Amin, *Empire of Chaos* (New York: Monthly Review Press, 1992); Arjun Appadurai, *Modernity at Large: Cultural Dimensions of Globalization* (Minneapolis: University of Minnesota Press, 1996); Manuel Castells, *The Rise of the Network Society* (Malden, Mass., and Oxford: Blackwell Publishers, 1996); Castells, *The Power of Identity* (Malden, Mass., and Oxford: Blackwell, 1997); Castells, *End of Millennium,* 2nd ed. (Malden, Mass., and Oxford: Blackwell Publishers, 2000); Inderpal Grewal and Caren Kaplan, *Scattered Hegemonies: Postmodernity and Transnational Feminist Practices*

(Minneapolis: University of Minnesota Press, 1994); Michael Hardt and Antonio Negri, *Empire* (Cambridge, Mass., and London: Harvard University Press, 2000); Hardt and Negri, *Multitude: War and Democracy in the Age of Empire* (New York: Penguin Press, 2004); David Harvey, *The Condition of Postmodernity: An Enquiry into the Origins of Cultural Change* (Cambridge, Mass.: Blackwell, 1989); David Held and Anthony G. McGrew, *Globalization/Anti-Globalization* (Cambridge: Polity, 2002); Fredric Jameson and Masao Miyoshi, *The Cultures of Globalization* (Durham, N.C.: Duke University Press, 1998); Anthony D. King, ed., *Culture, Globalization, and the World-System: Contemporary Conditions for the Representation of Identity* (Minneapolis: University of Minnesota Press, 1997); Naomi Klein, *No Logo: Taking Aim at the Brand Bullies* (New York: Picador, 2000); Lisa Lowe and David Lloyd, *The Politics of Culture in the Shadow of Capital: Post-Contemporary Interventions* (Durham, N.C.: Duke University Press, 1997); Subcomandante Marcos, *Our Word Is Our Weapon: Selected Writings*, ed. Juana Ponce de León, 1st ed. (New York: Seven Stories Press, 2001); Aihwa Ong, *Flexible Citizenship: The Cultural Logics of Transnationality* (Durham, N.C.: Duke University Press, 1999); Saskia Sassen, *The Global City: New York, London, Tokyo* (Princeton, N.J.: Princeton University Press, 1991). For one concise argument about the inadequacies of the term *globalization,* I point the reader to the chapter "Globalization" in Doug Henwood, *After the New Economy* (New York: New Press, 2003). I adopt "age of globalization" here not only because the term has become so ubiquitous in popular and scholarly discourse, but also because it is the category that Denning uses to mark the transformations in culture and cultural study beset by the post-1989 demise of the second world.

7. Denning, *Culture,* 28–29.

8. Address by George D. Woods, The Canadian Club, Toronto, Canada, November 9, 1964, "The Development Century." Box 13; Series 4117; WB IBRD/IDA 23; Records of the Office of External Relations, IPA Press Releases, World Bank Group Archives.

9. The influential special issue of *Social Text* on third world and postcolonial issues published in 1992 (10, no. 31/32) may be seen as an important marker in this disciplinary evolution. That is, the articles published in this issue (including the Anne McClintock essay discussed below) demonstrate an awareness of the emergence of Postcolonial Studies (capital *P,* capital *S*) as a discipline. However, one also finds in these essays a simultaneous and at times contradictory antidisciplinary energy, which attempts to avoid the static rigidities of a "body of knowledge" in part by sketching out a new set of global political exigencies and by insisting that postcolonial scholarship wrestle with the contemporary moment in its relation to an older colonial archive.

10. Anne McClintock, "The Angel of Progress: Pitfalls of the Term 'Post-Colonialism,'" *Social Text* 10, no. 31/32 (1992) (this essay was reprinted in a slightly different form in the introduction and postscript of Anne McClintock, *Imperial Leather: Race, Gender, and Sexuality in the Colonial Conquest* [New York: Routledge, 1995]); Aijaz Ahmad, *In Theory: Classes, Nations, Literatures* (London: Verso, 1992); Masao Miyoshi, "A Borderless World? From Colonialism to Transnationalism and the Decline of the Nation State," *Critical Inquiry* 19, no. 4 (1993): 726–51; Arif Dirlik, "The Postcolonial Aura: Third World Criticism in the Age of Global Capitalism," *Critical Inquiry* 20 (1994).

11. Henwood charts the number of articles printed in the *New York Times* and *The Washington Post* that contain the word *globalization* and points to the monumental spike in that term's usage between 1996 and 2000. Although I have no statistical data to support the claim, my suspicion is that a similar spike exists within postcolonial scholarship, and that references to the World Bank become more frequent in a roughly proportionate ratio. Henwood, *After the New Economy,* 146.

12. Mahasweta Devi, *Imaginary Maps: Three Stories,* trans. Gayatri Chakravorty Spivak (New York: Routledge, 1995); Spivak, *Critique of Postcolonial Reason.*

13. Amitava Kumar, ed., *World Bank Literature* (Minneapolis: University of Minnesota Press, 2003).

14. Carl E. Pletsch, "The Three Worlds, or the Division of Social Scientific Labor, Circa 1950–1975," *Comparative Studies in Society and History* 23 (1981): 565–90.

15. Arturo Escobar, *Encountering Development: The Making and Unmaking of the Third World* (Princeton, N.J.: Princeton University Press, 1995); Wolfgang Sachs, *The Development Dictionary: A Guide to Knowledge as Power* (London: Zed Books, 1992).

16. Spivak, *Critique of Postcolonial Reason,* xiii.

17. Kumar, *World Bank Literature,* xix–xx.

18. For example, see the chapters by Subir Sinha, Keneth Surin, Joseph Medley and Lorrayne Carrol, Suzanne Bergeron, and see, to a lesser degree, my own contribution to Kumar's collection.

19. Rosemary Hennessy "¡Ya Basta! We Are Rising Up! World Bank Culture and Collective Opposition in the North," in *World Bank Literature,* ed. Kumar, 41.

20. Like the term *globalization, antiglobalization* has predictably come under scrutiny and critique. Many social movement activists argue that they are not against globalization per se—indeed, they intend to globalize resistance—but rather against a particular form of *corporate globalization* or against capitalism as a global system. Their choice of terms such as *counterglobalization* or *alterglobalization* attempts to

address such concerns. These discussions, obviously connected to the debates over the term *globalization* itself, can be found in numerous places. They are nicely crystallized in the forewords and "proem" by Irene Santiago, Hilary Wainwright, and Jai Sen in *World Social Forum: Challenging Empires, ed.* Jai Sen et al. (New Delhi: The Viveka Foundation, 2004).

21. *World Bank Literature*, ed. Kumar, xix.

22. Ibid.

23. Bruce Robbins, "Afterword," in *World Bank Literature*, ed. Kumar, 299, 300.

24. Spivak, *Critique of Postcolonial Reason*, 372–73.

25. Ibid., 200–201.

26. Ibid., 380. This reference is a revised claim from her afterword to *Imaginary Maps*, in which she points to the "connection, indeed complicity, between the bourgeoisie of the Third World and migrants in the First" as the "traffic line in Cultural Studies"(198–99).

27. Gayatri Chakravorty Spivak, afterward, in Devi, *Imaginary Maps*, 200.

28. Spivak, *Critique of Postcolonial Reason*, 379.

29. Can she mean this in the Derridean sense of "supplement?" It seems unlikely that she would attribute to academic work from the North the paradoxical centrality vested in the Derridean notion of the supplement that completes the whole: a supplement that is in no way extraneous or beyond, but is in fact necessary and foundational. Spivak, needless to say, chooses her words with care. Thus the degree to which the mainstreaming contribution of academic labor is taken in this account as central or as peripheral to her "Globe Girdling Movements" hinges on one's reading of *supplement* in relation to, say, *moonlighting*.

30. My examination of public documents comes both by choice and by necessity. Because I am interested in the World Bank's changing public image—the way it constructs and conveys an institutional identity in response to specific social pressures—the speeches, press releases, annual reports, oral histories, and publications afford much insight into the ways that the Bank is crafting particular rhetorical responses for specific audiences and contexts. All of the primary sources that I cite in the coming chapters were gathered during time spent researching at the World Bank Archives located in the Bank's Washington, D.C., headquarters; all are publicly available for researchers and require no special permissions or authorization. The Bank will, upon special request, make available internal memoranda, correspondence, and other documents. Although access to these materials would have been useful—if only to draw attention to the ways the institution's public rhetoric

has mirrored or departed from the debates taking place behind closed doors—permission to use these documents is granted only on the condition that the Bank be given authorization over the final manuscript. Thus, even though I have no reason to believe that the Bank would have refused to allow my publication of any materials, I chose to forego its layer of editorial control. Any internal debates or positions that I cite, therefore, have been published elsewhere.

31. For those interested in a more comprehensive treatment, several admirable histories already exist—both official, generally laudatory accounts, and critical or counterhegemonic versions. The World Bank commissioned the Brookings Institution to publish institutional histories on the occasions of the Bank's twenty-fifth and fiftieth anniversaries. See Edward S. Mason and Robert E. Asher, *The World Bank since Bretton Woods: The Origins, Policies, Operations, and Impact of the International Bank for Reconstruction and Development* (Washington, D.C.: Brookings Institution, 1973), and Devesh Kapur, John Prior Lewis, and Richard Charles Webb, *The World Bank: Its First Half Century,* 2 vols. (Washington, D.C.: Brookings Institution, 1997). These two monumental histories—roughly three thousand pages between them—constitute by far the most detailed, comprehensive account of the Bank's operations. Critical at times, they are nonetheless marked by political and economic centrism and written with a fair amount of empathy for the Bank. In Noam Chomsky style, I prefer to rely most heavily on these two officially commissioned histories both because of their thoroughness and to avoid the impression of cherry-picking materials from more critical sources. There are of course numerous critical histories of the Bank. Most notable are Walden F. Bello, *Deglobalization: Ideas for a New World Economy* (London; New York: Zed Books, 2002); Rich, *Mortgaging the Earth*; Cheryl Payer, *The World Bank: A Critical Analysis* (New York: Monthly Review Press, 1982); Catherine Caufield, *Masters of Illusion: The World Bank and the Poverty of Nations* (New York: Henry Holt, 1996); Danaher, *50 Years Is Enough*; Michael Goldman, *Imperial Nature: The World Bank and Struggles for Justice in the Age of Globalization* (New Haven, Conn.: Yale University Press, 2005); Patrick Bond, *Against Global Apartheid: South Africa Meets the World Bank, IMF, and International Finance,* 2nd ed. (Lansdowne, South Africa: University of Cape Town Press, 2003); Susan George and Fabrizio Sabelli, *Faith and Credit: The World Bank's Secular Empire* (Boulder: Westview Press, 1994).

32. Stephanie Black, "Life and Debt" (New York: distributed by New Yorker Films, 2001).

33. To greater and lesser extents, this is the pattern of the volumes by Caufield, George and Sabelli, Goldman, and Rich.

1. Imaginative Ventures

1. This argument implicitly builds upon a Gramscian notion of hegemony, understood not solely in terms of producing consent and collaboration, but also in terms of the contested claims by both dominant and subaltern blocs in their struggle over social relations. Hegemony in this sense is always historical, emerging in response to specific pressures and relying upon specific forms of prestige and persuasion. Moreover, consent always exists in careful balance with coercion; it is when the intellectual work of producing supposedly spontaneous consent fails that the coercive apparatus of the state must reveal itself.

2. Two recent examples (among many) indicating the range and relevance of new and important scholarship being published in this area include the detailed archival analysis in Betty Joseph's *Reading the East India Company 1720–1840: Colonial Currencies of Gender* (Chicago: Chicago University Press, 2004) and the rhetorical analysis of legal protection afforded to prisoners by the Geneva Conventions (and denied by the Bush administration) in Judith Butler, *Precarious Life: The Powers of Mourning and Violence* (London: Verso, 2004).

3. Terry Eagleton, *Literary Theory: An Introduction* (Oxford: Basil Blackwell, 1983), 206. For a concise and useful introduction to the long-standing debate between those who see rhetoric as obfuscation and those who see it as socially productive (or, in Fish's terms, between rhetoric and philosophy), see Stanley Fish, "Rhetoric," in *Critical Terms for Literary Study*, ed. Frank Lentriccia and Thomas McLaughlin (Chicago: University of Chicago Press, 1990), 203–22. See also Raymond Williams, *Communications* (New York: Barnes and Noble, 1967); Stuart Hall, "The Rediscovery of 'Ideology': Return of the Repressed in Media Studies," in *Culture, Society, and the Media,* ed. Tony Bennett, Michael Gurevitch, James Curran, and Janet Woollacott (London: Methuen, 1982), 56–90.

4. Frequently cited examples of the textual turn include Arturo Escobar, *Encountering Development: The Making and Unmaking of the Third World* (Princeton, N.J.: Princeton University Press, 1995); Wolfgang Sachs, *The Development Dictionary: A Guide to Knowledge as Power* (London: Zed Books, 1992); James Ferguson, *The Anti-Politics Machine: "Development," Depoliticization, and Bureaucratic Power in Lesotho* (Cambridge and New York: Cambridge University Press, 1990); Gustavo Esteva, "Development," in *The Development Dictionary.*

5. For a useful corrective to some of the excesses of the textual turn, see J. S. Crush, *Power of Development* (London and New York: Routledge, 1995).

6. Escobar, *Encountering Development,* 4.

7. Esteva, "Development," 7.

8. Escobar, *Encountering Development*, 84.

9. Ibid., 225. It should be said that, although *Encountering Development* appears to privilege discursive hybridity and the politics of representation, Escobar's other work, including his theorization of the World Social Forum (which I will examine in the final chapter of this book), places more emphasis on social movements and radical organizing—a position that I see as more politically promising.

10. Ibid.

11. Walden F. Bello, *Deglobalization: Ideas for a New World Economy* (London and New York: Zed Books, 2002); Patrick Bond, *Against Global Apartheid: South Africa Meets the World Bank, IMF, and International Finance*, 2nd ed. (Lansdowne, South Africa: University of Cape Town Press, 2003); Catherine Caufield, *Masters of Illusion: The World Bank and the Poverty of Nations* (New York: Henry Holt, 1996); Kevin Danaher, *50 Years Is Enough: The Case against the World Bank and the International Monetary Fund* (Boston: South End Press, 1994); Julia Elyachar, "Empowerment Money: The World Bank, Non-Governmental Organizations, and the Value of Culture in Egypt," *Public Culture* 14, no. 3 (2002); Cynthia H. Enloe, *Bananas, Beaches, and Bases: Making Feminist Sense of International Politics* (London: Pandora, 1989); Ferguson, *Anti-Politics Machine*; Susan George and Fabrizio Sabelli, *Faith and Credit: The World Bank's Secular Empire* (Boulder, Colo.: Westview Press, 1994); Teresa Hayter, *Aid as Imperialism* (Great Britain: Penguin Books, 1971); Rosemary Hennessy, *Profit and Pleasure: Sexual Identities in Late Capitalism* (New York: Routledge, 2000); Naila Kabeer, *Reversed Realities: Gender Hierarchies in Development Thought* (London and New York: Verso, 1994); Naila Kabeer, *The Power to Choose: Bangladeshi Women and Labour Market Decisions in London and Dhaka* (London and New York: Verso, 2000); Maria Mies, *Patriarchy and Accumulation on a World Scale: Women in the International Division of Labour* (London and Atlantic Highlands, N.J.: Zed Books, 1986); Timothy Mitchell, *Rule of Experts: Egypt, Techno-Politics, Modernity* (Berkeley and Los Angeles: University of California Press, 2002); Chandra Talpade Mohanty, *Feminism without Borders: Decolonizing Theory, Practicing Solidarity* (Durham, N.C.: Duke University Press, 2003); Mohanty, Ann Russo, and Lourdes Torres, *Third World Women and the Politics of Feminism* (Bloomington: Indiana University Press, 1991); Cheryl Payer, *The Debt Trap: The IMF and the Third World* (New York: Monthly Review Press, 1975); Payer, *The World Bank: A Critical Analysis* (New York: Monthly Review Press, 1982); Bruce Rich, *Mortgaging the Earth: The World Bank, Environmental Impoverishment, and the Crisis of Development* (Boston: Beacon Press, 1994); Vijayendra Rao and Michael Walton, *Culture and Public Action* (Stanford, Calif.: Stanford University Press,

2004); Vandana Shiva, *Biopiracy: The Plunder of Nature and Knowledge* (Boston, Mass.: South End Press, 1997); Shiva, *Stolen Harvest: The Hijacking of the Global Food Supply* (Cambridge, Mass.: South End Press, 2000); Shiva, *Water Wars: Privatization, Pollution, and Profit* (Cambridge, Mass.: South End Press, 2002); Gayatri Chakravorty Spivak, *A Critique of Postcolonial Reason: Toward a History of the Vanishing Present* (Cambridge, Mass.: Harvard University Press, 1999).

12. For a thoughtful attempt to navigate between the disjunctures of official texts and their implementations in the field, see Subir Sinha, "Breaking the Waves: Reading World Bank and Social Movement Documents on the Global Fisheries," in *World Bank Literature,* ed. Amitava Kumar (Minneapolis: University of Minnesota Press, 2003), 111–27.

13. Indirectly, this section builds upon the methodological innovations of Ranajit Guha and the Subaltern Studies group, which uses a discursive historiography as a corrective to the exclusions of peasant resistances from the official history of British colonial occupation of India. See Ranajit Guha, *Elementary Aspects of Peasant Insurgency in Colonial India* (Delhi: Oxford University Press, 1983).

14. Edward S. Mason and Robert E. Asher, *The World Bank since Bretton Woods; The Origins, Policies, Operations, and Impact of the International Bank for Reconstruction and Development* (Washington, D.C.: Brookings Institution, 1973), 458.

15. Arundhati Roy has written eloquently about the devastating effect of big dams in the Narmada River Valley. See Arundhati Roy, *The Cost of Living* (New York: Modern Library, 1999), 7–90, and *Power Politics* (Cambridge, Mass.: South End Press, 2001), 1–86. See also Caufield, *Masters of Illusion,* 5–29. At the March 31, 2005, meeting of executive directors in which Paul Wolfowitz's nomination as new Bank president was accepted, the Bank also announced its approval of the Nam Theun 2 dam project in Laos (a project initiated under the Wolfensohn presidency).

16. Mason and Asher, *World Bank since Bretton Woods,* 51.

17. George and Sabelli, *Faith and Credit,* 249.

18. Louis Althusser, "Ideology and Ideological State Apparatus," trans. Ben Brewster, in *Lenin and Philosophy and Other Essays* (New York: Monthly Review Press, 2001), 123.

19. Devesh Kapur, John Prior Lewis, and Richard Charles Webb, *The World Bank: Its First Half Century,* 2 vols. (Washington, D.C.: Brookings Institution, 1997), 77.

20. Address by John J. McCloy before the Foreign Policy Association, Cincinnati, Ohio, Tuesday, June 1, 1948. Box 4; Series 4117; WB IBRD/IDA 23 Records of the Office of External Relations, IPA Press Releases, World Bank Group Archives.

21. Reminiscences of George Martin (August 3, 1961), in the Co-

lumbia University Oral History Research Office Collective (hereafter CUOHROC), 23.

22. Ibid.

23. Reminiscences of Eugene R. Black (August 6, 1961) in the CUOHROC, 13.

24. Caulfield argues that the Treasury Department hired "New York public relations whiz" Randolph Feltus to head up an "organized propaganda effort" in 1945, a tactic it repeated fifty years later when the Bank hired "media guru" Herb Schmertz to develop a public relations response to environmental critics, particularly targeting Bruce Rich's book *Mortgaging the Earth*. Caufield, *Masters of Illusion*, 44, 274.

25. Or, following Jacques Derrida, we could say that such confidence-building work is precisely *supplemental*, for the very same reason of its centrality.

26. Mason and Asher, *World Bank since Bretton Woods*, 250–51.

27. Speech of Honorable J. W. Beyen, executive director for Holland and Union of South Africa of the International Bank for Reconstruction and Development, to the Savings Bank Association of the State of New York at its annual meeting, Chateau Frontenac, Quebec, Canada, October 14, 15, and 16. Box 4; Series 4117; WB IBRD/IDA 23 Records of the Office of External Relations, IPA Press Releases, World Bank Group Archives.

28. The reference here is to the seminal work on nationalism, Benedict Anderson's *Imagined Communities: Reflections on the Origin and Spread of Nationalism* (London: Verso, 1991).

29. Describing the Bank's early years, its officials repeatedly use the metaphor of a bridge. Among many other instances are Black's recollection, in a 1961 interview, that "the Bank was looked on as a sort of bridge between war and peace," and McCloy's description of the Bank as "essentially a bridge between intergovernmental lending and private investment." Never content to rely on the inherent ambiguity of metaphor, and always prone to rhetorical equivocation, the presidents used such qualifiers as, in these examples, "sort of" and "essentially." Reminiscences of Eugene R. Black (August 6, 1961), in the CUOHROC, 20, and address by John J. McCloy before the Foreign Policy Association, Minneapolis, Minnesota, Wednesday, January 19, 1949, Box 5; Series 4117; WB IBRD/IDA 23 Records of the Office of External Relations, IPA Press Releases, World Bank Group Archives.

30. Klaus Knorr, "The Bretton Woods Institutions in Transition," *International Organization* 2 (1948): 35–36.

31. Quoted in Mason and Asher, *World Bank since Bretton Woods*, 59.

32. Ibid., 12.

33. Among the purposes of the Bank listed in Article I are: "To assist in the reconstruction and development of territories of members by facilitating

the *investment of capital for productive purposes,* including the restoration of economies destroyed or disrupted by war, the reconversion of productive facilities to peacetime needs and the *encouragement of the development of productive facilities and resources in less developed countries"* and "To conduct its operations with due regard to the effect of international investment on business conditions in the territories of members, and in the immediate post-war years to assist in bringing about a s*mooth transition from a wartime to a peacetime economy"* (Articles of Agreement, International Bank for Reconstruction and Development [Washington DC: U.S. Department of Treasury, 1944], 51–52).

34. Mason and Asher, *World Bank since Bretton Woods,* 2.

35. Kapur, Lewis, and Webb, *World Bank,* 95. The passage they quote is from C. A. Knowles, *The Economic Development of the British Overseas Empire,* 2nd ed., (London: Routledge, 1928), vii.

36. World Bank Charter, Article I (iii), 52.

37. Ibid., 59–60.

38. Kapur, Lewis, and Webb, *World Bank,* 62.

39. Ibid., 69.

40. Mason and Asher, *World Bank since Bretton Woods,* 28. This curious use of "Anglo-Saxon," presumably a racialized inflection of "Anglo-American," appears with some regularity in early Bank materials, and is picked up by historians such as Mason and Asher.

41. Ibid., 2.

42. Of course, "one nation, one vote" is another antidemocratic mechanism, disregarding as it does the distribution of global population, and bolstering a system in which the nation state is taken as the only legitimate organizational form to stand as a political representative for the world's peoples.

43. Articles of Agreement, Article V. Sec. 3. (a), 67.

44. It was not until 1989 that the U.S. voting share dipped below the 20 percent needed to veto any changes to the Bank Charter, at which point the Charter was amended to maintain the U.S. veto by lowering the threshold to 15 percent.

45. It is worth noting that, unlike the United Nations, the Bank designated English its official language.

46. *Questions and Answers on the Fund and Bank* (Washington D.C.: U.S. Department of Treasury, March 15, 1945), 7, 8, 15.

47. Ibid., 15. The 32 percent total is down from the original 35 percent as a result of the addition of several new member nations in the period between Bretton Woods and this publication.

48. Mason and Asher, *World Bank since Bretton Woods,* 1. See also Richard N. Gardner, "The Political Setting," in *Bretton Woods Revisited; Evaluations of the International Monetary Fund and the Inter-*

national Bank for Reconstruction and Development, ed. Keith Acheson, J. F. Chant, and Martin F. J. Prachowny (Toronto: University of Toronto Press, 1972).

49. The 1945 *Questions and Answers* booklet works to assuage this public fear, assuring Americans who might be concerned that their local savings would be jeopardized by risky foreign investment. In response to the question, "Will membership in the Bank mean an expansion of Government control over the banking system?" the Bank/Treasury offers an unambiguous assurance: "No" (15).

50. Quoted in Gardner, "Political Setting," 24.

51. Cited in Caufield, *Masters of Illusion,* 50.

52. *Questions and Answers on Bank for Reconstruction and Development* (Washington D.C.: U.S. Department of Treasury, 10 June, 1944), 37.

53. Address by Honorable John J. McCloy at the Seventh Annual Forum of Social and Economic Trends, April 18, 1947, "International Investment of Capital," April 16, 1947. Box 4; Series 4117; WB IBRD/IDA 23 Records of the Office of External Relations, IPA Press Releases, 2; World Bank Group Archives.

54. Mason and Asher, *World Bank since Bretton Woods,* 1.

2. Imperial Burden

1. Edward S. Mason and Robert E. Asher, *The World Bank since Bretton Woods: The Origins, Policies, Operations, and Impact of the International Bank for Reconstruction and Development* (Washington, D.C.: Brookings Institution, 1973), 36.

2. As stipulated in Article III, Section 4, the Bank may lend money to "any member [i.e., nation state] or *any political subdivision thereof*" (emphasis added) provided that the member government is willing to fully guarantee repayment. In this case, the loan to Crédit National was guaranteed by the French government.

3. Address by John J. McCloy, Broadcast over Station CFCF, Montreal, Canada, under the Auspices of the Canadian Club of Montreal, 1:30 P.M., E.S.T., Wednesday, February 18, 1948. Box 4; Series 4117; WB IBRD/IDA 23 Records of the Office of External Relations, IPA Press Releases, World Bank Group Archives.

4. Mason and Asher, *World Bank since Bretton Woods,* 125.

5. Address by Mr. Robert L. Garner at the Meeting of the National Association of Mutual Savings Banks, Hotel Statler, Boston, Mass., May 6, 1947, "What Is This International Bank?" Box 4; Series 4117; WB IBRD/IDA 23 Records of the Office of External Relations, IPA Press Releases, 2, World Bank Group Archives.

6. *Articles of Agreement, International Bank for Reconstruction*

and Development (Washington D.C.: U.S. Department of Treasury, 1944), 51

7. Address by W. A. B. Iliff of the United Kingdom before the World Trade Week Convention, Masonic Temple, Detroit, Mich., Thursday, May 20, 1948. Box 4; Series 4117; WB IBRD/IDA 23 Records of the Office of External Relations, IPA Press Releases, World Bank Group Archives.

8. Catherine Caufield, *Masters of Illusion: The World Bank and the Poverty of Nations* (New York: Henry Holt, 1996), 242–43.

9. Press release: Third Annual Report, September 29, 1948. Box 1; Series 4117; WB IBRD/IDA 23 Records of the Office of External Relations, IPA Press Releases, World Bank Group Archives.

10. Address by Eugene R. Black before the Thirty-Sixth Annual Meeting of the Investment Bankers Association, Hollywood, Fla., Tuesday, December 2, 1947. Box 4; Series 4117; WB IBRD/IDA 23 Records of the Office of External Relations, IPA Press Releases, World Bank Group Archives.

11. Address, John J. McCloy, February 18, 1948. 4-4117-23, 3.

12. Almost every major investment portfolio, including those held by most universities and pension plans, now includes World Bank bonds. This has led to some marginally successful social movement campaigns, based in part on the divestment strategies used to censure apartheid South Africa, to boycott World Bank Bonds. See http://www.worldbank-boycott.org.

13. *International Bank Notes* 1, no. 7 (July 25, 1947): 1. The cartoon appears on the same page.

14. Press release: "International Bank Completes Third Year," June 26, 1949. Box 1; Series 4117; WB IBRD/IDA 23 Records of the Office of External Relations, IPA Press Releases, World Bank Group Archives.

15. Karl Marx and Frederick Engels, "Capital," vol. 1, in *The Marx-Engels Reader,* ed. Robert C. Tucker (New York: Norton, 1978), 333. Throughout this book, I quote, when possible, from *The Marx-Engels Reader* for consistency's sake and to make it simpler for readers to locate the relevant passages. Moreover, as others have pointed out, Tucker's translations often emphasize the literary quality of Marx's prose.

16. Ibid., 334.

17. Devesh Kapur, John Prior Lewis, and Richard Charles Webb, *The World Bank: Its First Half Century,* 2 vols. (Washington, D.C.: Brookings Institution, 1997), 125.

18. Ibid., 122.

19. Reminiscences of Paul Rosenstein-Rodan (August 14, 1961), in the CUOHROC, 7.

20. Kapur, Lewis, and Webb, *World Bank,* 81.

21. IBRD Articles of Agreement, 57–58.

22. Ibid., 65.

23. Quoted in Kapur, Lewis, and Webb, *World Bank*, 76. This has been the de facto definition of nonpolitical throughout the Bank's history. Although Bank lending may not have the atrocious record of political coercion and manipulation that bilateral lenders such as USAID have amassed, this lending has undeniably been influenced (as how could it not have been?) by political considerations. In addition to the litany of expected critiques of Bank political lending that can be found in Susan George and Fabrizio Sabelli, *Faith and Credit: The World Bank's Secular Empire* (Boulder, Colo.: Westview Press, 1994); Caufield, *Masters of Illusion*; Michael Goldman, *Imperial Nature: The World Bank and Struggles for Justice in the Age of Globalization* (New Haven, Conn.: Yale University Press, 2005); Patrick Bond, *Against Global Apartheid: South Africa Meets the World Bank, IMF, and International Finance,* 2nd ed. (Lansdowne, South Africa: University of Cape Town Press, 2003); Bruce Rich, *Mortgaging the Earth: The World Bank, Environmental Impoverishment, and the Crisis of Development* (Boston: Beacon Press, 1994). Kapur, Lewis, and Webb, the officially sanctioned Bank historians, point to obvious U.S. political influence in Bank lending decisions about India (101), Ethiopia (102), Nicaragua (103), Guatemala (103), Yugoslavia 103), Iraq, Iran (104), and Indonesia (106), to name but a few.

24. Address by John J. McCloy before the First Annual "Forecasting" Conference of the Chamber of Commerce of Philadelphia, Warwick Hotel, Philadelphia, Penn., Thursday, January 15, 1948, "Europe's Home for Recovery." Box 4; Series 4117; WB IBRD/IDA 23 Records of the Office of External Relations, IPA Press Releases, World Bank Group Archives.

25. Address, W. A. B. Iliff, May 20, 1948. 4-4117-23.

26. Press release: Summary of Fifth Annual Report, September 8, 1950. Box 1; Series 4117; WB IBRD/IDA 23 Records of the Office of External Relations, IPA Press Releases, World Bank Group Archives.

27. Ibid.

28. Address by Mr. John J. McCloy before the Thirty-Fifth National Foreign Trade Convention, Grand Ballroom, Waldorf-Astoria, New York, Monday, November 8, 1948, "The International Bank and World Trade." Box 4; Series 4117; WB IBRD/IDA 23 Records of the Office of External Relations, IPA Press Releases, World Bank Group Archives.

29. The conservative McCloy and Black had a strong aversion to nationalized economies in the Bank's early years. This waned during McNamara's regime, but was reasserted even more aggressively as a policy of privatization during the mid-1980s in the political context of Reagan/Thatcher–era conservatism.

30. Summary of Fifth Annual Report, September 8, 1950. 1-4117-23.

31. The relation between power and "experts" is famously theorized by Foucault in, among other places, *Discipline and Punish: The Birth of the Prison* (New York: Pantheon Books, 1977). The notion of expertise informs any number of insightful critiques of the Bank, including Arturo Escobar, *Encountering Development: The Making and Unmaking of the Third World* (Princeton, N.J.: Princeton University Press, 1995); James Ferguson, *The Anti-Politics Machine: "Development," Depoliticization, and Bureaucratic Power in Lesotho* (Cambridge, England, and New York: Cambridge University Press, 1990); Timothy Mitchell, *Rule of Experts: Egypt, Techno-Politics, Modernity* (Berkeley and Los Angeles: University of California Press, 2002); Rich, *Mortgaging the Earth*; Arundhati Roy, "The Ladies Have Feelings, So. Shall We Leave It to the Experts?" in *Power Politics* (Cambridge, Mass.: South End Press, 1991).

32. Lorrayne Carroll and Joseph E. Medley have pointed to similar medical tropes in more recent World Bank/IMF discourse having to do with the Asian financial crisis. See "Whooping it Up for Rational Prosperity: Narratives of the East Asian Financial Crisis," in *World Bank Literature*, ed. Amitava Kumar (Minneapolis: University of Minnesota Press, 2002).

33. Quoted in Kapur, Lewis, and Webb, *World Bank*, 65–66.

34. Meyer submits his resignation on December 4, 1946, to be effective beginning December 18. His speech is dated December 9 and delivered December 13.

35. Address by Eugene Meyer, President, International Bank for Reconstruction and Development at the Annual Meeting of Life Insurance Association of America, Hotel Waldorf-Astoria, New York, December 13, 1946, December 9, 1946. Box 4; Series 4117; WB IBRD/IDA 23 Records of the Office of External Relations, IPA Press Releases, World Bank Group Archives.

36. Address by Mr. Eugene Meyer at the Annual Meeting of the Academy of Political Science, Hotel Astor, New York, November 7, 1946. Box 4; Series 4117; WB IBRD/IDA 23 Records of the Office of External Relations, IPA Press Releases, World Bank Group Archives.

37. Statement by Mr. Eugene Meyer, June 4, 1946, Box 4. Series 4117; WB IBRD/IDA 23 Records of the Office of External Relations, IPA Press Releases, World Bank Group Archives.

38. Amartya Kumar Sen estimates the figure could be as high as 3.048 million deaths. See his classic text on the politics of famine, *Poverty and Famines: An Essay on Entitlement and Deprivation* (Oxford: Oxford University Press, 1981).

39. Address, Eugene Meyer, November 7, 1946. 4-4117-23.

40. Quoted in Vladimir Ilyich Lenin, "Imperialism, the Highest Stage of Capitalism," in *The Lenin Anthology,* ed. Robert C. Tucker (New York: Norton, 1975), 236.

41. Interestingly, the export of "surplus" population from overpopulated regions of Europe is an issue that the Bank considers in some of its early materials. Given the Malthusian rhetoric of population control in the underdeveloped world that likely reaches a high point during McNamara's presidency in the late 1960s and early 1970s, the idea of an underpopulated South American continent depicted in the following quote from a McCloy speech in 1948 is striking: "In some of the governments of our member countries in the South American Continent serious consideration was being given to schemes of immigration and settlement whose object would be to receive into their countries from the over populated areas of the European Continent immigrants and settlers of the type who could be relied upon to carve out their homes and their opportunities in new lands. Schemes of this sort require careful preparation and organization and they also require some financing. . . . It is a field in which much can and should be done, in my judgment, and is one in which the International Bank with the cooperation of the countries involved may be able to help."
Address by John J. McCloy before the Foreign Policy Association, Cincinnati, Ohio, Tuesday, June 1, 1948. Box 4; Series 4117; WB IBRD/IDA 23 Records of the Office of External Relations, IPA Press Releases, World Bank Group Archives.

42. Lenin, *Lenin Anthology,* 209.

43. Marx and Engels, *Marx-Engels Reader,* 336.

44. Quoted in Kapur, Lewis, and Webb, *World Bank,* 98.

45. Press release, Summary of Sixth Annual Report, September 10, 1951. Box 1; Series 4117; WB IBRD/IDA 23 Records of the Office of External Relations, IPA Press Releases, World Bank Group Archives.

46. Statement of Principal Activities of the IBRD, July 1, 1951 through March 31, 1952, April 15, 1952. Box 1; Series 4117; WB IBRD/IDA 23 Records of the Office of External Relations, IPA Press Releases, World Bank Group Archives.

47. The Belgian Congo gained independence, nine years after the Bank loans, as the nation of Zaire in 1960. The northern portion of Southern Rhodesia gained independence from Britain in 1964 and became Zambia. The southern portion of the colony, which upon independence would become known as Zimbabwe, remained under British rule until 1980.

48. Joseph Conrad, *Heart of Darkness,* ed. Robert Kimbrough, 3d ed., Norton Critical Edition (New York: W. W. Norton and Company, 1988), 8.

49. Address by John J. McCloy before the Foreign Policy Association,

Minneapolis, Minn., Wednesday, January 19, 1949. Box 5; Series 4117; WB IBRD/IDA 23 Records of the Office of External Relations, IPA Press Releases, World Bank Group Archives.

50. Address by John J. McCloy, April 18, 1947. 4-4117-23.

51. Ibid., 5.

52. Press release, Colombia Mission, June 30 1949. Box 5; Series 4117; WB IBRD/IDA 23 Records of the Office of External Relations, IPA Press Releases, World Bank Group Archives.

53. The analogy is imprecise, of course, but it does suggest that the fruitful postcolonial critiques of anthropology could be extended and developed by transnational cultural studies to expose the ways the World Bank missions provided intellectual and ideological justification for the economic paradigms of the World Bank.

54. See especially George and Sabelli, *Faith and Credit,* and Rich, *Mortgaging the Earth.*

55. Rudyard Kipling, "The White Man's Burden," *McClure's Magazine* 12 (February 1899), http://www.boondocksnet.com/ai/kipling/kipling.html. In Jim Zwick, ed., *Anti-Imperialism in the United States, 1898–1935,* http://www.boondocksnet.com/ai/ (October 6, 2005).

56. Address by W. A. B. Iliff, May 20, 1948. 4-4117-23.

57. Cited in Lois Alward Raphael, *The Cape-to-Cairo Dream; a Study in British Imperialism* (New York: Octagon Books, 1973), 71.

58. Address by Eugene R. Black before the Annual Convention of the Savings Banks Association of the State of New York aboard the Nieuw Amsterdam, October 23, 1949. Box 5; Series 4117; WB IBRD/IDA 23 Records of the Office of External Relations, IPA Press Releases, World Bank Group Archives.

59. Consider the following assessment from Macaulay's "Minute on Indian Education": "But when we pass from works of imagination to works in which facts are recorded, and general principles investigated, the superiority of the Europeans becomes absolutely immeasurable. It is, I believe, no exaggeration to say, that all the historical information which has been collected from all the books written in the Sanscrit language is less valuable than what may be found in the most paltry abridgments used at preparatory schools in England. In every branch of physical or moral philosophy, the relative position of the two nations is nearly the same." Barbara Harlow and Mia Carter, *Imperialism and Orientalism: A Documentary Sourcebook* (Malden, Mass.: Blackwell Publishers, 1999), 58.

60. Address by Eugene R. Black, October 23, 1949. 5-4117-23.

61. Ibid.

62. Ibid.

63. Ibid.

3. Uncomfortable Intimacies

1. Remarks of Eugene R. Black on the occasion of the Inauguration of Dr. John A. Logan, Jr., as President of Hollins College, Roanoke, Va., April 14, 1962. Box 2; Series 4117; WB IBRD/IDA 23 Records of the Office of External Relations, IPA Press Releases, 6; World Bank Group Archives.

2. Remarks by Eugene Black on the occasion of Founder's Day at the University of Virginia, Charlottesville, Va., April 13, 1962. Box 2; Series 4117; WB IBRD/IDA 23 Records of the Office of External Relations, IPA Press Releases, 5-6; World Bank Group Archives.

3. It is perhaps worth noting, Kapur, Lewis, and Webb conclude, that after fifty years of the Bank, "poverty alleviation" is the only consistent principle around which the Bank's operations cohere. They ultimately advocate for the Bank to refocus its institutional mission around poverty alleviation (primarily through the encouragement of economic growth), and forego "special interest" distractions such as health, the environment, education, women in development, etc., that, according to these authors, have stretched the Bank too thin in recent years. Devesh Kapur, John Prior Lewis, and Richard Charles Webb, *The World Bank: Its First Half Century*, 2 vols. (Washington, D.C.: Brookings Institution, 1997), 1215–16.

4. Membership to the Bank is conferred on any nation state that becomes a signatory to the Bank's Charter of Principles (including the provision that any member of the Bank must also be a member of the IMF) and that pays its initial capital subscription, calculated according to the relative size of the national economy.

5. For voting rights changes and for specific country breakdowns, see the useful tables in Mason and Asher (on pages 65 and 800, respectively). Edward S. Mason and Robert E. Asher, *The World Bank since Bretton Woods: The Origins, Policies, Operations, and Impact of the International Bank for Reconstruction and Development* (Washington, D.C.: Brookings Institution, 1973).

6. Ibid., 400–1.

7. Catherine Caufield, *Masters of Illusion: The World Bank and the Poverty of Nations* (New York: Henry Holt, 1996), 106.

8. Reminiscences of J. Burke Knapp (July 1961) in the CUOHROC, 36–37.

9. For an academic parallel, see John Guillory's critique of "rigor" as a reaction to the integration of the university and the expansion of the canon for literary studies in John Guillory, *Cultural Capital: The Problem of Literary Canon Formation* (Chicago: University of Chicago Press, 1993).

10. Mason and Asher, *World Bank since Bretton Woods*, 380.

11. Kapur, Lewis, and Webb, *World Bank*, 1128.

12. Ibid., 170.

13. Quoted in Ibid., 154.

14. Remarks by Eugene Black at Closing Joint Session of the Boards of Governors, September 22, 1961. Box 2; Series 4117; WB IBRD/IDA 23 Records of the Office of External Relations, IPA Press Releases, 2; World Bank Group Archives.

15. Kapur, Lewis, and Webb, *World Bank*, 1145.

16. See the many critiques of the influence of Oxfam upon the 2005 G8 debt relief announcements. Patrick Bond's many books and articles are an excellent reference to some of the most radical Southern social movements. See, for instance: Patrick Bond, Dennis Brutus, and Virginia Setshedi, "When Wearing White Is Not Chic, and Collaboration Not Cool," *Foreign Policy In Focus* (Silver City, N.M., and Washington, D.C.) (June 16, 2005); Katharine Quarmby, "Why Oxfam Is Failing Africa," *New Statesman* (May 30, 2005); and John Pilger, "The G8 Summit: A Fraud and a Circus," *New Statesman* (June 24, 2005). See, too, the incisive critique of NGOs as tools of imperialism, in James F. Petras and Henry Veltmeyer, *Globalization Unmasked: Imperialism in the Twenty-first Century* (New York: Palgrave, 2001). More radical social movement critiques of debt, international finance, privatization of resources, and, more broadly, the role of the Bank in the world are many and vibrant. For just a few examples, see Jubilee South, http://www.jubileesouth.org; World Bank Bond Boycotts, http://www.econjusticenet.org/wbbb; Fifty Years Is Enough, http://www.50yearsisenough.org; IFIs Out!, http://www.ifi-out .org; Our World Is Not For Sale, http://www.ourworldisnotforsale.org; The Development Gap, http://www.developmentgap.org; Focus on the Global South, http://www.focusweb.org; Via Campesina, http://www .viacampesina.org; Narmada Bachao Andolan and Movimiento Sem Terra, http://www.mstbrazil.org.

17. Kapur, Lewis, and Webb, *World Bank*, 161.

18. Address to the UN Economic and Social Council by Mr. George D. Woods, United Nations, New York, February 25, 1966. Box 13; Series 4117; WB IBRD/IDA 23 Records of the Office of External Relations, IPA Press Releases, 5–7; World Bank Group Archives.

19. Ibid., 6.

20. Speech by Mr. George Woods to the Société Francaise de Géographie Economique, Paris, January 24, 1967. Box 13; Series 4117; WB IBRD/IDA 23 Records of the Office of External Relations, IPA Press Releases, 6; World Bank Group Archives.

21. Address to the UN Economic and Social Council by Mr. Robert S. McNamara, United Nations, New York, December 5, 1968. Box 13; Se-

ries 4117; WB IBRD/IDA 23 Records of the Office of External Relations, IPA Press Releases, World Bank Group Archives.

22. Mason and Asher, *World Bank since Bretton Woods*, 718–19.

23. Kapur, Lewis, and Webb, *World Bank*, 111.

24. Speech by Eugene Black, University of Hamburg, Germany, January 19, 1962, "The Spirit of Europe." Box 2; Series 4117; WB IBRD/IDA 23 Records of the Office of External Relations, IPA Press Releases, World Bank Group Archives.

25. Raymond Williams, *Keywords: A Vocabulary of Culture and Society* (New York: Oxford University Press, 1976). See also the more recent account in Terry Eagleton, *The Idea of Culture* (Oxford: Blackwell, 2000).

26. Address by George D. Woods, The Canadian Club, Toronto, Canada, November 9, 1964, "The Development Century." Box 13; Series 4117; WB IBRD/IDA 23 Records of the Office of External Relations, IPA Press Releases, 8; World Bank Group Archives.

27. Vijayendra Rao and Michael Walton, *Culture and Public Action* (Stanford: Stanford University Press, 2004), vii.

28. Ibid.

29. For examples of important ethnographic case studies that highlight local experiences with Bank development, see Julia Elyachar, "Empowerment Money: The World Bank, Non-Governmental Organizations, and the Value of Culture in Egypt," *Public Culture* 14, no. 3 (2002); James Ferguson, *The Anti-Politics Machine: "Development," Depoliticization, and Bureaucratic Power in Lesotho* (Cambridge and New York: Cambridge University Press, 1990); Timothy Mitchell, *Rule of Experts: Egypt, Techno-Politics, Modernity* (Berkeley and Los Angeles: University of California Press, 2002).

30. Woods, "Development Century."

31. Black, Remarks at Closing Joint Session of the Boards of Governors, September 22, 1961. 2-4117-23.

32. Woods, "Development Century."

33. Woods, Address to UNESCO, February 25, 1966. 13-4117-23.

34. Apocalyptic predictions about population expansion are nothing new. See Paul Ehrlich, *The Population Bomb* (New York: Ballantine Books, 1971); Betsy Hartmann, *Reproductive Rights and Wrongs* (Boston: South End Press, 1995); Bret Benjamin, "Under Control: Reading the Facts and Faqs of Population Control," in *World Bank Literature*, ed. Amitava Kumar (Minneapolis: University of Minnesota Press, 2003).

35. McNamara, Address to UNESCO, December 5, 1968. 13-4117-23.

36. This might be seen as yet another iteration of the dialectic between expansion and contraction that structures so much of Marx's analysis of capitalism in *Capital*.

37. Address by Eugene R. Black before the Pilgrims, London, May 5, 1959. Box 2; Series 4117; WB IBRD/IDA 23 Records of the Office of External Relations, IPA Press Releases, 2; World Bank Group Archives.

38. Remarks of Mr. George D. Woods to the Ministerial Meeting of the Development Assistance Committee of OECD, Washington, D.C., July 20, 1966. Box 13; Series 4117; WB IBRD/IDA 23 Records of the Office of External Relations, IPA Press Releases, 4; World Bank Group Archives.

39. Ibid., 4–5.

40. Walter B. Wriston, *The Twilight of Sovereignty: How the Information Revolution Is Transforming Our World* (New York: Scribner, 1992), 9, 45, 59.

41. Writing in the same register, but from the opposite end of the political spectrum, Michael Hardt and Antonio Negri argue in *Empire* that we should harbor no nostalgia for the passing of the era of the sovereign nation state, which in their analysis has primarily served as the protector of capital and capitalists rather than of the proletariat. They argue, in fact, that the first political demand for the revolutionary multitude of empire is "global citizenship" (400) with the ability to control the movement of bodies and ideas including "free access to and control over knowledge, information, communication, and affects" (407). See, too, the final section of *Multitudes*, which elaborates on the authors' conception of democracy, outside the politics of representation. Michael Hardt and Antonio Negri, *Empire* (Cambridge, Mass., and London: Harvard University Press, 2000); Hardt and Negri, *Multitude: War and Democracy in the Age of Empire* (New York: Penguin Press, 2004).

42. Black, Remarks at Founder's Day, April 13, 1962. 2-4117-23.

43. Black, "The Spirit of Europe," January 19, 1962. 2-4117-23.

44. Ibid., 3.

45. Ibid.

46. Ibid., 4.

47. Ibid., 5–6.

48. This turn is often dated from a 1985 speech in Seoul by James Baker, U.S. Secretary of the Treasury under the Reagan administration.

49. Black, Remarks at Founder's Day, April 13, 1962 (2-4117-23). The example of Stalin and the Soviet state, presumably, is the yoke that allows Black to bind together, without so much as a word of justification, the seemingly antithetical notions of a greater good of a collective, and tyranny or despotism.

50. Woods, "Development Century."

51. McNamara, Address to UNESCO, December 5, 1968. 13-4117-23.

52. Ibid., 7.

53. Ibid., 2.

54. Black, Remarks at Closing Joint Session of the Board, September 22, 1961. 2-4117-23.

55. Text of the Second Lecture by Eugene R. Black, Stafford Little Series, Princeton University, May 8, 1962, "A Multilateral Approach to Aid." Box 2; Series 4117; WB IBRD/IDA 23 Records of the Office of External Relations, IPA Press Releases, 1–2; World Bank Group Archives.

56. Woods, Speech to Société Française de Géographie Economique, January 24, 1967. 13-4117-23.

57. I use the term *neo*imperialist not because I think the Bank's form of intervention is fundamentally novel—to the contrary, the transfer of wealth from South to North continues unabated—but rather because the interventionist project is predicated upon a rhetorical insistence that the era of empire has passed.

58. Black, Remarks at Founder's Day, April 13, 1962. 2-4117-23.

59. I know very little about this group. According to the Project for the Exposure of Hidden Institutions, an Internet site whose credibility I cannot vouch for, the Pilgrims Society is a secret "aristocratic Anglo-American dining club" that began in 1902 as a means of preserving the power of the British Empire and consisted of an extensive membership of the most influential executives and aristocrats from New York and London, linking among others Cecil Rhodes with J. P. Morgan, John D. Rockefeller, the Dulles Brothers, Bank presidents Eugene Meyer, John McCloy, and Eugene Black, Federal Reserves Chairpersons Paul Volker and possibly Allan Greenspan. Black does mention his "old friend Sir Rover Makins" in his address, a name that also appears on the Pilgrims Society Membership list provided by this website. A more extensive history is available at "Project for the Exposure of Hidden Institutions," http://home.planet.nl/~reijd050/organisations/Pilgrims_Society.htm (October 8, 2005).

60. Black, Address to Pilgrims, May 5, 1959. 2-4117-23.

61. Address by Robert S. McNamara to the Board of Governors of the World Bank, September 29, 1969. Box 13; Series 4117; WB IBRD/IDA 23 Records of the Office of External Relations, IPA Press Releases, 31–32; World Bank Group Archives.

62. Kapur, Lewis, and Webb, *World Bank*, 248.

63. Woods, "Development Century."

64. McNamara, Address to UNESCO, December 5, 1968. 13-4117-23.

65. Knapp, in a 1960 internal meeting, acknowledged that, from its inception, "IDA had that missionary function." Quoted in Kapur, Lewis, and Webb, *World Bank*, 161.

66. Hardt and Negri, *Empire*, 36–37. See also Petras and Veltmeyer, *Globalization Unmasked*, 128–38.

67. Hardt and Negri, *Empire*, 36–37.

68. Hardt and Negri, *Multitude,* 7. The problem of sovereignty and exceptionalism is the topic of much contemporary political theory. Most notably see: Giorgio Agamben, *Homo Sacer: Sovereign Power and Bare Life* (Stanford: Stanford University Press, 1998); Giorgio Agamben, *State of Exception* (Chicago: University of Chicago Press, 2005); Judith Butler, *Precarious Life: The Powers of Mourning and Violence* (London: Verso, 2004).

69. Black, Address to Pilgrims, May 5, 1959. 2-4117-23.

70. George D. Woods, "The Development Decade in the Balance," *Foreign Affairs* (January 1966): 206–15.

71. Woods, "Development Century."

4. Culture Underwritten

1. Michael Denning, *Culture in the Age of Three Worlds* (London: Verso, 2004), 2.

2. Ibid., 3.

3. Ibid., 1.

4. Matthew Arnold, "Culture and Anarchy," in *Culture and Anarchy, and Other Writings* (Cambridge: Cambridge University Press, 1993), 79.

5. Matthew Arnold, "The Function of Criticism," in ibid., 4.

6. Ibid., 35–36.

7. I am oversimplifying Arnold's claims here. In fact, he develops fascinating historical arguments about epochs of concentration versus epochs of revolution, epochs of creative genius versus epochs of critical clarity, and the like. Nevertheless, Arnold ultimately avers that the glasses of history and politics can only serve to cloud our perception of humankind's finest thought and expression.

8. As Fredric Jameson reminds us, the term "high culture," only comes to have meaning after the introduction of mass or "low" culture. The term is relational and has no historical specificity prior to modernism's aesthetic reaction against mass cultural commodification. Fredric Jameson, "Reification and Utopia in Mass Culture," *Social Text* 1 (1979).

9. This rarified Arnoldian notion of culture prompts Raymond William's critique "Culture is Ordinary," one of the important early statements of British cultural studies. Raymond Williams, "Culture Is Ordinary," in *Resources of Home* (London: Verso, 1958).

10. Edward Burnett Tylor, *The Origins of Culture,* vol. 1 (New York: Harper and Brothers, 1958), 1.

11. Ibid., 21.

12. Denning, *Culture in the Age of Three Worlds,* 79.

13. For examples of other cultural studies histories or genealogies, see Francis Mulhern, *Culture/Metaculture, New Critical Idiom* (London:

Routledge, 2000); Terry Eagleton, *Idea of Culture* (Oxford: Blackwell, 2000); Bill Readings, *The University in Ruins* (Cambridge, Mass.: Harvard University Press, 1996); Chris Barker, *Cultural Studies: Theory and Practice* (London: Sage, 2000); Barker, *Making Sense of Cultural Studies: Central Problems and Critical Debates* (London: Sage, 2002); Ioan Davies, *Cultural Studies and Beyond: Fragments of Empire* (London: Routledge, 1995); Richard Johnson, "What Is Cultural Studies Anyway?" *Social Text*, no. 16 (1987); Stuart Hall, "Cultural Studies and Its Theoretical Legacies," in *Cultural Studies,* ed. Lawrence Grossberg, Cary Nelson, and Paula Treichler (New York: Routledge, 1992); Patrick Brantlinger, *Crusoe's Footprints: Cultural Studies in Britain and America* (New York: Routledge, 1990); Patrick Brantlinger, *Who Killed Shakespeare? What's Happened to English since the Radical Sixties* (New York: Routledge, 2001).

14. Denning, *Culture in the Age of Three Worlds*, 2.

15. Ibid., 3.

16. Ibid., 18–19.

17. Meaghan Morris, "Banality in Cultural Studies," in *The Logics of Television,* ed. Patricia Mellencamp (Bloomington: Indiana University Press, 1990).

18. Readings, *University in Ruins,* 91.

19. Eagleton, *Idea of Culture,* 130.

20. Denning, *Culture in the Age of Three Worlds,* 155, 34, 50, 13.

21. Aijaz Ahmad articulates a similar conclusion in a book written just after the 1989 break. Aijaz Ahmad, *In Theory: Classes, Nations, Literatures* (London: Verso, 1992).

22. Denning, *Culture in the Age of Three Worlds,* 103.

23. Ibid., 150.

24. For a useful overview of Fordism and Post-Fordism see David Harvey, *The Condition of Postmodernity: An Enquiry into the Origins of Cultural Change* (Cambridge, Mass.: Blackwell, 1989), 144.

25. Antonio Gramsci, *Selections from the Prison Notebooks of Antonio Gramsci,* trans. Quintin Hoare and Geoffrey Nowell-Smith (New York: International Publishers, 1971), 302.

26. Connections abound. McNamara was the CEO of Ford Motor Company before joining the Kennedy administration. The Ford Foundation (along with the Rockefeller Foundation) has been a formal and informal partner with the Bank throughout its history, working on food, population, education, NGOs, and more. Looking ahead to the final chapter, I shall mention that the Ford Foundation also provided financial backing for the World Social Forum prior to that group's internal debates about corporate funding sources, debates that accompanied the 2003 meeting in Mumbai, India.

27. Harvey, *Condition of Postmodernity*, 133.

28. Address by Mr. Eugene Meyer at the Annual Meeting of the Academy of Political Science, Hotel Astor, New York, November 7, 1946. Box 4; Series 4117; WB IBRD/IDA 23 Records of the Office of External Relations, IPA Press Releases, World Bank Group Archives.

29. Ibid.

30. Vladimir Ilyich Lenin, "Imperialism, the Highest Stage of Capitalism," in *The Lenin Anthology*, ed. Robert C. Tucker (New York: Norton, 1975), 209. This splintering of the global proletariat—the unwillingness of European labor to see that its gains were won at the expense of labor in the South—is ultimately what prompts Césaire to resign from the Communist Party. See Aimé Césaire, "Letter to Maurice Thorez" (Paris: Présence Africane, 1957).

31. Address by W. A. B. Iliff of the United Kingdom before the World Trade Week Convention, Masonic Temple, Detroit Mich., Thursday, May 20, 1948. Box 4; Series 4117; WB IBRD/IDA 23 Records of the Office of External Relations, IPA Press Releases, World Bank Group Archives.

32. Address by W. A. B. Iliff, May 20, 1948. 4-4117-23.

33. Ibid., 5.

34. Address by Eugene R. Black to the Investment Bankers' Association, Waldorf-Astoria Hotel, New York, October 4, 1961. Box 2; Series 4117; WB IBRD/IDA 23 Records of the Office of External Relations, IPA Press Releases, World Bank Group Archives.

35. Gramsci, *Prison Notebooks*, 302.

36. Leslie Sklair, "Social Movements and Global Capitalism," in *The Cultures of Globalization*, ed. Fredric Jameson and Masao Miyoshi (Durham, N.C.: Duke University Press, 2001).

37. Address by W. A. B. Iliff, May 20, 1948. 4-4117-23.

38. Karl Marx and Friedrich Engels, *The Marx-Engels Reader*, ed. Robert C. Tucker, 2nd ed. (New York: Norton, 1978), 319–28.

39. Ibid., 58.

40. Address by Eugene Meyer, November 7, 1946. 4-4117-23.

41. Address by Honorable John J. McCloy at the 7th Annual Forum of Social and Economic Trends, April 18, 1947, "International Investment of Capital," April 16, 1947. Box 4; Series 4117; WB IBRD/IDA 23 Records of the Office of External Relations, IPA Press Releases, World Bank Group Archives.

42. Marx and Engels, *Marx–Engels Reader*, 476–77.

43. Max Horkheimer and Theodor W. Adorno, *Dialectic of Enlightenment* (London: Verso, 1979), 131.

44. Address by John J. McCloy before the Foreign Policy Association, Cincinnati, Ohio, Tuesday, June 1, 1948. Box 4; Series 4117; WB IBRD/

IDA 23 Records of the Office of External Relations, IPA Press Releases, World Bank Group Archives.

45. This argument can usefully be extended and updated to include the celebrated practice of microcredit, typified by the work of recent Nobel Prize winner Muhammad Yunus. Its own sort of development monument in Bangladesh, the Grameen Bank offers a more precise homology to the responsive culture industry, relying as it does upon a logic of small-scale lending tailored to the needs and desires of the masses. Hardly the dream factory it is often portrayed to be, microcredit, which typically targets women because of a perception that they are more responsible (read: docile) and thus more likely to repay loans, inculcates widespread indebtedness (often at usurious rates of interest) and effectively interpolates borrowers into capitalist relations of property.

46. McCloy, address, June 1, 1948.

47. Jameson, "Reification and Utopia in Mass Culture," 130–48.

48. Ibid., 144.

49. Address by Eugene R. Black before the Pilgrims, London, May 5, 1959. Box 2; Series 4117; WB IBRD/IDA 23 Records of the Office of External Relations, IPA Press Releases, World Bank Group Archives.

50. Frantz Fanon, *The Wretched of the Earth* (New York: Grove Press, 1963), 81.

51. Fanon's essay "This Is the Voice of Algeria" elaborates on this process of Algerian cultural appropriation of the radio during the short period between the massacres at Sétif and Guelma in 1945 (when less than 5 percent of the Algerian population owned a radio) and the airing of Voice of Algeria in 1956 (by which point, the device's presence was ubiquitous). He traces the radio's historical shift from a colonial technology that defined and sustained French identity in opposition to the "nonculture" of the Algerians, to a revolutionary technology the possession of which "seriously meant *going to war.*" Frantz Fanon, *A Dying Colonialism* (New York: Grove Press, 1967), 71, 93. See also Nigel Gibson, "Jammin' the Airwaves and Tuning into the Revolution: The Dialectics of the Radio in *L'An V de la Révolution Algériénne,*" in *Fanon: A Critical Reader,* ed. Lewis R. Gordon, T. Denean Sharpley-Whiting, and Renée T. White (Oxford: Blackwell, 1996).

52. E. J. Hobsbawm, *The Age of Extremes, 1914–1991* (New York: Pantheon Books, 1994). See especially chapters 12 and 15.

53. Eagleton, *Idea of Culture*, 63.

54. Truth be told, a sustained analysis of gender (or even of the role of women) is one of the weaker suits of this body of anticolonial cultural theory. This is not to downplay the significant role of women and women intellectuals in national liberation struggles, but only to suggest that for a variety of complicated reasons the most influential figures in

this tradition were men, for whom the category of gender was not the primary focus of investigation and critique. It was the related but nevertheless distinct *women's movement*—that other enormously consequential intellectual/political current that transformed the study of culture—that insisted upon the centrality of feminist thought and analyses of gender.

55. Denning, *Culture in the Age of Three Worlds*, 150–51.

56. Kwame Nkrumah, *Neo-Colonialism: The Last Stage of Imperialism* (New York: International Publishers, 1966), 67.

57. Ibid., 242.

58. Aimé Césaire, *Discourse on Colonialism*, ed. Robin D. G. Kelley, trans. Joan Pinkham (New York: Monthly Review Press, 2000), 76.

59. Ibid., 76–77.

60. Fanon, *Wretched of the Earth*, 66.

61. Lenin, "Imperialism," 226.

62. Fanon, *Wretched of the Earth*, 104.

63. Ibid., 153.

64. See Devesh Kapur, John Prior Lewis, and Richard Charles Webb, *The World Bank: Its First Half Century*, 2 vols. (Washington, D.C.: Brookings Institution, 1997), 289, 305, 420, 1148.

65. Fanon, *Wretched of the Earth*, 98.

66. Ibid., 102–03.

67. Ibid., 223–24.

68. Readers versed in British cultural studies will note my use of Raymond Williams's schema of dominant, residual, and emergent cultural formations, a topic that the following chapter considers in more detail.

69. Richard Wright, *The Color Curtain* (Jackson: University Press of Mississippi, 1956), 12.

70. Jules Sauerwein, "The Bandung Asian-African Conference," *Diario Popular*, Lisbon, Portugal, March 9, 1955, cited in *The Asian-African Conference: Views and News* (The National Committee for the Commemoration of the Thirtieth Anniversary of the Asian-African Conference, 1985), 23–24.

71. Robin D. G. Kelley, "A Poetics of Anticolonialism," in Césaire, *Discourse on Colonialism*, 7.

72. Kapur, Lewis, and Webb, 143.

73. Neil Larsen, "Imperialism, Colonialism, Postcolonialism," in *A Companion to Postcolonial Studies*, ed. Henry Schwarz and Sangeeta Ray (Oxford: Blackwell, 2000), 33.

74. C. L. R. James, *The Black Jacobins: Toussaint Louverture and the San Domingo Revolution* (London: Secker and Warburg, 1938).

75. "Speech by Prime Minister Nehru before the Political Committee of the Asian-African Conference, April 22, 1955," in George McTurnan Kahin, *The Asian-African Conference, Bandung, Indonesia, April 1955*

(Ithaca, N.Y.: Cornell University Press, 1956), 65. For an excellent analysis of this line and its national political context as well as its place within Three Worlds Theory, see Ahmad, 287–318.

76. *Daily Mirror,* March 19, 1955, Manila, in *Asian-African Conference: Views and News,* 14.

77. "The Solution," *The Manila Times,* February 17, 1955, Manila, in Ibid., 13.

78. Kahin, *The Asian-African Conference, Bandung, Indonesia, April 1955,* 3.

79. Ahmad, "Three Worlds Theory," in *In Theory: Classes, Nations, Literatures,* 287–318.

80. Lenin's assessment of imperialism seems apt: "the capital exporting countries have divided the world among themselves in the figurative sense of the term. But finance capital has led to the *actual* division of the world," Lenin, 229.

81. "Final Communiqué of the Asian-African Conference," in Kahin, *Asian-African Conference,* 76.

82. Cited in Kapur, Lewis, and Webb, *World Bank,* 103.

83. Kahin, *Asian-African Conference,* 77.

84. Unless otherwise noted, all quotations from the "Cultural Cooperation" section of the Communiqué are from ibid., 79.

85. Address by Honorable John J. McCloy at the Seventh Annual Forum of Social and Economic Trends, April 18, 1947 (April 16, 1947), 3.

86. Benedict Anderson, *Imagined Communities: Reflections on the Origin and Spread of Nationalism* (London: Verso, 1991).

87. Wright's title announces his indebtedness to W. E. B. DuBois's work on "the color line" from earlier in the century (*The Souls of Black Folks* was published in 1903). Susan Hegeman's work on the export of American modernism and culture provides a valuable pre-text for the midcentury turn theorized by Denning. As always, we find that culture moves incrementally, by fits and starts. Insurrectionary moments signal breaks and ruptures, to be sure, but they typically offer prisms or magnifications of previously articulated concerns or conceptions. The point of periodizing the global cultural turn as a postwar phenomenon is not to establish firm and clear chronological boundaries—earlier work such as DuBois's certainly exhibits shared theoretical concerns and helps shape the work of midcentury cultural radicals—but rather to highlight the ascendance of particular hegemonic tendencies. Susan Hegeman, *Patterns for America: Modernism and the Concept of Culture* (Princeton, N.J.: Princeton University Press, 1999).

88. Wright, *Color Curtain,* 12.

89. Fanon, *Wretched of the Earth,* 40. I take up this argument in more detail in chapter 7.

90. C. L. R. James, *Beyond a Boundary* (Durham, N.C.: Duke University Press, 1993), 66, 7.

91. Raymond Williams, *Marxism and Literature: Marxist Introductions* (Oxford: Oxford University Press, 1977), 131.

92. Wright, *Color Curtain,* 14.

93. Williams, *Marxism and Literature,* 128.

94. Fanon, *Wretched of the Earth,* 224.

95. Wright, *Color Curtain,* 28.

96. Ibid., 60.

97. Ibid., 12.

98. "Closing Speech by Prime Minister Nehru at the Asian-African Conference, April 24, 1955," in Kahin, *Asian-African Conference,* 65.

99. "Speech by President Soekarno at the Opening of the Asian-African Conference, April 18, 1955," in ibid., 46.

100. Wright, *Color Curtain,* 203.

101. Ibid., 140.

102. Ibid., 211.

103. Ibid., 213.

104. Ibid., 214–15.

105. Ibid., 216.

106. Ibid., 217.

107. Kahin, *Asian-African Conference,* 44.

108. Wright, *Color Curtain,* 51–52.

5. Success Stories

1. The brief historical overview that follows reduces the full complexity and significance of this event. For more substantive historical analyses of the debt crisis, see Cheryl Payer, *The Debt Trap: The IMF and the Third World* (New York: Monthly Review Press, 1975); Sue Branford and Bernardo Kucinski, *The Debt Squads: The U.S., the Banks, and Latin America* (London: Zed Books, 1990); Elmar Altvater et al., eds., *The Poverty of Nations: A Guide to the Debt Crisis from Argentina to Zaire* (London: Zed Books, 1987); John Walton and David Seddon, *Free Markets and Food Riots: The Politics of Global Adjustment,* Studies in Urban and Social Change (Oxford: Blackwell, 1994).

2. Quoted in Devesh Kapur, John Prior Lewis, and Richard Charles Webb, *The World Bank: Its First Half Century,* 2 vols. (Washington, D.C.: Brookings Institution, 1997), 297.

3. Quoted in ibid., 676–77.

4. Walton and Seddon, *Free Markets and Food Riots,* 39–40.

5. Patrick Bond offers a useful catalog of anti–World Bank/IMF/WTO actions that took place across the planet in the year following the Seattle protests, indicating the density and diversity of the opposition.

Patrick Bond, *Against Global Apartheid: South Africa Meets the World Bank, IMF, and International Finance*, 2nd ed. (Lansdowne, South Africa: University of Cape Town Press, 2003), 216–18.

6. The Bank's newly explicit investments in the category *culture* can be traced in large part to the scholarship of political philosopher Amartya Sen. See especially "Culture and Development," http://www.worldbank .org/wbi/B-SPAN/sen_tokyo.pdf (October 19, 2004), along with his Webcast lecture, "Cultural and Sustainable Development: An Economic Perspective," http://www.worldbank.org/wbi/B-SPAN/sub_sen_599.htm (October 19, 2004). See also the recent collection published in conjunction with the World Bank (including essays by such influential theorists as Sen, Arjun Appadurai, and Mary Douglas), Vijayendra Rao and Michael Walton, eds., *Culture and Public Action* (Stanford, Calif.: Stanford University Press, 2004).

7. Amitava Kumar, "Introduction," *World Bank Literature, ed.* Amitava Kumar (Minneapolis: University of Minnesota Press, 2003), xix, xvii. A version of the introduction was originally published as "World Bank Literature: A New Name for Postcolonial Studies in the Next Century," *College Literature* 26, no. 3 (1999): 195–204.

8. Ibid., xx. My answer is a definitive "no" (and I would venture to guess that Kumar himself would agree). As I suggested in the introduction, I am much more interested in the idea of World Bank literature as a rule-breaking critical constellation than as a field or discipline with its attendant budgetary and administrative apparatus. One of its great strengths, as I suggest below, is its ability to call into question various "institutions of literature."

9. Bruce Robbins, "Afterword," in *World Bank Literature,* ed. Kumar, 299–300.

10. Suggested boldly by Michael Hardt and Antonio Negri in *Empire* (Cambridge, Mass.: Harvard University Press, 2000), but echoed with various degrees of qualification by numerous other scholars. As they do with many of the boldest theoretical provocations in *Empire*, Hardt and Negri later qualify and refine their claims about the Bank and supranationalism. See the distinction between their analyses on page 31 and page 134.

11. Indeed, the increasingly visible and accepted critique of the Washington Consensus principles has produced some strange but effective bedfellows. First brought to mainstream U.S. public attention by the 1999 Seattle WTO protests, an intriguing solidarity has developed among social movements (from both North and South, including labor, environmentalism, indigenous groups, and many others), national leaders from indebted countries, intellectuals, and more. Public acceptance of the critiques leveled against the Washington Consensus has been bolstered by the participation of the former chief economist of the World Bank, Joseph

Stiglitz. See his *Globalization and Its Discontents*. (New York: Norton, 2002). Given Stiglitz's insider status, the presence of this eminent economist has done much to undermine what had until recently been an almost unassailable economic doctrine within the United States and Europe. Although this odd, informal collection of forces has proven effective in destabilizing the public's unquestioned faith in neoliberalism, it is important we not erase the substantial differences in positions staked out by the participants. Although the tactical alliance among these groups—materialized by their collective presence at the World Social Forum, where Stiglitz was a featured speaker in Mumbai—has been effective in focusing attention on the failures of the Washington Consensus, we must distinguish between the more radical critiques of global capitalism and the more accommodationist calls for kinder and gentler reforms. In addition to Stiglitz, Amartya Sen's influential *Development as Freedom* should be counted in the latter category.

12. World Bank, "10 Things You Never Knew about the World Bank" (Washington D.C.: 2002). An online Web version is also available, http://www.worldbank.org/tenthings (April 15, 2006).

13. "Press Conference with James D. Wolfensohn," April 19, 2002, http://web.worldbank.org/WBSITE/EXTERNAL/NEWS/0,,contentMDK:20040040~menuPK:34476~pagePK:34370~piPK:42771~theSitePK:4607,00.html (June 17, 2004).

14. Kumar, *World Bank Literature,* xvii.

15. For information on Schmertz and the publicity campaign, see Catherine Caufield, *Masters of Illusion: The World Bank and the Poverty of Nations* (New York: Henry Holt, 1996), 274. See also: World Bank, "The World Bank Current Questions and Answers," (Washington D.C.: World Bank, 1994); World Bank, "The World Bank in Action: Stories of Development," (Washington D.C.: World Bank, 2003); Robert Chambers, *Voices of the Poor: Crying Out for Change,* vol. 2 (Washington D.C.: World Bank, 2001); Deepa Narayan, *Voices of the Poor: Can Anyone Hear Us?* vol. 1 (Washington D.C.: World Bank, 2000). The *Voices of the Poor* set can be ordered in book format, or downloaded from the Bank's Website at http://www1.worldbank.org/prem/poverty/voices/index.htm (January 19, 2005). For a more multimedia-rich example, see the stories published by the Bank at "Development 360: Working toward the Millennium Development Goals," http://dev360.worldbank.org/ (April 15, 2006).

16. World Bank, "ICT Stories," http://www.iicd.org/stories/ (June 17, 2004). The ICT Stories project is only one example.

17. All quotes from Becky Wachera and Matthew Meyer, "Sole Comfort Dot-Com: Bridging the Global Income Gap through Hard Work,

Quality Sandals, and ICTs," April 14, 2002, http://www.iicd.org/base/ story_read?id=4909 (June 17, 2004).

18. This is a concept that Hardt and Negri explore in *The Labor of Dionysus: A Critique of the State Form* (Minneapolis: University of Minnesota Press, 1994) and develop in *Empire* and *Multitude*. McKenzie Wark's *The Hacker Manifesto* (Cambridge, Mass.: Harvard University Press, 2004) extends Hardt's and Negri's discussion specifically to information and digital media.

19. Address by John J. McCloy before the Foreign Policy Association, Cincinnati, Ohio, Tuesday, June 1, 1948. Box 4; Series 4117; WB IBRD/ IDA 23 Records of the Office of External Relations, IPA Press Releases, World Bank Group Archives.

20. Cynthia H. Enloe, *Bananas, Beaches, and Bases: Making Feminist Sense of International Politics* (London: Pandora, 1989), 166.

21. See, in addition to Enloe's, the work of Suzanne Bergeron, Inderpal Grewal, Rosemary Hennessy, Miranda Joseph, Naila Kabeer, Maria Mies, Chandra Talpade Mohanty, Vandana Shiva, and Gayatri Chakravorty Spivak. Suzanne Bergeron, *Fragments of Development: Nation, Gender, and the Space of Modernity* (Ann Arbor: University of Michigan Press, 2004); Inderpal Grewal, *Transnational America: Feminisms, Diasporas, Neoliberalisms* (Durham, N.C.: Duke University Press, 2005); Rosemary Hennessy, *Profit and Pleasure: Sexual Identities in Late Capitalism* (New York: Routledge, 2000); Miranda Joseph, *Against the Romance of Community* (Minneapolis: University of Minnesota Press, 2002); Naila Kabeer, *The Power to Choose: Bangladeshi Women and Labour Market Decisions in London and Dhaka* (London and New York: Verso, 2000); Maria Mies, *Patriarchy and Accumulation on a World Scale: Women in the International Division of Labour* (London; Atlantic Highlands, N.J.: Zed Books, 1986); Chandra Talpade Mohanty, *Feminism without Borders: Decolonizing Theory, Practicing Solidarity* (Durham, N.C.: Duke University Press, 2003); Vandana Shiva, *Biopiracy: The Plunder of Nature and Knowledge* (Boston, Mass.: South End Press, 1997); Gayatri Chakravorty Spivak, *A Critique of Postcolonial Reason: Toward a History of the Vanishing Present* (Cambridge, Mass.: Harvard University Press, 1999).

22. Address by Eugene R. Black before the Thirty-Sixth Annual Meeting of the Investment Bankers Association, Hollywood, Fla., Tuesday, December 2, 1947. Box 4; Series 4117; WB IBRD/IDA 23 Records of the Office of External Relations, IPA Press Releases, World Bank Group Archives.

23. Mohanty, *Feminism without Borders*, 234.

24. Caroline Moser, an academic at the University of London, was

apparently the driving force behind this shift to "Gender and Development" at the World Bank during the 1990s. See the Gender in Development section of the World Bank Website. "Gender and Development," August 17, 2004, http://www.worldbank.org/gender (April 15, 2006). See, too, Spivak's critique: Spivak, *Critique of Postcolonial Reason,* 200–201.

25. A useful overview of legal decisions can be found in Sanford A. Schane, "The Corporation Is a Person: the Language of a Legal Fiction," *Tulane Law Review* 67 (1987). A sophisticated reading of this issue was offered by Joseph Slaughter, "Incorporation: Or How International Law Personifies the Person" (paper presented at the Cultural Studies Association Conference, Boston, Mass., May 2004).

26. See, for two very different examples, Fredric Jameson, "Notes on Globalization as a Philosophical Issue," in *The Cultures of Globalization,* ed. Fredric Jameson and Masao Miyoshi (Durham, N.C.: Duke University Press, 2001), and Shiva, *Biopiracy.*

27. Hardt and Negri, *Empire,* 57.

28. Ibid.

29. Although I would insist that all labor is material, I understand the distinction that Hardt and Negri are trying to make. (I take up the theoretical question of affective or immaterial labor in the following chapter in my discussion of Arundhati Roy's novel.) Indeed, their notion of immateriality may perhaps be read as another form of marshalling the *literary.* That is, although immateriality—and particularly this notion of a networked communicability of singularities—seems altogether too simple as a political program, the term is richly suggestive as a theoretical figure for a future-looking construction of collectivity. *Theory* here is not a synonym for the unreal. Hardt's and Negri's is a suggestive example of the ways in which theory not only is informed by, but also informs, the work of social movements. Witness the celebrity of these two political theorists at the World Social Forum and elsewhere in the movements for global justice and solidarity.

30. All Raymond Williams quotations from Raymond Williams, "Dominant, Emergent, and Residual," in *Marxism and Literature* (Oxford: Oxford University Press, 1977), 121–27.

31. Michael Denning, *Culture in the Age of Three Worlds* (London: Verso, 2004), 162–63.

32. See, for instance, Fredric Jameson's seminal essay, "Postmodernism; or, The Cultural Logic of Late Capitalism," *New Left Review* 146 (July–August 1984): 59–92.

33. That is, "arts and culture" in precisely the sense that Williams argues against in "Culture Is Ordinary," *Resources of Hope* (London: Verso, 1958).

34. "Press Conference with James D. Wolfensohn," April 19, 2002.

35. The caricature offered in Jagdish N. Bhagwati, *In Defense of Globalization* (Auckland, Australia: Oxford University Press, 2004).

36. Naomi Klein, "Reclaiming the Commons," *New Left Review* 9 (2001). This piece is republished in *A Movement of Movements*, ed. Tom Mertes (London: Verso, 2004).

37. João Pedro Stedile, "Brazil's Landless Battalions" (34), and Chittaroopa Palit, "Monsoon Risings" (91), in *Movement of Movements*. Interestingly, the first quotation goes on to say that Salgado's *Terra* exhibition "gave the Sem Terra Movement a global visibility in the field of the arts, without the need for an ideological discourse," suggesting that some of the alterglobalization social movements also, at times, understand the arts as functioning as a kind of transparent communication that takes place outside of ideology. At least to judge from these two interviews, the MST and NBA acknowledge the importance of artists like Salgado and Roy, but see their contributions in terms of publicity and financial support. I raise this point only to suggest some of the complexities involved with an argument that posits the work of Salgado, Roy, and others as fully emergent forms of cultural opposition. With these artists, as well as with the alterglobalization movements generally, I would apply at best the cautiously optimistic *pre-emergent* to some of the more radical practices.

38. This is in contrast to the main World Bank Website, portions of which are now published in eighteen languages.

39. See Naomi Klein, *No Logo: Taking Aim at the Brand Bullies* (New York: Picador, 2000).

40. In addition to Kumar's *World Bank Literature,* see the recent special issue of *Social Text* 22, no. 2 (2004), "Turning Pro: Professional Qualifications and the Global University," ed. Stephano Harney and Randy Martin. See, too: Stanley Aronowitz and Henry A. Giroux, *Education under Siege: The Conservative, Liberal, and Radical Debate over Schooling* (South Hadley, Mass.: Bergin and Garvey, 1985); Henry A. Giroux and Stanley Aronowitz, *Education Still under Siege* (Westport, Conn.: Bergin and Garvey, 1993); Michael Berube and Cary Nelson, *Higher Education under Fire: Politics, Economics, and the Crisis of the Humanities* (New York: Routledge, 1995); Jennifer Gore, *The Struggle for Pedagogies: Critical and Feminist Discourses as Regimes of Truth* (New York: Routledge, 1992); Bill Readings, *The University in Ruins* (Cambridge, Mass.: Harvard University Press, 1996); Sheila Slaughter and Larry L. Leslie, *Academic Capitalism: Politics, Policies, and the Entrepreneurial University* (Baltimore, Md.: Johns Hopkins University Press, 1999); Evan Watkins, *Work Time: English Departments and the Circulation of Cultural Value* (Stanford, Calif.: Stanford University Press, 1989).

41. Never more emphatically or successfully than in "Culture," her profoundly nuanced final section of *A Critique of Postcolonial Reason*.

6. Literary Movements

1. All subsequent citations from Arundhati Roy, *The God of Small Things* (New York: Random House, 1997). Subsequent references abbreviated as *GOST*. Roy's novel makes extensive use of italicization, nonstandard capitalization, spelling, and mechanics. All quotes are faithful to the original unless otherwise noted.

2. Michael Denning, *Culture in the Age of Three Worlds* (London: Verso, 2004), 103.

3. Terry Eagleton, *The Idea of Culture* (Oxford: Blackwell, 2000), 52.

4. Gayatri Chakravorty Spivak, *A Critique of Postcolonial Reason: Toward a History of the Vanishing Present* (Cambridge, Mass.: Harvard University Press, 1999), 112.

5. Terry Eagleton, "Just My Imagination," book review of Russell Jacoby's *Picture Imperfect: Utopian Thought for an Anti-Utopian Age*, *The Nation*, June 13, 2005, 23–24.

6. This frequently quoted line appears to originate from an interview with David Barsamian in the April 2001 issue of *The Progressive*, available online at http://www.progressive.org/intv0401.html.

7. Denning, *Culture in the Age of Three Worlds*, 70.

8. See Stuart Hall, "The Meaning of New Times," in *New Times: The Changing Face of Politics in the 1990s*, ed. Stuart Hall and Martin Jacques (London: Lawrence and Wishart, 1989).

9. Frantz Fanon, *The Wretched of the Earth* (New York: Grove Press, 1963), 40.

10. Arjun Appadurai, *Modernity at Large: Cultural Dimensions of Globalization* (Minneapolis: University of Minnesota Press, 1996), 178–99.

11. Joseph Conrad, *Heart of Darkness*, ed. Robert Kimbrough, 3rd ed.: Norton Critical Edition (New York: W. W. Norton and Company, 1988), 8.

12. This, of course, has many similarities with orthodox Marxist ideology critique, which seeks to invert appearance and reality to make visible the materialist foundations of metaphysical and superstructural expression.

13. Film, of course, opens up different modes of interpretive ambiguity. I take Roy's comments to suggest an awareness of the specificity of different media, rather than an effort to privilege print over film as inherently more demanding of its audience. The two media demand differently.

14. "Scimitars in the Sun: N. Ram interviews Arundhati Roy on a writer's place in politics," *Frontline* 18, no. 1 (January 6–19, 2001), http://www.flonnet.com/fl1801/18010040.htm.

15. See, for instance, Roy's comments from her "Scimitars in the Sun" interview with *Frontline*: "When I was writing *The Greater Common Good* I was acutely aware of two things: One, [. . .] I was not going to write on 'behalf' of anyone but myself because I think that's the most honest thing to do—in our society particularly, the politics of 'representation' is complicated and fraught with danger and dishonesty. Two, I was not writing an anthropological account of the lifestyles of people that I knew very little about. I was writing about social justice, about the politics of involuntary displacement, about what happens to people who are forcibly uprooted from an environment they know well and dumped in a world they know nothing about—a world in which, instead of a forest and a river and farmlands, they have unemployment and a tin shack. It's an unfair, unequal bargain for anybody—Adivasi or Aggarwal. At no point in my essay have I even attempted to describe Adivasi lifestyle, let alone romanticise it."

16. In part, this is what Jameson has referred to as the "problem of political art." Fredric Jameson, "Reification and Utopia in Mass Culture," *Social Text* 1 (1979): 139.

17. Richard Wright, *The Color Curtain* (Jackson: University Press of Mississippi, 1956), 94; ellipses in original.

18. Michael Hardt and Antonio Negri, *Multitude: War and Democracy in the Age of Empire* (New York: Penguin Press, 2004), xiv.

19. Ibid.

20. Ibid., 108.

21. Ibid., 110.

22. Césaire writes, "and the determination of my biology, not a prisoner to a facial angle, to a type of hair, to a well-flattened nose, to a clearly Melanian coloring, and negritude, no longer a cephalic index, or plasma, or soma, but measured by the compass of suffering." Aimé Césaire, Clayton Eshleman, and Annette Smith, *Notebook of a Return to the Native Land* (Middletown, Conn.: Wesleyan University Press, 2001), 43.

23. The twins' scene is described as "But very quiet" (310) rather than "A little quiet."

24. Benedict Anderson, *Imagined Communities: Reflections on the Origin and Spread of Nationalism* (London: Verso, 1991), 24.

25. Hardt and Negri, 192–93.

26. Ibid., 194.

7. Minimum Agendas

1. Of course, 1994 is only a convenient marker, not a definitive break; for instance, the 1988 Bank meetings in Berlin featured massive protests, and the Midnight Notes Collective was publishing ideas about the "new enclosures" and the privatization of the global commons in 1992 and earlier.

My point is simply that 1994 functions as a convenient marker for a convergence of global anticapitalist resistance. See Midnight Notes Collective, *Midnight Oil: Work, Energy, War, 1973–1992* (Brooklyn: Autonomedia, 1992). Michael Denning's attempts to periodize the era of globalization inform the analysis in this section as a whole. See especially Michael Denning, *Culture in the Age of Three Worlds* (London: Verso, 2004), 35–50.

2. A wonderful timeline of these events from 1994 to 2003 can be found online at the site "We Are Everywhere: The Irresistible Rise of Global Anticapitalism," http://weareeverywhere.org (April 18, 2006). See too the printed book from Notes from Nowhere, *We Are Everywhere: The Irresistible Rise of Global Anticapitalism* (London; New York: Verso, 2003).

3. For a further articulation of the cultural turn's theorizing of class, gender, race, and national "formations," see Denning, *Culture in the Age of Three Worlds*, 151–52.

4. World Social Forum Charter of Principles, June 2001, Item 6. The charter, reprinted in many places, is available on the Web at http://www.forumsocialmundial.org.br.

5. WSF Charter, Item 9.

6. Ibid.

7. Boaventura de Sousa Santos, "The World Social Forum: Toward a Counter-Hegemonic Globalization (Part 1)," in *World Social Forum: Challenging Empires,* ed. Jai Sen et al. (New Delhi: Viveka Foundation, 2004), 235.

8. Michael Hardt, "Today's Bandung?" *New Left Review* 14 (2002): 112, 113.

9. Ibid., 113.

10. For a brief but thoughtful history of the WSF, see the introduction to William F. Fisher and Thomas Ponniah, eds., *Another World Is Possible: Popular Alternatives to Globalization at the World Social Forum* (New York: Zed Books, 2003), 1–20. The best collection of essays in print is *World Social Forum*). Probably the most complete collection of writings about the WSF can be found online in the Library of Alternatives on the WSF Website, http://www.forumsocialmundial.org.br.

11. WSF Charter, Item 1.

12. To my mind, this is a welcome development, one that indicates an awareness on the part of the International Council of the centrality of major social movement actors to the WSF process. Teivo Teivainen, a longtime commentator on the WSF, discusses the implications of this decision in a blog entry about the 2006 IC meetings, http://www.nigd.org/nigd-wsf-area/world-social-forum/categories/wsf-international-council-meeting-october.

13. Chico Whitaker, "The WSF as Open Space," in *World Social Forum*, 111–21.

14. John Keane, *Global Civil Society? Contemporary Political Theory*. (Cambridge: Cambridge University Press, 2003), 210.

15. Whitaker, "WSF as Open Space," 113.

16. Among the many critiques of civil society, see especially Denning, *Culture in the Age of Three Worlds*, 209–26; Miranda Joseph, *Against the Romance of Community* (Minneapolis: University of Minnesota Press, 2002), 69–118; Gayatri Chakravorty Spivak, *A Critique of Post-colonial Reason: Toward a History of the Vanishing Present* (Cambridge, Mass.: Harvard University Press, 1999).

17. Whitaker, "WSF as Open Space," 115.

18. WSF Charter, Item 4.

19. Ibid., Item 1, 11

20. World Bank Group Website, "Defining Civil Society," http://web .worldbank.org/WBSITE/EXTERNAL/TOPICS/CSO/0,,contentMDK: 20101499~menuPK:244752~pagePK:220503~piPK:220476~theSitePK: 228717,00.html (December 13, 2004).

21. World Bank, "Civic Engagement Newsletter," January 2004: 2–3.

22. Hardt, "Today's Bandung," 117.

23. Arturo Escobar, "Other Worlds Are (Already) Possible: Self-Organization, Complexity, and Post-Capitalist Cultures," in *World Social Forum*, 350–51.

24. de Sousa Santos, "The World Social Forum," 241.

25. M. M. Bakhtin, *The Dialogic Imagination: Four Essays*, ed. Michael Holquist (Austin: University of Texas Press, 1981), 294.

26. Richard Wright, *The Color Curtain* (Jackson: University Press of Mississippi, 1956), 51–52.

27. Arundhati Roy, "Confronting Empire," address to the World Social Forum, delivered Janurary 2003 in Porto Alegre, Brazil, reprinted in *World Social Forum*, 51. Subsequent citations are referenced with in-text parenthetical page numbers.

28. For their argument about the "incommunicability of struggle," see Michael Hardt and Antonio Negri, *Empire* (Cambridge, Mass. and London: Harvard University Press, 2000), 54–56.

29. Naomi Klein, "The Hijacking of the WSF," January 30, 2003, No Logo Website http://nologo.org/newsite/detail.php?ID=133.

30. Ibid.

31. Enloe's question, "Where are the Women?" resonates in this context as well. Although Roy's presence on the podium is a far cry from Enloe's analysis of Margaret Thatcher as, in a revealing photograph, the lone woman head of state, feminist critiques offer among the most useful

analyses to guard against any betrayal of the democratic and egalitarian practices and objectives of the WSF.

32. Subcomandante Marcos, "The Fourth World War Has Begun," in *The Zapatista Reader,* ed. Tom Hayden (New York: Thunder's Mouth Press/Nation Books, 2002), 284.

33. The formulation "one 'no' and many 'yeses'" appears to have come out of the second National Encuentro of Civil Society in May 1999, and appears frequently in analyses of the Zapatistas, including Paul Kingsnorth's 2004 book by that name, *One No, Many Yeses: A Journey to the Heart of Global Resistance* (New York: Free Press, 2004). For Klein's references, see Naomi Klein, "The Unknown Icon," reprinted in *The Zapatista Reader,* 119.

34. Hugo Chavez appears now the figure on the political Left with whom the cult of personality critiques are most typically associated, perhaps assuming the mantle from Lula, who took it from Marcos, who took it from Che or Fidel. . . .

35. Fredric Jameson, "Notes on Globalization as a Philosophical Issue," in *The Cultures of Globalization,* ed. Fredric Jameson and Masao Miyoshi (Durham, N.C.: Duke University Press, 2001), 74.

36. Naomi Klein, "Reclaiming the Commons," *New Left Review* 9 (2001).

37. For a probing analysis of just this question, see McKenzie Wark, *Virtual Geography: Living with Global Media Events* (Bloomington: Indiana University Press, 1994).

38. Arundhati Roy, "Do Turkeys Enjoy Thanksgiving?" World Social Forum address delivered in Mumbai, India, January 14, 2004, reprinted in *An Ordinary Person's Guide to Empire* (Cambridge Mass.: South End Press, 2004), 94. Subsequent references cited parenthetically in the text.

39. Gopal Balakrishnan, "The National Imagination," *Mapping the Nation,* ed. Gopal Balakrishnan (London: Verso Press, 1996), 208, 210.

40. Quoted in Devesh Kapur, John Prior Lewis, and Richard Charles Webb, *The World Bank: Its First Half Century,* 2 vols. (Washington, D.C.: Brookings Institution, 1997), 101.

41. Patrick Bond, *Against Global Apartheid: South Africa Meets the World Bank, IMF, and International Finance,* 2nd ed. (Lansdowne, South Africa: University of Cape Town Press, 2003), 283.

42. Walls, bridges, buildings, and makeshift canvases throughout the city of Mumbai were painted with MR slogans such as "globalization cannot be humanized," "Debate alone cannot build another world," and "Imperial capital cannot be reformed. It must be smashed," making the MR disdain for liberal humanist arguments about civil society and the public sphere perfectly clear to all WSF participants.

43. I have quoted this paragraph from a version of Roy's speech pub-

lished online, because this version includes the specific invitation to MR participants that for some reason has been excised from the published version in *An Ordinary Person's Guide to Empire*. Roy's speech is reproduced in numerous online venues. Here I cite copy using the slightly different title "Turkey Tales," located on *Infochange WSF 2004*, which contains links to numerous other related documents from the Mumbai gathering, http://www.infochangeindia.org /infochange_wsf15.jsp?wsf15 (July 17, 2005).

44. Patrick Bond has responded point by point to the manifesto. This provocative dialogue is available online at http://www. zmag.org/ Sustainers/Content/2005-02/22bond.cfm (April 17, 2006).

45. Hardt and Negri, *Empire*, 57.

46. Terry Eagleton, *The Idea of Culture* (Oxford: Blackwell, 2000), 88, 131.

47. Denning, Culture *in the Age of Three Worlds*, 28–29.

Index

Adorno, Theodor: and Max Horkheimer, 106–10
affective labor, 153, 182, 183–88, 195, 209–12, 224n29. *See also* immaterial labor
Ahmad, Aijaz, xvii, 120
Albert, Michael, 209
Ali, Mohamed, 118
alterglobalization movements: affirmative platform of, 23; debates over terminology, 225–26n20; opposing the World Bank, xx, xxiv, xxviii, 135–44, 189–92, 257–58n1; as pre-emergent cultural formations, 158–60, 164, 255n37; problems of representation, 173–80, 193–202, 207–8; utopic vision of, 186–89, 209–12, 220–21; World Social Forum and, xxxii–xxxiii, 165–67, 173, 186–88, 189–221
Althusser, Louis, 8
Anderson, Benedict, 185–86, 215
Another World Is Possible: World Social Forum and, 166–67, 187, 192–202, 208

anticapitalist movements, 158–60, 169–74, 189–221. *See also* social movements
anticolonial intellectuals: alterglobalization legacies and, 189–92, 212–19; Bandung and, 123–34; compared with Roy, 169–73, 174, 176–78; contributions to postcolonial and cultural studies, 98, 110–11; midcentury radicals and the World Bank, 110–19, 135; nonalignment and, 117–19; third world and, 176–78. *See also* anti-imperialist critique; Césaire, Aimé; Fanon, Frantz; Wright, Richard
antiglobalization. *See* alterglobalization movements
anti-imperialist critique: Bandung and, 123–34; Roy and, 169–74; World Bank and, 55–89, 110–19, 135; World Social Forum and, 189–92, 204, 212–21
Arnold, Matthew, 84, 90–92, 123–24, 156, 165, 220, 244n7
Asian-African Conference

Bret Benjamin is associate professor of English at the University at Albany, State University of New York. He has published essays on an eclectic array of topics within transnational cultural studies, including sanitation and hygiene in Northern Ireland, population control programs in Indonesia, and links between reality television and the phenomenon of embedded reporting during the 2003 U.S. invastion of Iraq.